ART
CAN
KILL

STORIES OF
ART WORLD CROOKS,
CLOWNS & CONNOISSEURS

BRYAN COOKE

Inquiries concerning book purchases may be made through
the Publisher's website—www.ArtWorldPublishing.com

Owned and Published by Art World Publishing Inc.

Hardcover ISBN: 979-8-9865560-0-0
Paperback ISBN: 979-8-9865560-1-7
Ebook ISBN: 979-8-9865560-2-4

Library of Congress Catalog Number: 2022912379

Cover Design Concept by Bryan Cooke
Cover Design by Joseph DePinho, DePinho Design
Interior Design by Jess LaGreca, Mayfly Design

Editor: Donna Frazier Glynn

Copy Editor: Suzanne Coner

Printed in the United States of America

For My Wonderful Family
Amazing Wife Aileen, Son Kevin & His Spouse Kat,
Daughter Emily Cheatham & Her Husband Mike,
& Two Beautiful Grandchildren Aubrey & Isla

Contents

Introduction

Moving Art

THE HISTORY OF ART belongs to the survivors. The works that outlast natural disasters or wars. The ones unscathed by carelessness, malice, and neglect. It's the record of the lucky ones that survived the perils of being moved across continents—or across the street—that have been able to take their place in the timeline of history, remembered, recognizable, essence intact. When I look at art in a gallery, a collector's home, or a museum, I can't help but see not just the pieces themselves but all that might've befallen them. In a half-century of moving and handling art, I've learned quite a bit about what survives and how easily it might not.

The hands of fate often belong to unsung blue-collar types who haul precious objects from one place to another. Insurance companies specializing in art will tell you that most damage claims occur while art is being moved and installed. It's handling mistakes like poor packing methods and inadequate crating and shipping that cause the greatest risks to art's survival. Thus it has always been. One of the great unseen corners of the art world is the tense arena where the workers who handle art beat back the forces that threaten not just the objects but even the handlers' lives. It may sound far-fetched to someone standing in a hushed museum gallery looking at paintings or sculptures bathed in serene pools of light, but art can kill—and it's astonishingly easy to "kill" art as well.

When art was being painted on cave walls 20,000 years ago, it couldn't be moved, which proved to be one of the ultimate survival strategies. Risk ratcheted up when the designs for ancient Egyptian, Greek, and Etruscan tombs sometimes required massive stones and plasters to be transported from other locations, often at a great cost of human endeavor. In modern times, conquest and thievery have uprooted art created in situ. This has sent works like the Elgin Marbles—friezes from the Parthenon carved by the brilliant Phidias in his workshop and moved to the Acropolis building site—on journeys unimaginable to their creators. Looted from Greece in the early nineteenth century by an art-loving Brit named Lord Elgin, who wanted to "protect" them by installing them in his own home, the Marbles were packed and sent by a sailing ship to London. And I can't help but wonder: What if they had been damaged by the craftsman who hacked them out of the Parthenon? What if the ship had foundered and sunk?

Moving art has always revolved around developing strategies to reduce the possibility of damage. Stones used to construct the fluted temple columns of Gothic cathedrals were carved at the construction site because damaging an unfinished block during transport was far less costly than damaging a completed work. As human activities expanded in cities and towns, more art was made in locations apart from where it finally rested. Few records exist to tell us how this art was transported because "mere logistics" rarely warranted a mention—despite the skill needed to safely deliver paintings or sculptures across great distances on lousy roads and often in poor weather conditions. The laborers responsible for their safekeeping were largely unseen, unremembered, and uncredited. How was a painting by Rubens or Goya protected while tied to a donkey's back traversing rough trails between Renaissance cities? What buffered it from the elements and kept it out of the hands of thieves? In every instance, someone had to assess the risks and make the many consequential decisions that would let them safely transport the art entrusted to them.

The enormous quantities of art spanning many centuries displayed in today's museums reflect the outcome of careful and skillful handling. And equally important, a sense of responsibility honed by a keen awareness of what the loss of a work could mean.

Think, for instance, of how much value—both economic and intangible—would have been lost if Michelangelo's magnificent sculpture *David* had been damaged or destroyed during the many times it was handled and manipulated before its final installation in Florence.

First, there was the expense of quarrying the pure, white Carrara marble from a mountainside and shaping it into a block. *David* is seventeen feet high by six and a half feet wide. The block it was carved from likely exceeded eighteen feet by eight feet and could have weighed forty tons or more. The cost of moving that huge chunk of rock eighty miles out of the mountains to Florence over dirt roads and across rivers had to be high. I have driven up the narrow, steep roads to the Carrara quarries, and it's clear that the prospect would be daunting even for heavy trucks on modern, paved roads. For workers using teams of oxen or horses, the job would have been many times more arduous and fraught with danger. The marble sat for several years in Florence, as several sculptors accepted commissions to carve it and then backed out. One claimed that the block was of inferior quality, and another had already begun carving a hole through the spot where David's legs would be before giving up. That would have weakened the stone, making it even more difficult and expensive to move to the studio of the young Michelangelo, who was just twenty-six when he took on the project.

Before he could begin, the stone needed to be raised from horizontal to vertical so he could carve 360 degrees around it. Since there were no cranes in those days, someone had to build a hoisting structure using timbers capable of supporting the weight—and then assemble a large team of men who'd use block and tackles to raise it. Modern chain hoists have a built-in ratchet system to prevent an object from "unspooling," but Michelangelo's team would've had to maintain continuous control of the lifting rope, a fatiguing task. The lifting ratios of the pulleys would be short, requiring them to be reset multiple times until the stone was upright. Once it was upright, it would've been in danger of falling over, and wood cribbing or earth would have to be placed underneath to support it. All this time-consuming engineering and labor added to the costs. Then Michelangelo carved and completed his sculpture, working steadily for two years and likely employing apprentices, which would have layered on even more expense.

The finished *David* needed to be transported from the studio to the Florence Plaza where it would be installed. Though it was a short journey, as recounted by one of Michelangelo's neighbors, an amateur historian, it was full of travails. The sculpture was too tall to pass through the archway over the artist's courtyard entrance, so that had to be torn down. Then the six-ton sculpture was moved on rollers across the city—which took days—and hoisted onto a pedestal. At each juncture, the fate of this masterpiece was in the hands of "art movers"—ones who could make no mistakes and had to rely on careful planning, great skill, and extensive knowledge to ensure that one of the world's greatest works of art would endure and be seen. The pressures of working with such stakes and challenges are enormous. And from Michelangelo's time to the present, art handlers have faced them almost every day.

Contemporary art moving requires skills ranging from truck and forklift driving to carpentry, along with an extensive knowledge of tools and engineering principles. But unlike any other blue-collar occupation, it also demands a knowledge of art history, techniques, and materials, as well as the ability to be comfortable working for and talking with a wealthy and powerful clientele. For all their expertise, art handlers are servants, and servants must always say yes. If a client's request is too stupid to safely or reasonably comply with, art handlers must practice servant psychology—ensuring clients never lose face and always believe that the conclusion they've been steered toward was their idea. Along with such diplomatic skills and guile, handlers must also have a kind of fearlessness that lets them work with high-value paintings and sculptures without dwelling on the high cost of any misstep, lest they lose their nerve.

My youthful experiences living close to poverty and working as a farm laborer toughened me up to survive in this environment. Art school and gallery training gave me an appreciation of what I was handling and a grounding in the rules of provenance and archiving. Working as a studio assistant to Richard Diebenkorn gave me a window into genius. I've needed all of that and more to navigate the perils and personalities in this business. I have watched masterpieces in the making and have been the last person to see a work intact before it was lost forever. I've pulled off impossible installations and have been pulled into crime scenes and near disasters. Somehow, I've lived to tell the tale.

In the fifty-plus years I've been an art handler, I've witnessed the phenomenal growth of art galleries, expansions of museums, and increased art collecting worldwide. I have moved or stored entire museum collections and some of the world's most expensive works of art, including masterpieces such as Gainsborough's *The Blue Boy* and Monet's *Lily Pond* paintings, as well as Rembrandts, a Leonardo da Vinci, and Rodin and Calder sculptures. The individual paintings I have stored and shipped have broken world sales records—including a Jackson Pollock painting valued at $155 million, a $167 million Picasso, and recently a David Hockney painting that sold for $90 million, a record for a living artist. My company even moved the

$1.2 billion collection of paintings assembled for the *Van Gogh's Van Goghs* exhibition at the Los Angeles County Museum of Art, which our trucks delivered from LAX under the heavily armed watch of the Los Angeles Police Department's SWAT team.

Each time, any misstep could have changed the history of art.

While many people, including some of our clients, tend to think of art moving as a rote "muscle job," it's actually a high-skill, high-risk occupation where failure is not an option but is always lurking close by. Every day in this business, we take the high-stress risks that come with protecting fragile art that's often of inestimable financial or intrinsic value—work that cannot be replaced. And not infrequently, we put our wellbeing and even our lives on the line to do it.

This book is a look into some humorous, harrowing, and dark corners of the art world I've seen while "invisibly" moving and handling art. It's a collection of weird and outrageous events involving extremely expensive art, high-powered and important art collectors, and strange occurrences over the past fifty years. I don't tell these stories to besmirch the many wonderful people I have known and have been honored to do business with. This world is full of connoisseurs. But there are others who casually put great works in peril or try to enrich themselves by cheating the system, the "clowns and crooks" looking for shortcuts or easy money who assume that art is a game full of fools they can play.

I started in the early days of art handling when it was dominated by the van and storage companies that move household goods. It quickly became clear that the brute ability to lug couches and refrigerators does not translate into careful art handling services. Over time, the specialists who emerged amassed tremendous experience and established the professional standards, rules, and ethics that guide us today. Some of the wilder behavior and "cowboy" solutions in these stories would rarely happen now. But human nature hasn't changed. Greed, impatience, and short-sightedness haven't disappeared. And the massive egos and quirky personalities of those who populate the art world haven't either.

Artists, collectors, gallerists, and art experts at the top of the food chain are generally the ones who document the scene and present themselves as knowledgeable and sophisticated to their peers. But a truer view might be the one I've gotten from the bottom—where ignorance and potentially lethal bad behavior sit side by side with all of that acclaim and sophistication.

Case in point: the day we installed Marcia Weisman's backyard Richard Serra.

Art Can Kill

IN 1984, Marcia Weisman breathlessly called to tell me that she had just purchased "a masterpiece by Richard Serra" from Larry Gagosian in New York. At the time, Marcia was campaigning to establish the Museum of Contemporary Art in Los Angeles. She and her husband Frederick had one of LA's notable collections of modern art. This new piece would be the grandest of the lot. She wanted me to take care of the shipping and installation arrangements.

"Call Larry!" she said. "He will tell you where to go get it."

Gagosian told me the Corten steel structure measured eight feet high by twelve feet wide by six inches thick, and it weighed 16,000 pounds. It was at a sculpture fabricator's up in Connecticut.

I made an appointment with a crane company to meet me at Marcia's Angelo Drive residence in Beverly Hills to determine what size crane we would need for the installation. Marcia showed us a location in the backyard where she wanted to place the sculpture. It would sit near her garage, close to the swimming pool, where a hedge directly behind the spot would backdrop the sculpture nicely. The crane estimator said we'd need a seventy-five-ton, self-propelled hydro crane. It would have to be set up on the street to lift the sculpture over the single-story garage and installed on a concrete pad Marcia's contractor was pouring.

I arranged to have the piece trucked in from the East Coast, scheduled the crane, and gave Marcia a cost estimate. Unfortunately, the Los Angeles Olympic Games were scheduled to begin at the same time, so we couldn't obtain the required permits to drive the truck and crane through LA into Beverly Hills. We postponed the installation date until after the games.

Five months later, I called my crane operator to remind him about the job. He said he would go back to look at Marcia's house again. It sounded like a waste of time to me, but he insisted. The next morning, he called to report that the garage was *two* stories high, and we would need a much larger crane to lift the sculpture over it. I argued with him—we both knew the garage was only one story high. We'd seen it together. He must have gone to the wrong address. But he was adamant he had gone to the right place and said I should go take a look. He added that we'd now need additional tractor-trailers to deliver the crane and gave me a much higher estimate. I wasn't sure Marcia would want to pay.

I went over to the house, and sure enough, Marcia had added a second room on top of the original garage during the Olympics. "Frank designed it for me," she said when I arrived. I took that to mean Frank Gehry. My assumption was confirmed when she showed me the stairs that curved from the garden to the new upstairs room. They were clad in the galvanized sheet metal Gehry was beginning to use in his architecture and sat only a few feet from the concrete pad where the Serra sculpture, also curved, would rest. Marcia explained that Frank had seen a photo of the Serra and designed the stairs to "complement" the sculpture. But the clash of styles was going to look terrible.

I knew Serra wouldn't be happy, but I hid my apprehension and tried to persuade Marcia that the sculpture should be relocated to another part of her garden. She rebuffed the suggestion as "nonsense."

On a clear, chilly fall morning, the crane arrived. It was accompanied by truckloads of boom sections and the massive weights we would need to counterbalance the heaviness of the Serra to prevent the crane from tipping over. We set up barricades blocking each end of Angelo Drive. By the time the flatbed trailer carrying Serra's sculpture pulled in, we had five large trucks parked up and down the street. The massive sculpture was too unstable to ride upright, so it was supported on a frame of steel girders at a 45-degree angle. This kept it braced, low and legal for driving across the United States.

Richard Serra showed up to supervise the unloading and set-up. He was in a good mood, joking with my employees and me while inspecting his sculpture as we discussed our installation plans. As the crew assembled the crane, Serra walked around the garage to the backyard. I followed a few minutes later and saw him standing on the sculpture pad with his hands stuffed into his pockets, staring unhappily at Frank Gehry's staircase. He looked sullen and pissed off. It wasn't a good sign.

I went back out to the street to watch the progress of the crane and noticed a line of Bentleys, Rolls Royce's, and Mercedes sedans forming inside our street barricades. They were parking between the trucks and near the crane. Women dressed in afternoon cocktail attire got out of the cars and began walking through our work area to Marcia's front door—completely oblivious to the dangers posed by the crane parts being hoisted overhead.

When the crane was almost set up, with its outriggers straddling the cribs of timbers that were keeping it level on the sloping street, I returned to the backyard. I saw that a party was in progress. Marcia had invited all of her friends to watch the installation. They sat at cloth-covered tables set with silverware and fine china. A butler dressed in tails was serving cocktails and finger sandwiches. The crowd swelled to around twenty women, boisterous and talking excitedly. Serra was still standing gloomily on his empty sculpture pad, looking down at his feet instead of the party on the other end of the lawn. Marcia had not invited him to meet her friends or join the party. She was pointedly ignoring him.

Trying to control the apprehension growing in my stomach, I returned to the street as the riggers were attaching "dogs"—large clamps that grip steel plates—to the top of the sculpture. The dogs dangled from steel cables attached to a spreader bar hanging from the crane hook. They were positioned so they would grip the sculpture a foot in from each end to keep it balanced while the crane lifted it. The clamps squeezed together like salad tongs, working on the principle that the heavier the weight, the greater the gripping pressure. Much like putting your fingers into one of those novelty Chinese finger traps. The harder you pull, the more difficult it is to get free.

Once the sculpture was safely airborne, the riggers and I rushed around the garage and into the backyard to wait for it to descend so we could guide it into position. The crane operator was on the opposite side of the house and couldn't see us, so one of the riggers used a walkie-talkie to give him directions. I watched in awe as eight tons of steel gracefully swung high above a house filled with millions of dollars of paintings and sculptures.

The sculpture came overhead and slowly moved down until it was a few feet from the ground in front of the concrete pad. We were just about to tell the crane operator to stop lowering it so we could swing it into position when I heard Marcia shouting, "Yoo-hoo! Yoo-hoo! Richard! Oh, Richard! Could you turn the sculpture in the other direction so we can see how it looks?" The request was absurd because it could only face one way, but she was posturing in front of her friends, trying to show them that her purchase gave her power over the artist.

This was a huge miscalculation. Serra straightened up with a glare and yelled: "Lady, I'd rather shove it up your fat ass!"

Immediately chaos broke out. Marcia's friends jumped up, knocking over chairs and spilling champagne glasses and china on the lawn. "How dare you talk to her that way!" they screamed at him. Serra stood his ground with his chin jutting forward and yelled back at the crowd.

The abruptness of the uproar distracted us, and the rigger forgot to radio the crane operator to stop letting out cable. I had turned my back on the sculpture and was looking toward Marcia when suddenly the whole thing fell over. The massive steel plate brushed my shirt sleeve on the way down. Had it come an inch or two closer, it could've cut off my arm or crushed me to death. It fell with the dogs still attached, suspending it at an angle about twenty-four inches off the grass, where it began violently yo-yo-ing up and down. I looked up. The crane boom was tilting dangerously over Marcia's house and bouncing in rhythm with the steel.

My heart pounded, but I was completely calm. I ran—fast—underneath the wavering boom and out to the street. The crane was tilted at an angle with its outriggers sticking up in the air. It was barely balancing and within mere inches of toppling onto the house. The crane operator, in fear for his life, had jumped out and was standing a hundred feet down the street, visibly upset and wide-eyed. I yelled at him to get back in the crane and let out cable until the crane lowered itself back into position. Reluctantly, he climbed back into the cab and reset the crane while I raced back around the house where the hubbub was still going on. I got the attention of the riggers, and we lifted the sculpture and set it on the concrete pad in the correct orientation. In the heat of their fight, neither Marcia nor Serra noticed how close we had come to a complete disaster. If the crane had fallen, it would have destroyed the house and perhaps killed several of us, including Serra, who was standing on the pad underneath the boom.

Once the adrenalin began to subside, I could see that the sculpture was a wonderful piece. It was shaped in an arc, and when it sat on the pad, it tilted forward, balancing on the front points of the bottom corners with the rear of the curve elevated several inches off the concrete. The balance was so perfect you could shove a finger against it, and 16,000 pounds of steel would gently rock back and forth. It was by far the greatest Richard Serra I had ever seen. A passing breeze would set it in motion.

Finally, things quieted down, and in the midst of her friends, Marcia attempted to make peace. "Richard, would you help me break a bottle of Dom Perignon over your sculpture to christen it?"

Serra wasn't in the mood. "I would rather break a bottle of beer on the goddamn thing," he said. That brought the party to an abrupt ending, and the guests began heading to the exit.

Carried by a rush of exhilaration—We'd pulled off the save! The piece, the house, and all of us had come out unscathed!—I managed to persuade Richard to sit down with Marcia in an attempt to get them to talk. I felt like the adult trying to get two squabbling children to make up and act in a civilized manner. Marcia had her butler open the bottle of christening champagne and serve glasses to her and Richard. Still, the artist was having none of this rapprochement and sat in angry silence—his gaze shifting between his sculpture and the Frank Gehry staircase next to it.

The next morning Marcia telephoned me. "Bryan! Did you hear how that man talked to me? Did you hear what he said? I want you to get that sculpture out of my yard now! I am not going to look one more day at that thing! Get it out!"

I told her she should wait until things cooled down, that it was a fantastic piece, and she could still change her mind. Removing it was going to cost just as much as installing it, I added, hoping that would slow her down. "I don't care!" she said. "Get it out of my yard!" She hung up. A week later, we went back to take the Serra away.

Twenty years after those events, I finally developed several rolls of black and white film that one of my employees had taken during the installation. There in the midst of Marcia's coiffed friends, stood Frank Gehry. I hadn't noticed him that day. He was laughing his head off.

I got more insight into what was going on when the *New Yorker* ran a long article about Richard Serra in 2002. Calvin Tomkins interviewed both Gehry and Serra. He described their competitive relationship and the sculptor's assertion that architects are not artists. The piece also delved into the Marcia Weisman incident from Gehry's viewpoint. The evening following the near disaster, Gehry called Serra and suggested he send Marcia a dozen roses to make amends. Several hours later, a dozen roses were instead delivered to Gehry with the note: "Shove these up *your* ass!"

I could see how Frank Gehry might have enjoyed goading Richard Serra with the curved staircase—but what stayed with me was how they were so absorbed in the theatrics of their one-upmanship that neither of them noticed when it nearly turned fatal.

Gehry became a client of mine over the following decades, and as his career grew, we crated, shipped, and stored hundreds of his models. In the early days, he called me directly to discuss the work he wanted done. But as his reputation grew, the contacts were always through his employees. One morning, I was waiting at the reception desk in his architecture offices in Santa Monica when he walked in, ignoring me as he strode past. "Good morning, Frank," I said politely. But his shoulders stiffened as if he were deeply offended, and without acknowledging me, turned his back and walked away. Would he have cared if I had died because of his curved staircase?

But Serra was different. A rigger had been killed in the 1970s when one of Serra's lead sculptures fell on him at the Walker Art Museum. It was a tragedy that deeply affected Serra, and I believe he would have cared a lot. I never had an opportunity to work with him again directly, but I've moved and installed his sculptures on other occasions—always very cautiously.

Education

IT TAKES A COOL HEAD to react quickly to avert a tragedy. And it requires tremendous grit to do so amidst irreplaceable art objects and volatile personalities. I could salvage the Serra episode and many more because of a toughness that was beaten into me from my experiences working as a farm laborer and attending a rough high school. Survival didn't allow any room for weakness.

I was twelve years old when my parents took office jobs at Dunlap Ranches in Thermal, California, the agricultural center of the Coachella Valley, where abandoned packing sheds lined the railroad tracks. Thermal was a small town of decrepit trailer parks, junky houses, a gas station, grocery store, and a lumberyard. Each summer, it could become the hottest place on Earth, surpassing the temperatures of the Sahara Desert and Death Valley—a hellish phenomenon caused by its location 138 feet below sea level in a desert. Without fondness, I called Thermal the "armpit of the world."

During World War II, Gen. George S. Patton trained his troops there for desert warfare. He expanded a nearby small airfield to fly in personnel and supplies and train air support for his soldiers. Patton commanded motorized army divisions and specialized in tank warfare. Before that, he was a horse soldier in the US Cavalry under Gen. John J. Pershing of World War I fame. Patton accompanied

Pershing's raid into Mexico in pursuit of Poncho Villa. One of Patton's friends, the pioneering female aviator Jacqueline Corcoran, kept her airplane at the Thermal airport. Knowing Patton was an avid and skilled polo player, she installed a polo field at her ranch south of town for him to use. Those polo grounds are now where an expensive golf resort is located.

Our lives had no trace of that glamorous history. We lived at the southern end of town in cramped ranch housing where the units were separated by common walls through which sounds easily carried. Within a few weeks of moving in, I was home alone after school when the married couple next door began fiercely arguing. I could hear them yelling and cursing at each other until a door slammed and footsteps ran away. Looking out my window, I saw the husband jump into his car, desperately backing down the dirt road. His wife ran into the street carrying a revolver and began firing it at the retreating vehicle. She was one hell of a shot. The next day the car was parked outside again with a tight pattern of six bullet holes in the windshield, all of them aimed at the passenger's side, deliberately missing him. I knew then that I needed to get out of that existence, and a college education was the way to escape. To pay for it, I would need to work and save.

My first summer job, at age 13, was building pallets at the local lumberyard for a contractor. The yard had precut all the wood, and the pallet contractor had made a jig that positioned the wood pieces for nailing. The automatic nail gun had not yet been invented, so nailing was still done the old-fashioned way—with a heavy framing hammer. By the end of my first day, my hand was swollen and bleeding from blisters. I soaked it in the evening, but the next day it was still so sore that I couldn't grip my hammer. So I taped my hand to the handle and went back to work.

The following summer, I started working in the fields picking grapes. But that came to a quick end after Cesar Chavez began organizing the farmworkers and picket lines formed outside the gates. I pedaled my bicycle to work at five each morning through a gantlet of shouting strikers, uncertain what to do because I sympathized with them but badly needed to work. The dilemma was solved when my employer contracted Filipino pickers from Fresno to replace local labor. With picking jobs taken, I began "swamping" trucks—loading them with packed 27-pound lugs of grapes. Swamping involved picking the boxes off the ground and tossing them up to a stacker who stood on the deck of a flatbed truck. The stacker then piled them on pallets—seventy-two lugs per pallet, sixteen pallets per truck, and eight to ten trucks per day. I was fourteen years old, weighed 120 pounds, and was repeatedly tossing twenty percent of my body weight from the ground to a fellow worker above my head. I started at 5:30 a.m. and often worked until 10 p.m., seven days a week without rest in heat that routinely rose to 115 degrees. To counter dehydration, we drank gallons of water and took handfuls of salt pills. At the end of each day, my clothes were stiff, caked white with salt from sweat. Adding to the discomfort were thousands of gnats, tiny flies attracted to the moisture in eyes, noses, and mouths. To keep them away, we smoked small Toscanelli cigars, which looked like twisted black roots and were hard as rocks. Their tar-like consistency kept them smoldering for hours, and the foul taste was worth enduring to avoid the torture inflicted by the insects.

Pickers finished around noon, leaving hundreds of boxes for us to load. After lunch, the Filipinos would send a delegation of young toughs to make sure we were filling up the trucks fast enough—because if the fruit sat in the sun too long, it would be ruined, and they wouldn't get paid. They always pulled out switchblades and brandished them at us to make their point.

During the last several years working in the fields, and before leaving for college, I became a driver. I drove a truck along the rows as the lugs of grapes were stacked and then transported the loaded truck to a chilling plant. I then used a forklift to move the pallets into a chiller. One day I was standing behind my truck cinching a rope to secure my pallets before heading to the plant, and I noticed that another driver had backed in behind me. After tying on his load, he started his truck, never shifting out of reverse. Suddenly, I was being squeezed between the chest-high beds of the two trucks. Fortunately, I was able to yell before my chest was so compressed it cut off my breathing, but swiveling my head, I could see the other driver looking at me in his side mirror, laughing at the joke he was playing. He pulled forward in response to my yell, but if his foot had slipped on the clutch, or the truck had rolled as he shifted into forward gears, I would have ended up in a wheelchair for life.

High school also toughened me up and taught me to deal with adversity. There were daily fights at Coachella Valley Union High School, and I was always looking over my shoulder. Even shop period wasn't safe. My nickname for one notorious student, a guy named Desuetta, was "Desuetta the Humper." Whenever I, or any other slightly built student, was bent over a table saw, feeding a board through, Desuetta would sneak behind, grab ahold and begin pumping his hips. Several times his violent shoving almost pushed my hand through the saw blade. The shop teacher just laughed and walked away.

I knew what I was in for as soon as the school bus picked me up on the first day of my freshman year. The ranch where we lived was the last stop on the bus before it drove to the high school several miles away. It was coming from Mecca, a hardscrabble town where people lived in rundown trailers, some without indoor plumbing or air conditioning. Mecca still pops up in the news once in a while because its location near the polluted Salton Sea causes adverse health problems. The state of California periodically cracks down on their deplorable living conditions, including sanitation issues and unclean, arsenic-tainted water supplies. Most of Mecca's residents were Mexican or Native American, and the students from there had a reputation for being the worst of the bad. They came from families who survived on seasonal farm work at low pay, and many of the students were behind in their schooling because they'd taken time off to work the fields or came from Mexico, where standards lagged behind California's. A good number of them were eighteen or older.

The bus came into view, climbing over the bridge that spanned the dry creek next to our ranch. As it pulled closer, I could hear yelling and cheering and wondered what was going on. The bus stopped with hissing air brakes, and its door flew open—but the driver didn't look at me or acknowledge my presence as I stepped on. As soon as I got to the top of the steps, I could see the bus was full of big bodies packed three to a seat, all staring at me. The driver slammed the door shut, and before I could get my bearings, he took off, throwing me off balance. I stumbled down the aisle, accidentally bumping into one of the riders.

"*Puto!*" the kid erupted in rage. "Fucking asshole! Stay off of me!" He stood up and violently shoved me across the aisle into another student, who reacted with a punch. This set off a maelstrom of punches, kicks, and curses from all directions, propelling me almost to the windshield, where I stood next to the driver. He was hunched over the steering wheel, white-faced and staring ahead. Although he was a big guy in his forties, I realized he was scared out of his brains and wasn't going to help me. Oddly, I wasn't frightened. I was upset, angry, and uncertain how to react. I understood they hated me because I was the only white guy on the bus, a symbol of the oppressor they could punish. The cheering I heard as the bus approached had been jeering—provoked when the passengers saw a wimpy, blond kid in glasses waiting by the roadside. This abuse continued for weeks. To stay out of reach and avoid additional beatings, I stood the entire way to school each day in the square foot of space near the stairs that kept me out of kicking range.

There are those who say the way to deal with bullies is to punch them in the nose, and I considered that but held back. Did my avoidance strategy make me a coward? I got my answer on the third day when two big toughs began fighting. One knocked the other onto the bus floor with a crisp punch, climbed on top, and relentlessly beat his stunned opponent to a pulp. The entire bus was an uproar of laughing, cheering spectators urging him on. No one intervened, and the driver kept the bus moving. Fight back? Right.

Finally, the driver quit. He was replaced by a diminutive, middle-aged woman wearing glasses, hair tied back in a ponytail. When I walked up the stairs, she ordered me to find a seat and kept the bus idling. Then, as I walked down the aisle and the kicking and punching began, she stood up, took an aggressive step forward, and started barking orders: "This bus doesn't move until he is seated! Give him a seat now! Any of you idiots who act up is getting off my bus and can walk to school! Do you understand me? Do you?" No one said a word, and I was able to sit in strained peace on the edge of a seat, with one cheek on and the other precariously cantilevered over the aisle.

I found the art classroom to be a place of peace and solace. The teacher, Mr. Pierce, was a World War II veteran who had served in an Army Mountain Ski Division, fighting the Nazis in the Italian Alps. He had gone to the Rhode Island School of Design on the G.I. Bill. He was tougher than any of the high schoolers, having endured terrible combat, but he exuded calm and tranquility. The love of art he fostered in me and the friends I made in his class changed the course of my life. One of his older students, Ramses Noriega, was a talented artist who later attended UCLA and worked on murals around Southern California. Ramses' family lived in Mexicali, and he invited me to visit for a week in the summer. It was an eye-opening experience. They lived in an adobe and corrugated metal shack on the banks of the Mexicali River, a creek-sized open sewer.

I was used to being poor, but in reality, I saw now, I was lucky. Our hardships were nothing compared to the appalling poverty and slum conditions just south of the US border. One afternoon, we drove out of the city to visit "Laguna," a lake on the Mexicali River. We passed a stream of street urchins dressed in rags who were walking there and trying to hitch rides. Laguna, it turned out, was less of a lake than a widening of the Mexicali River where several hundred kids and some adults were splashing and playing to seek relief from the mind-numbing afternoon heat. I wasn't sure if we were upstream or downstream from the city, but I wasn't going to chance getting into the murky water. Soon I was glad I hadn't. While we were there, one of the street kids drowned. No one noticed until it was too late. A group of kids waded over to his floating body, and after arguing in Spanish, they hauled it out, leaving the boy sprawled face-up on the sloping mud bank with his feet still submerged, eyes staring into the sun. I was surprised by the way they ran back into the water and resumed splashing and raucously laughing and insulting each other. I learned then that life can be very cheap and decided I would appreciate every opportunity it gives.

Bill

I made my escape to college—the University of Redlands—and paid my way by working summers in the fields and then taking a job at a gas station. My experiences at the station taught me lessons about business that have served me well in my career. And thanks to my boss there, Bill, I got a good education in dealing with crooks. Bill was porcine. His eyes seemed too small in proportion to the mass of his head, and he had a malevolent glare. He was so overweight his eyes were embedded inside fat, swollen cheeks, and his complexion was bright red, maybe from high blood pressure. How did someone become so fat? Overeating? French fries? Too much beer? His starched white uniform accentuated the redness of his skin. His neck fat bulged over his collar giving the impression the uniform's necktie was strangling him.

Bill was the manager of the Standard Oil gas station in Indio, California. It was a busy, 24/7, full-service stop at the junction of Highway 66 and the Blythe highway. This was before the I-10 freeway bypassed Indio, and most businesses failed.

His assistant manager, Woody, had gotten his girlfriend pregnant several years earlier, forcing him to drop out of college. He was a bitter man. Assistant gas station manager was likely as high as Woody would go. People like him migrated to California looking for the golden life, but the high cost of living bounced many off the coast—landing them in the desert—where vacant land was plentiful, and the rent was cheap in desolate trailer parks. For the poor, the desert has always been a last resort, the misery of scraping by made worse by the merciless glare of the hot sun.

My first encounter with Bill was his version of boot camp. Four of us new hires had completed a training course and arrived dressed in starched white uniforms for the first day of work. Bill told us to line up an arm's length apart and stand with our hands behind our backs. He announced that he was a retired Air Force sergeant and warned that he wouldn't tolerate slackers. Bill focused his beady eyes on me and suddenly grabbed the back of my neck with a sweaty hand. "College boy!" he screamed in my ear, yanking me over to the station's office door. Bending my head into a bow, he shoved it within inches of a sign on the door's bottom, screaming, "What does it say?"

I read the words out loud, "Bill Aloysius Daily, Manager."

He slammed my head into the door and yanked it back. "Are you stupid? What the fuck does it say, college boy!"

I was confused. My head was hurting, and the compression in my chest from bending over made it hard to breathe. He cocked his left middle finger against the side of my nose and brushed across it to point at the first letter, then the second and third letters. "What does that say, college boy?"

"B.A.D., sir!"

"That's right, asshole! BAD! And don't you ever forget it! Now get to work!"

The Standard Oil Company trained its service station attendants to sell accessories to customers. In the 1960s, gasoline was cheap, thirty-five cents a gallon, so there was greater profit in selling a quart of oil or a tire. Standard gave new hires a five-day course in sales techniques and taught us how to persuade customers to purchase accessories and services by looking for anything on their cars that might require maintenance—and then suggest remedies like oil changes, new tires, windshield wipers, or antifreeze. This sales training would prove helpful throughout my life.

The station attendants were expected to reach specific weekly and monthly sales goals. While there was no extra pay or reward for meeting or even exceeding the targets, Standard played on our competitiveness by posting the weekly sales totals for each employee. The side-by-side comparisons could be humiliating if your name was on the bottom of the list. Better to hustle customers than suffer needling by more successful peers. Attendants who lacked charm and an honest face had to rely on scams to meet their goals. "Short sticking" in a gas station had nothing to do with hockey. It was the practice of pulling the oil dipstick out of a hot engine while holding a rag and deftly removing enough oil from below the full line to make it appear to the customer that her car was a quart low. The perpetrator would hold the dipstick up to the driver's side window so the customer could see and launch into a spiel about the dangers of ruining an engine by driving with low oil. This worked on drivers' anxieties about crossing miles of hot desert, running out of engine fluids, and becoming stranded. It made sales easy. Once the victim agreed to purchase a quart of oil, the attendant would bring out an empty can, his rag covering the holes. He would set it on the ground in front of the car, out of the customer's sight, and insert the pouring spout into the existing holes. He would then make a show of pouring the contents into the engine. Customers never realized they had been fleeced.

I frequently had the best weekly sales. I was motivated because it was better to get a car up on a lift inside the service bays for changing oil or tires than to work outside in the blistering sun. It also kept Bill off my back. Bill and Woody were supposed to work alongside the rest of us, but instead, they sat in the shade outside the station, barking orders and insults. Since they couldn't see me from outside, I could work at my own pace. Exceeding the station's sales quotas also brought Bill and Woody kudos from Standard's upper management, another reason they left me alone while I was working on car tires and oil changes.

I worked the day shift for several weeks. The work was incessant, and the flow of cars never stopped. Unhappy drivers lined up for gas in the boiling desert sun, with their overtaxed engines and bug-splattered windshields, which they demanded to be cleaned while they ran to the restrooms with their kids. It took a lot of elbow grease to dislodge gooey remnants of bugs that had glued themselves to the glass. And after a day of dipping sponges into soapy water, my hands retained the sour smell of insect death that couldn't be washed away. It was amazing how the hot, barren desert could spawn so many flying bugs.

One afternoon, as I completed my shift, Bill and Woody called me into the office and announced they were moving me to the 10 p.m. to 6 a.m. night shift. They both smiled as if they were doing me a big favor. I was happy about the change because working at night would be less hot—and they wouldn't be around to harass and humiliate me. But I arrived the next evening at ten and discovered I would be the only person there. This was not just a violation of Standard's policy, which stated there should be several employees on night duty for security and safety reasons. It also meant that I would be running around all night pumping gas and cleaning windshields, while my sales quotas suffered from a lack of time working in the shop.

By the end of my first overnight shift, I was exhausted, and I was happy when Bill and Woody arrived at 6 a.m. But then, they called me into the office and said I couldn't leave because the night guy also had the responsibility of reconciling the station's books for the previous twenty-four hours.

"It should be easy for a college boy," Bill sneered. "And you won't get paid for doing it, so you better get moving!"

Reconciling involved counting all the credit card receipts and register cash, inventorying tires and oil cans, and dipping the four underground gasoline tanks. Dipping was a method of checking the amount of gasoline left in each tank. It involved opening the ground-level access ports, dropping a long pole to the bottom of the tank, and quickly lifting it out. The wet portion on the pole marked how much fuel remained in the tank. I wrote those figures on a worksheet and used them to reconcile the gallons sold and order tanker shipments to replenish the tanks.

It took me several hours to complete the tasks. I was dog-tired. It was difficult reconciling all of the credit card and cash receipts, but I added them three times until I was confident the results were correct. I handed this work to Bill. He looked it over and stared at me. "Stealing?" he said.

I was stunned by his accusation and decided it would be safer to say nothing.

"You're five dollars short. If you can't account for it, we are going to be taking it out of your pay."

Standard's starting wage was a dollar sixty an hour. Docking my pay five dollars meant I lost half my night's wages. And that didn't count the two unpaid hours I spent working on the books—a task the manager or assistant manager was supposed to do each day.

The same thing happened the next two days. There was money missing, my bosses said, and I was on the hook to make it up. On the fourth night, though, traffic was slow and I had time to reconcile the receipts before Bill and Woody showed up. This also gave me time to figure out what to do. The "shortages" were happening every day, and it was obvious something wasn't right. They had me working alone, which made me the fall guy for anything that went wrong and set me up to be fired or even arrested for stealing. It also seemed very likely that Bill and Woody were picking the till and using my pay to make up for it. I felt stuck. There weren't many jobs in the Coachella Valley, except in agriculture, and those didn't pay as well. I needed to save money to pay for college, so I couldn't quit. But I suddenly realized I didn't have to let them fleece me—there was a variable I could use to adjust the books in my favor. Oil cans and tires could be easily checked for inventory accuracy because they were sitting exposed on the station's shelves. On the other hand, measuring the gasoline levels was less precise, and the tanks were out of sight below ground. Bill and Woody were lazy and unlikely to want to breathe gas fumes in the heat of the day. And dipping the tanks was routinely done early in the morning before the heat rose, causing the gasoline to expand and making measurements less accurate. I knew they were happy to let me do it, and they would never bother to check my work.

Altering those numbers was feasible. The shortage that day was six dollars. Six dollars divided by 35 cents a gallon came to eighteen gallons. To balance the books, we'd have to "sell eighteen gallons more." I "adjusted" the tank levels by showing eighteen gallons of extra gas on the ledgers. Spread over four tanks, this amounted to only four and a half gallons per tank. I knew that while I was doing all the work of reconciling the station ledgers, Bill or Woody signed the reconciliation each day, so their superiors wouldn't know they had been forcing the tasks on me. If there was going to be trouble—and I knew it was coming—it would belong to them.

When Bill and Woody arrived in the morning, I showed them the balanced ledger. They exchanged surprised glances, which gave them away. Now I knew they were dirty.

I continued making adjustments for the rest of the week and wondered when they would discover what I had been doing. But judging by their bewildered glances at each other, I knew they couldn't figure it out. As I "balanced" the books for the rest of summer, Bill and Woody thought they had a good thing going. The till shortage amounts steadily increased. More and more phantom gasoline was on the books, while less was actually underground. Bill and Woody didn't learn the ramifications until a few days before I left work to return to college.

One morning, an auditor from Standard Oil arrived for a routine quarterly examination of the station's books. I had finished my shift, and instead of leaving, I decided to hang around and watch to see what would happen. The auditor finished counting oil and tires and took his clipboard and the dipstick out to the tanks. He unscrewed the first tank cover lid, dropped the stick in, and pulled it out. He looked at the stick and down at the clipboard and seemed confused. He lowered the stick into the tank again and compared results. He stood there for a long moment and then dipped the other tanks, each time checking and rechecking. I could see the expression on his face changing. Auditors live to find discrepancies that will justify their jobs. Bill and Woody watched out the station window looking increasingly worried.

The auditor finished, stood for a moment, apparently making up his mind, and walked with purpose back to the office. I watched as he showed them his measurements, pointing at the discrepancies on his worksheet. I already knew the tanks were more than 1,400 gallons short, and there was no logical way to explain this. Bill and Woody both looked stunned and fearful. Their signatures were on the station's books, making them solely responsible for the losses. Shortly afterward, both were fired. It made me appreciate that a college education enhanced one's ability to think of solutions and solve difficult problems.

College

I paid my way through the University of Redlands by continuing to pump gas throughout the summer. During the school year, I took a job as a preparator for the university art gallery, where I learned to install art, adjust lights, and inventory collections. Redlands is a small, conservative college with high academic standards, and I quickly realized that my high school education lagged behind the other students. I wound up concentrating on art because art classes were a way to keep my GPA high, and I loved learning about art techniques and history. Our course work took us through many painting and drawing methods in Ralph Mayer's *The Artist's Handbook of Materials and Techniques*—including outmoded techniques like silverpoint drawing and little-used mediums like egg tempera paints. By contemporary art standards, this was a dated, classical art education. But it became invaluable for later art handling and especially condition reporting—the art handler's "CYA" (Cover Your Ass!) mantra. Condition reporting is integral to surviving in the art moving business. It relies on a chain of documents tracking the custody of a work of art as it passes from its owner through multiple hands and shippers to a final destination. A condition report establishes what preexisting damages or changes were present in the artwork when someone in the chain received it. Thoroughness is critical because once the paperwork is signed, any damage or irregularity found becomes the potential responsibility of the art moving company. Numerous times, a painting has hung for years on a collector's wall with an existing damage issue. Perhaps someone brushed past it and left scuff marks. Or the cleaning lady's mop handle scratched it. Or the paint was cracking because the artist used improper techniques. Often the collector was shocked when I pointed out the flaw. In other cases, I've returned a painting or sculpture that had been away for some time in a traveling exhibition, and the collector noticed damage and demanded an insurance claim. Having an original condition report showing that the damage was old, not new, puts a stop to that.

However, despite all precautions taken, there will be instances where hidden condition problems come to light during handling and shipping. For example, one summer several years ago, my company transported a large, framed Roy Lichtenstein lithograph on paper from a collector's Malibu beach house to his home at a Rancho Mirage country club in the Coachella Valley. Several days later, the collector called me in an agitated state, saying the print was torn in two. It turned out the framer had incorrectly mounted it by gluing all four corners to a backboard. The beach air had been moist, and paper, being absorbent, had expanded. When the print was hung in the desert where the air was very dry, the paper contracted, and the glued corners prevented it from adjusting, so the print pulled apart.

I got my understanding of such basics in my undergrad classes. After Redlands, I went into the MFA program of Claremont Graduate School, which encompassed a small network of related campuses. In exchange for tuition, I'd be a teaching assistant in Scripps College printmaking classes. Claremont was quiet, and most of the art professors were on sabbatical or leave—except David Gray, a minimalist sculptor who taught courses at Pomona College. One of his undergraduate students, Chris Burden, gained renown as an experimental artist when he had himself intentionally shot in the arm. He also crucified himself on a Volkswagen Bug, with nails hammered through his hands, impaling him to the car's roof. But that came later. When I first encountered Burden on the Pomona College lawn, he was constructing a large, yellow minimalist sculpture. It was immediately clear that although he was still an underclassman, he was far more advanced as an artist than those of us working on MFAs.

Despite the presence of Gray and Burden, though, I found Claremont to be stupefying. So I talked my way into receiving a full-ride to transfer to the MFA program at the University of Southern California, where my real art world immersion began.

Dennis

Most people fail to recognize an opportunity when it is in front of them. Or they won't act—out of timidity or fear of failing. Opportunity is rare. It is even rarer to experience a series of events that, when linked together, end up being an invitation to a new world and a new possibility of success. But that's what I got when I roomed with a guy named Dennis, aka "Dead Hair." He was a fellow MFA student known for the wiry, kinky bush that stuck up from his head.

Dennis and I rented an apartment in a neighborhood known then as The Jungle. It was an area east of La Cienega Boulevard and just below Baldwin Hills. Hundreds of Black families lived there in dozens of cookie-cutter apartment buildings, all two stories high and built around a courtyard with a swimming pool. Successful Black men and women lived up in Baldwin Hills, while poorer families lived in The Jungle, and the even poorer ones lived in Watts—which was the site of the Watts riots several years earlier. We were the only two white guys around.

"Bob the Cop" and his chubby, light-skinned wife lived in the second-floor apartment directly across from ours. Bob was a Black LAPD patrol officer whose patrol beat included South Central Los Angeles, an impoverished area with a high crime rate. Before coming to LA, he had been fired from the Saint Louis PD. I never found out why, but I suspect the cause was his unstable, borderline psychotic personality. On warm weekends, Bob would lie on a chaise lounge by the pool in his bathing suit and a shoulder holster. Whenever he saw me walking by, he would pull out his gun, yell, "Hey Whitey!" and point the pistol at me, pulling the trigger multiple times screaming, "Bang! Bang! You're dead!" while laughing at his big joke. The pistol was unloaded, but what if he had forgotten to empty the chamber?

One afternoon, I came home to find five police cars parked at cockeyed angles in front, many with engines running and doors open. Cops were milling around in front of Bob's apartment, excitedly talking to his wife. They were looking for Bob, who had beaten a handcuffed suspect while on patrol in Watts and taken off in the patrol car with the suspect—leaving his partner alone on the street. The cops were trying to find him before he killed his prisoner. Whatever happened, I didn't see Bob again. And his wife moved out a few days later.

Staring down the barrel of Bob's pistol desensitized me to fear in later years when police aimed guns at me and clients spun out of control.

"Coping with cops and psychos" wasn't on the MFA curriculum, but maybe it should've been. It gave me graduate-level skills in functioning under duress, invaluable on the business end of art. I was getting other practical skills as well. Just as I had at Claremont and Redlands, I worked in the university galleries to pay my way through

USC. These jobs taught me the fine points of moving, tracking, and installing paintings and sculptures and sparked my interest in making a career in art handling.

Knowing I had that experience, my roommate Dennis asked me to help him deliver a large abstract canvas he sold to a woman living in Pacific Palisades. We carried it from the painting studios to his car and placed it face-up on the roof. I told Dennis we needed rope or clothesline to tie it on, but instead, he brought a ball of twine because it was cheaper. I was dubious and told him we should wait until we found some rope. When he insisted, I said I would have to wash my hands of the consequences.

We rolled down the car windows, ran a spiderweb of twine through the windows and around the painting's stretcher bars, and headed west on the I-10 freeway. We were speeding along at sixty miles per hour, and Dennis was happily chattering away when something caught my eye in the passenger-side mirror. The painting had gone airborne behind us. It briefly stuck upright against the grill of a following car before getting sucked underneath and flying out the rear. Other cars swerved, trying to avoid running it over. I opened my mouth to tell Dennis but realized he would likely jam on his brakes and jump onto the freeway to save his artwork, so I stayed quiet. Stopping was just too dangerous.

When we arrived at the house in Palisades, the buyer came out the front door to greet us. Dennis excitedly jumped out of the car, giving her a big smile and a wave before turning around to untie the painting. A look of bewilderment crossed his face as he realized it was gone. This taught me an important art handling lesson: movement causes damage. There is constant movement while carrying, trucking, and shipping works of art. To be successful, you have to mitigate that movement with proper packing and careful handling methods and techniques. For starters, rope, not twine. And maybe not tying the art to the roof at all.

Later, if somehow things went awry anyway, I knew I'd stick to my newly minted freeway rule: if the choice is between rescuing the art or saving yourself, all's forgiven if you choose yourself.

Hammer

Some rules of the art handling game seem clear enough—protect the work, keep records to keep yourself out of trouble—but some come in the form of unspoken "understandings" between parties that you blunder into at your peril. Which is how I wound up wrestling a painting out of the hands of Dr. Armand Hammer—founder of Occidental Petroleum and the UCLA Hammer Museum—at the USC Fisher Galleries, where I was a preparator.

Fisher Galleries was constructed in 1939 and named after the founding donor, Elizabeth Fisher. Elizabeth not only financed the building but also donated a few dozen Dutch and Flemish Old Master paintings to the university. One of her stipulations was that only her collection could be displayed in one of the galleries. It was never to be moved. I don't know if this was the cause of all the malaise, but the Fisher galleries were rundown and dingy. The lighting system, always a critical element for exhibiting art, hadn't been upgraded since the original 1930s construction. Instead of track lighting and floodlights, the galleries were woefully illuminated by incandescent light bulbs behind glass diffusion lenses mounted in a ceiling box in the center of each room. Making things worse, a number of the bulbs had burned out, and the ceiling height made it difficult to replace them, so maintenance and upkeep didn't happen very often. The brooding quality of light in the galleries was accentuated by a burlap wall covering—painted in layers of yellowing, off-white paint so thick the surface was lumpy.

Paintings were hung on rods that descended from a channel installed along the top of each wall, another old-fashioned installation system. Fluted green stone wainscoting covered the bottom portion of each wall in a band forty inches high. That may have been appropriate when paintings were small enough to carry under one's arm, but in the 1960s, enormous, billboard-sized art was coming out of New York, and the wainscoting ate so much wall space it got in the way of hanging anything of consequence. The architect's original intent was to give the galleries a Classical Greek appearance, keeping with the academic tastes of the period. But thirty years later, the overall effect was funereal and depressing.

When I was hired by the Fisher, the director, Dr. Roy Peck—a Second World War Army vet who had worked alongside the Monuments Men—assigned me to take inventory of the USC collections in the gallery's basement storage and the holdings that were placed in offices around the campus over the years. I started by looking at the inventory records, kept on three-by-five cards stored in metal file boxes. The handwritten, occasionally typed, information on each card was basic, giving a simple description of the artwork, donor's name, dates, and where an item had gone if it was on loan. I took the boxes with me to the basement art storage vaults, and over many weeks, I verified which art was still there and what condition it was in. I set aside notes indicating which paintings and objects had been loaned over the years. Some were on loan to various professors and administrators to hang in their offices, while other entire collections were being stored in university warehousing facilities—some of which were located off-campus in other areas of Los Angeles. If I couldn't find the artworks in the basement rooms, or there wasn't enough information indicating when and where they had gone, I added them to my notebook for later searching.

Once I finished the vault inventory, I attempted to track down the art on loan to faculty and administrators. Most of these loans transpired years and even decades earlier, and many of the borrowers had long since retired or passed away. Virtually none of the paintings remained in the original offices. In a few instances, I tracked down retired profs or their surviving relatives, but every single person denied knowledge of the missing art. Most of the former professors claimed to have left the art hanging in their offices when they had retired. A few questioned my authority to investigate and shut their doors in my face. Much of the missing work was mediocre, but some missing pieces had become very valuable.

Next, I visited the off-campus storage areas looking for the larger collections. One of the Fisher galleries had been named the Quinn Jade Gallery. The walls of that room were still lined with built-in glass showcases that once housed an extensive collection of exquisitely carved Chinese jade objects. While searching through the dusty file cabinets in the basement, I found black and white photographs of those beautiful jades as they'd originally been installed. The USC inventory records indicated that they had all been packed into dish-pack barrels and sent to off-campus storage around six years earlier. But the record did not include any receipts that could link the shipments to an individual at the storage warehouse. I went to the warehouse and asked if anyone knew about the jade, but no one responded, so I walked through the building looking everywhere without success.

Once I completed my inventory survey, it was painfully obvious that the USC art collections had been extensively looted, and the monetary losses were substantial. I couldn't help but notice the Old Master paintings donated to the university by Armand Hammer. It was recorded that nearly forty paintings had been given in the 1950s, including additional donations, typically single paintings since then. Nearly all measured less than three feet, and most were Dutch and Flemish, whose listed values were substantial. A number of the Hammer paintings were missing, some of which had been donated only a few years earlier. This alarmed me because it suggested that there had been recent art thefts and perhaps an insider with sticky fingers. But when I reported this to Dr. Peck, the gallery director, and his secretary Doris Kent, they didn't seem concerned.

Several weeks later, I was sitting alone guarding the galleries at lunchtime when someone began loudly pounding on the front door.

I grabbed the key and walked over, asking who was there. "Dr. Armand Hammer," an authoritative voice on the other side announced. I unlocked and opened the door. Standing on the other side was a gray-haired, balding man with a bulbous nose, conservatively dressed in a dark navy pin-striped suit with a burgundy tie. He briefly looked me over with owlish eyes behind black-rimmed glasses, then barged past and disappeared into a side gallery. I looked outside at his black limousine. It was illegally parked on the street, the rear door being held open by a muscular chauffeur dressed in full livery, including jodhpur pants, a multi-buttoned jacket, high riding boots, and a small peaked cap. I thought he looked ridiculous. He may have read my mind because the hard eyes staring back at me from under the cap's rim carried a hostile glint flashing "bodyguard" and a veiled threat: "Don't mess with me!" Not wanting to get too close to him, I locked the door and followed Dr. Hammer into the gallery, only to find that he was removing a painting from the gallery wall.

His audaciousness was shocking. He walked in like he owned the place and was helping himself to what he wanted.

"What are you doing?" I challenged him. "You can't take that painting."

He turned, painting in hand, and quickly walked past me toward the front door.

"Young man," he declared, "I own this painting, and I'm taking it."

I ran after him, wondering if I should tackle him, grab the artwork back, or call the cops. If I called the campus police, who were slow, he probably would have time to escape. If I attempted to wrestle the painting back from him, it could get damaged. I was in charge of protecting the collections, and how would I explain letting a valuable work walk out the door?

I tried to reason with him by saying, "The painting belongs to the university—you donated it!" This stopped him momentarily, and I could see confusion in his eyes as he pondered how a student would know about his past donations and what the possible ramifications would be if he took the painting. I reached for it, and he yanked it away, heading toward the door as we did a weird waltz— me reaching for the painting, first on his right and then on his left as he kept moving and twisting to hold it away. He lunged for the door and tried shouldering it open. Then, realizing it was locked, he turned back and angrily confronted me.

"Young man! You open this door immediately!"

He was tightly clutching the fragile, ornate frame in both hands, and I worried he would damage it, so I tried grabbing it again. He turned toward the door and stood holding the painting inches from it, with his back toward me to prevent me from getting it.

"Look, Dr. Hammer," I said, "you can't take the painting, and I'm not going to unlock the door until you take it back and rehang it on the wall."

After a long minute of blustering and threatening, he gave up, and with a look of resignation, walked back and rehung it. I escorted him to the entrance and let him outside. He turned back and yelled, "I am going to have you expelled from this university!"

The chauffeur was still waiting by the limo, and I quickly relocked the door, so I wouldn't have to deal with him too.

When Dr. Peck and Doris Kent returned from their lunch, I told them what had happened. They were shocked—not because Hammer grabbed the painting off the wall, but because I had stood in his way. Apparently, this was an accepted practice. He donated paintings to the USC collections, came to carry some of them back home, and the university had always turned a blind eye. Dr. Peck confided that Hammer would take a tax write-off for donating paintings with high appraised values, wait several years, and then retrieve them. USC went along with the arrangement, Peck said, because Hammer promised future donations, which the university didn't want to lose by offending him.

That was my introduction to the dance of perks and privileges that come with being a major donor or collector, but also to the man who, strangely enough, would become one of my earliest and most significant clients when I started my art moving business. Our wrestling match didn't seem like an opportunity then, but it might have been a premonition.

Cart & Crate

AFTER GRADUATING FROM USC, I found myself unemployed and living in my car. The federal equal opportunity employment laws had just been passed, and the teaching job offers I received from Kent State, Temple Tyler University, and Cal State Dominguez Hills were suddenly withdrawn and given to women or minorities. I was eating two meager meals a day to save money.

During the 1960s, most of the major art galleries in Los Angeles were on La Cienega Boulevard between Melrose and Santa Monica. On Monday evenings, they would host a "gallery walk" with free wine, cheese, and other finger foods, which took the edge off my hunger. Snacking in the Molly Barnes Gallery, I bumped into my old roommate Dennis. When I told him I needed a job, he said he was working at an art moving company called Cart & Crate. They were looking to hire an art handler. He would recommend me, he added. This was an opportunity I recognized.

The job interview was bizarre. The manager, Gene Kazor, had black eyes and hair, a heavy beard, and a sour, irritable disposition. He invited me into his office, where he sat with his back to the wall. I took a chair that faced both his desk and an open door to the outer office, where a woman with stumpy, varicose-tattooed legs worked behind a desk a few feet away. The desk didn't have a vanity front, and I could see that she was wearing a very short miniskirt with no underwear. She flashed me while demurely smiling. This was my rude and crude introduction to the business.

Most of the art handlers working at Cart & Crate were skilled people who took pride in their work, and I learned a lot from them. Many were artists like Dennis and me, and most of us were hippies. The office personnel were another matter. A quart mason jar full of pills—uppers, downers, and whatever—was kept on a shelf for the office personnel to help themselves, and many seemed stoned each day. It was the end of the 1960s, and a lot of people were experimenting with drugs, some of them ruining their lives as a result. The paperwork the bleary office staff handed us was often incorrect. On one occasion, two of us drove all the way to Santa Barbara, ninety miles away, only to find that the bill of lading should have said Santa Monica. It was an excellent education on how not to run a business, which served me well when I started my company.

John

One of the old-timers at Cart & Crate was an art handler named John, who was a bit eccentric. The first thing you'd notice about him were his glasses, octagonal-shaped and held in place with thin wire rims. The thick plastic lenses were always covered with fingerprints and smudges, making it difficult to see his eyes. And the frames were usually bent out of shape, causing them to sit topsy-turvy on the bridge of his nose. For some unknown reason, the right lens had yellowed, adding to his crazy "gear-loose goose" appearance. I wondered how he viewed the world through the mess attached to his face. John had shoulder-length brown hair and a heavy beard. The hair was often dull and lifeless, and his expression was similar— deadpan and rarely showing any emotion.

I was assigned to work with him during my first couple of weeks of employment so he could train me, and from him, I got an unforgettable look at how badly things can go wrong in this business. Our first assignment was to drive to the La Jolla Museum of Art, pick up works from an exhibition, and return them to multiple lenders. I arrived at work on time, but John had not shown up. After half an hour, Gene, the brooding and surly manager, handed me the truck keys and ordered me to go to John's house in Echo Park.

I drove from West Los Angeles to the house—a small, decrepit, Craftsman-style bungalow. I walked across the squeaky porch and knocked on the front door. This caused an uproar inside of barking dogs, crying children, and a woman shouting for quiet. I backed up a few steps as John's wife Gloria opened the door, and immediately several scruffy, growling mutts attempted to lunge past her legs toward me. She cursed and began kicking the dogs out of the way. She wore a faded brown robe that covered a pink negligée, and a set of pink curlers adorned her head. A lit cigarette hung from her lips. As she stood glaring at me, a clump of tobacco ash separated and gently spiraled down, landing near a big toe sticking out of a pink slipper. I watched its path downward and noticed that the pink polish on her toes was worn and uneven. Three young children poked their heads around her butt, excited that the monotony of their morning routine had been disrupted. She knew why I was there but stared unforgivingly, waiting for me to make the first move.

"Is John here?" I asked in as polite a tone as I could muster.

"No!" she yelled. "How the hell would I know where he is? Sonofabitch didn't come home last night! Try the garage!"

She slammed the door in my face, and the dogs began barking. I heard a yelp as she kicked them again.

I opened the side gate and carefully walked back toward the garage, keenly aware of the dogs and worried that Gloria would open the back door and turn them loose. The garage was an old wooden structure, a relic dating from the Model T era. It was even more dilapidated than the house and listed to the right, which caused the two wooden doors to shift out of alignment. One was jammed into the ground and looked like it hadn't been opened in years. The other rode high enough to let me swing it open.

My eyes began adjusting to the gloom, and in a few moments, I saw the outline of what had to be John lying in a fetal position on the concrete floor. He was covered with sheets of newspaper for warmth against the morning chill. He didn't move, and for a brief second, I thought he was dead.

"John! Hey, wake up, John! Wake up!"

He groaned and rolled onto his knees, slowly rising off the floor. I detected a whiff of stale beer.

"Come on, John, we have to drive down to La Jolla, and it's getting late."

He stumbled outside, covering his eyes against the glare of bright sunshine. "Can you believe the fucking bitch locked me out? What the hell's wrong with her? Goddammit! I need some coffee!"

I drove the truck to a nearby donut shop and waited until John grabbed a cup of coffee. We headed south on the Santa Ana Freeway, and John sat in the passenger seat, sullenly staring at the floor of the truck, saying nothing until we were passing through Anaheim. He looked up, suddenly alert.

"Get off at the next ramp and turn right!"

I followed his directions to an industrial park, the kind that has small abutting units with roll-up garage doors. We parked next to one and walked inside. This was Doug's studio. Doug was an artist friend of his and a former classmate from Otis Art Institute. John didn't introduce me, and Doug didn't look my way. They began talking, and after a few minutes, Doug walked over to a shoulder-high shelf, reached behind some cans of paint, and pulled out a small metal film canister. He spooned some white powder onto the shelf and began chopping it with a razor blade. After dividing it equally into a couple of lines, they took turns snorting through a straw. When they were done, he chopped more cocaine with the razor blade. The loading door to the parking lot was still wide open, and we were in the heart of Republican John Birch Orange Country. I decided it would be safer to wait outside.

Twenty minutes later, John walked out. He was amped up. "Give me the keys," he said. "I'm driving."

It was late morning, and we were way behind schedule. John drove the truck toward San Diego with intensity and concentration. I later found out he road-raced motorcycles, and when I crewed for him once at a raceway, I saw the control he would exert on a bike speeding around the winding track. He may have been high, but his concentration remained solid.

We arrived in La Jolla and backed into the museum loading dock. The museum, which has since been renamed the San Diego Museum of Contemporary Art, was on a bluff overlooking the beach. While the main entrance faced the street, the loading dock was behind the museum on a lower level facing the ocean. It was a beautiful location. The sun was shining, and in the distance, we could see surfers bobbing in the sparkling water waiting for the next perfect wave.

Mary was the museum registrar. She was sweet, smart, and never took long between cigarettes. She greeted us warmly in her raspy smoker's voice and apologized that her co-workers were not around to help us load the artwork. I could tell John was unhappy that our job was going to take longer.

Mary led us inside the loading dock and down a hallway. We followed it to a corridor that ended at the roll-up of the museum's art storage vault. Mary opened the vault and began showing us the artworks, which were sitting on shelves lining the vault walls. She started checking items off an inventory list while we carried them out to our truck and secured them for our trip back.

It was a long list, and walking between the storage vault and our truck took time. John kept glancing at his watch, becoming agitated. "Come on! Come on! Get a move on it!" he whispered in a low voice. I knew he was worried that if we got back to West Los Angeles late, Gene Kazor would get pissed off. I was a new employee and didn't want trouble with my boss, but I also didn't want to damage any art by mishandling it.

We were about halfway loaded when Mary said she needed to make a call in her office, which I took as meaning she wanted to smoke. She handed John the inventory list and left us alone.

As soon as she left, John began running back and forth to the truck carrying paintings and small sculptures. I struggled to keep up, being careful not to drop a work of art. We were both gasping for breath when we located the last piece, which lay wrapped in moving blankets on a shelf. It was a large sculpture, a long piece of cast glass, wedge-shaped like a paper airplane—a thirty-six by twelve by seventy-two-inch-long diamond that tapered to a sharp point at one end. It was also heavy—at least 100 pounds.

We retrieved a four-wheel furniture dolly from our truck and carefully balanced the sculpture on top. Balancing meant that the heavier end was centered on the dolly while the lighter tapered portion stuck further out. We began rolling it into the hallway. The dolly was only eight inches high, and the sculpture sat low to the ground. This forced us to crabwalk alongside while awkwardly stooping over to keep a hold of it.

"Hurry! Hurry up! We gotta get going!" John ordered. And with a crazed look he began shoving the sculpture faster down the hall. His boots loudly slapped the tiled floor, and the sound echoed in the hallway. The tapered end of the sculpture was sticking out four feet in front of the dolly, and every shove caused it to lurch back and forth. I desperately hung on, trying to keep up, fearful the sculpture was going to fall. We neared the end of the corridor, where it turned left to the loading dock, and I could see we were going too fast to safely make the turn.

"John! We need to slow down! Come on, John, take it easy," I begged him.

Too late, John realized the point was going to swerve into a wall and tried to correct the dolly's direction by grabbing the tapered end. This caused the sculpture to abruptly swivel and slide off the dolly. It hit the floor, breaking into two pieces.

John stared down at it for a moment. "Fuck!" He leaned over. "Give me a hand!"

We loaded the two pieces back on the dolly.

"Hurry, Goddammit! Hurry! Hurry!"

We rushed back to the storage room and placed both parts of the sculpture back on the shelf, carefully fitting the pieces together and covering them with a blanket. John looked at the museum's inventory list and began counting, "Fifty-six pieces total." He took a pen and wrote fifty-five pieces on our bill of lading, and we walked to the registrar's office to find Mary. My stomach was churning while I tried to look as nonchalant as possible. John was expressionless as Mary signed our bill of lading receipt. She thanked us for doing a great job and waved with a big smile on her face as we walked to our truck and drove away.

Although I was only a trainee, I always felt guilty about what happened. Ten years later, I called Mary to apologize. She thought it was a hilarious story and roared with laughter.

John didn't seem to suffer from guilt, no matter how egregious his actions could be. Whenever I worked with him, the conversations weren't about his kids and certainly not about his wife, Gloria. They were always about his three dogs, especially Charlie. Charlie was the smartest dog, the leader, the alpha male dominating the other mutts. John always had funny, heartwarming stories about the cute things his dogs had done the evening before. "I love those dogs," he would often say with pride.

Then one day, while we were driving to a customer's house, he casually mentioned his family was moving over the weekend, and the landlord there didn't allow animals. I thought about the dogs and wondered what he would do with them. On a Monday, we teamed up on another project, and while John drove our truck, I asked about the dogs, expecting to hear he had found good homes for them. He chuckled.

"You wouldn't believe how funny it was," he said. "I put the three of them in my pickup truck and drove to the top of Topanga Canyon. We all got out, and I grabbed a ball and threw it down the hill. Charlie took off chasing after it, and the other two were trying to keep up with him. Charlie was always the fastest! I jumped into my truck and took off down the other side of Topanga. I thought I had lost them, but when I looked in the rearview mirror, there they were . . . right behind my truck. I kept driving faster, and they ran faster. I was almost at the bottom of the canyon when I finally lost them!" I was stunned by this admission.

Another time, after delivering an exhibition to the UC Berkeley Art Museum, John drove to a sleazy bar he knew in Oakland and ordered beers. There were a bunch of drunk Hells Angels in the place, playing 8-Ball on a small, threadbare pool table and cursing at each other. I kept my eyes averted to avoid eye contact, which was difficult because there were attractive young women hanging around, all wearing Hells Angels colors to show who they "belonged to." They all had big breasts—which must have been a requirement for hanging with the bikers.

A dumpy, middle-aged woman came in the door and sat down on the stool next to John. After spending less than five minutes talking with her, he announced we were leaving. The three of us walked out to our truck. John opened the rear doors, climbed into the cargo box, and leaned over to help her up. He tossed me the keys.

"You drive!" he ordered. "Lock us in and let us out when you get to LA."

I did as instructed and drove south all night. It was dawn when I opened the rear doors. The woman climbed down without saying a word and walked away.

John's general philosophy seemed to be *always keep moving*—letting the chips, art, and consequences fall where they may. Stories about him were legion. On another trip, he was delivering a Wayne Thiebaud painting to a residence near the town of Delta, a small farming community in the Sacramento River Delta. He arrived after sundown. Streetlights in this rural area were scarce, and he had taken several wrong turns in the darkness before locating the mailbox at the end of the consignee's driveway. He decided to reconnoiter the area, parking his truck on the side of the main road and walking down a long driveway to the house. It was a beautiful Victorian home with an expansive covered porch that stretched across the front and curved around the sides. He could see wicker furniture on the porch.

There were no lights on inside or out, indicating no one was home. So John walked back to the main road in the dark. He decided to wait for the homeowners to return and began slowly backing his truck through the gate and down the driveway. Suddenly he heard a loud crunch and the truck jolted. He had run into something. John stopped, jumped down, and walked behind the truck. He had hit the corner post supporting the veranda roof. The post was cracked and splintered but still standing upright—so he decided it would be prudent to leave before the owners returned.

As John pulled the truck away, he heard a rumbling sound, followed by a loud crashing and splintering wood. He stopped and walked back again. The entire porch roof had collapsed, demolishing the outdoor furniture along with sections of the porch railing.

John drove to the nearby small town and found a bar. After nursing some beers for a couple of hours, he called the house from a payphone, and the homeowner answered. In the background, John heard the growling whine of chainsaws. He identified himself and said he wanted to deliver the painting.

"Not now, son!" said the homeowner, agitated and excitedly yelling over the background commotion. "You will need to come back another time. We have a real emergency here! Our porch collapsed from termites! We are damn lucky it happened when we weren't home, or we could have been killed!"

John's quick and dirty style meant that whenever I worked with him, we were never too far from trouble—even on the incidental side jobs we did, like a quick wall-painting gig at the Irving Blum Gallery. Blum represented a roster of blue-chip and soon-to-be blue-chip artists. After we made a delivery there, Irving mentioned he was closing the gallery for the summer and offered each of us $100 to paint it over the weekend. He let us in on Saturday morning and left us to it. Since I had more patience than John, I did the fastidious brushwork while he rolled the walls. The gallery had been emptied of art, but as I worked under the reception counter, I bumped into an Andy Warhol soup can wastebasket where someone had overlooked four rolled drawings by Richard Serra and Carl Andre, which stuck out of the can. I set the can aside to get it away from my wet paint and kept working.

At noon, John wanted to leave to get food. I thought he'd take too long, so I told him I would go instead. When I returned and we finished eating, I crawled back under the counter and noticed the soup can was empty. John had found it, and without looking, he had laid the drawings on the floor to catch paint drips from his roller. The drawings were ruined, and Blum kept our pay.

Malcolm

Another memorable Cart & Crate character, out of many, was Malcolm. Malcolm had a big mop of long curly red hair and was in the US illegally from England. He had been given a free plane ticket to Canada in exchange for working in a logging camp for two years, but after six months, he decided it was too hard and ran away to Los Angeles. He'd taken up with a fifteen-year-old girl and crashed at the apartment of a rock band he befriended. The band members were shooting heroin, Malcolm became addicted, and one day came back to the apartment to find the band had moved out without telling him, likely tired of his mooching. Forced to go cold turkey, Malcolm installed a padlock on a closet door and told his girlfriend to lock him in for a week and not let him out, no matter how much he begged. He got himself off the heroin, and like many addicts, rebounded to another extreme by only eating foods purchased at a health food store. He got a job with Cart & Crate, and after working for six months, he heard his girlfriend's mother was actively searching for her. Malcolm began looking for an escape plan. He learned that Australia was recruiting workers to emigrate there and would provide documents, a job, and a free one-way plane ticket in exchange for a work commitment. Malcolm signed up to go.

Like many Englishmen, Malcolm had bad teeth, likely made worse by his heroin use. In preparation for his new life, he made his first trip to a dentist in many years, where he learned his mouth would need months of extensive work. He was only five weeks away from his escape to Australia, so he decided to pull all of his teeth, get fitted with dentures, and be gone before the bill arrived. One morning, he came to work with his face so badly swollen his head was pear-shaped, and he had difficulty talking. As days progressed before his departure, the swelling began to subside, but he was running out of time and insisted on being measured for his false teeth before he had fully recovered. They fit at first, but as the swelling went down, the dentures got so loose they were prone to falling out when he stooped down to pick up a work of art or crate. One day, we were wrapping a painting and had it lying flat across a work table when Malcolm sneezed, sending his teeth skittering across the painted surface. Luckily, they didn't cause any damage—as it would have been difficult explaining to an insurance adjuster that the painting was bitten by false teeth. A few days later, Malcolm and his girlfriend left for Australia, narrowly missing a bill collector who wanted cash for the loose chompers and the girl's mother, who'd come to look for her.

Butler

In the five years I worked for Cart & Crate, we moved many seminal works of art and exhibitions. We worked for brilliant artists, some who became mainstays—not only of the art world—but of my career as I moved or installed their work again and again. One of the weirdest and smelliest jobs I had was picking up dozens of suitcases filled with cheese from the downtown produce market on Central Avenue. I delivered them to Eugenia Butler Gallery on La Cienega, where Dieter Roth turned it into his singular 1970 work, *Staple Cheese.* Eugenia was a fascinating woman who often told us stories about being a Marine Corps master sergeant. At first, I thought she was putting us on, but she *had* been a tough-ass Marine, as well as a mother of eight and an avid collector with an incredible intellect. She found and exhibited great talent—people like John Baldessari—who were at the vanguard of LA's vibrant, creative art scene. She championed conceptual art with exhibitions that were far ahead of her time when Los Angeles was still a backwater compared to New York. *Staple Cheese* and shows like it were pure Eugenia innovation.

We found Dieter and his cheese-stuffed array of luggage at the wholesale market, where it was already beginning to smell pretty ripe. When we got everything to the gallery, he showed us where to put the cases, telling us to open some of them to expose the fast-rotting cheese. The suitcases were so heavy and full of cheese I was concerned they would burst their seams, or the handles would fail and yank out. If a suitcase full of smelly cheese came apart, would it be considered damaged art? To avoid that possibility, we grabbed the cases in bear hugs, and soon our clothes reeked. Each time we opened one, the stench was like a slap in the face. The off-gassing made our eyes water and sting, and our sinuses itched. We began to sneeze and had to run outside to gulp fresh air. It was tough, exhausting work, in part because it took so much effort to hold down our retching. I remember thinking how amazing and audacious this show was. But I also wondered what collector would be willing to purchase it and stink up his house. Would a buyer take the whole reeking arrangement home or purchase a license to recreate it? It often seemed that Eugena Butler was more interested in the art and the artists than profits. The health department tried to shut down the show, but it bowed to the pressure of Eugenia's lawyer—her husband—who argued that it should remain open because of its artistic merit.

For some, *Staple Cheese* was a hard taste to acquire. But it had a powerful impact on artists like Allen Ruppersberg, who told *KCET* in a 2011 interview that he considered it to be "one of the main works that was ever shown here in LA, period, and certainly is in all the memories of the artists who were there at the time." I was knocked out by the effect of it—and I'll never forget the smell.

Kienholz

Ed Kienholz had such an active presence in the Los Angeles art world that I crossed paths with him repeatedly. He was always intense—I rarely saw him laugh or smile—and he reminded me of a simmering volcano, ready to explode at any moment. There is an oft-told story of how Ed and his first wife, Lynn, purchased a Tiffany lamp in New York City and wanted to carry it on their return flight to Los Angeles but were forced by Trans World Airlines to check it in baggage. By the time they arrived at LAX, the lamp was smashed. When Kienholz couldn't get satisfaction from the airline after repeated attempts, he took matters into his own hands. Accompanied by a photographer and reporter from the *LA Times*, he marched into TWA's offices at the Los Angeles Airport with a double-bladed lumberman's axe and chopped the company president's desk into kindling. The resulting bad publicity caused TWA to pay for the lamp.

Ed was unflappable, with the kind of single-mindedness that let him tune out anything but his focus of the moment. When his seminal piece *Barney's Beanery* was being moved out of his Hollywood Hills compound—which stood high on a hill overlooking La Cienega Boulevard—portions of it were too large to fit through the doors of his house. The piece was a walk-in assemblage that recreates the look, sounds, and smells of the Beanery—an artists' hangout. He filled it with sculptures of customers, who all have clocks for faces. To move the sculpture's oversize sections, a crew had to lift them out of an inner courtyard, set them on the roof of the house, hand-carry them across it, and lower them to the ground on the other side. While all this was going on, Ed was in his living room meeting with a critic from the *New York Times* and several museum curators. They were sitting around a coffee table when one of the art handlers fell through a skylight and crashed onto the table, demolishing it and scattering coffee cups. Kienholz didn't blink an eye and continued talking as if nothing happened.

When Cart & Crate shipped *Barney's Beanery* to the Stedelijk Museum in Amsterdam in the 1970s, I vividly remember packing the crates amid the odors of stale mustard and cigarette ashes mingled with the chemical-smelling resins Ed coated everything with. He'd somehow managed to capture the distinctive olfactory qualities of a cheap dive bar, making the piece even more powerful. But in 2019, an art handlers' conference—for the professional association cleverly known as PACCIN: Preparation, Art Handling, Collections Care Information Network—took me to Amsterdam, and I had a chance to pay homage to the *Beanery*. It looked great, but the smells were gone, and the piece didn't seem complete. I mentioned this to the Stedelijk registrar, suggesting that the museum try to reintroduce the "scent profile" of the *Beanery* as Kienholz had intended, but she looked at me like I was either nuts or pulling her leg.

I first met Kienholz in 1970, when Cart & Crate sent me to pick up a framed drawing for an art collecting client. It was one of a series of drawings he had produced that acted as forms of currency. Each one described a tool or object Kienholz wanted, and if you gave it to him, you received the drawing as payment. It was hard to tell if he created the pieces as a tongue-in-cheek joke or if he was serious. To me, the process didn't seem equitable because a three-dollar screwdriver could be traded for a drawing worth $750. But Kienholz enjoyed it.

I lugged the collector's end of the exchange—a chainsaw still in its box—up to Kienholz's front door, and when I set it down inside, he handed me a chainsaw drawing. It had a zinc galvanized steel frame, adding to its utilitarian appearance, and said "Chainsaw" in penciled lettering that was traced on using a stencil. I noticed a label on the back stating that the art could not be altered or restored without the artist's authorization. It also said that if a collector resold the artwork, the artist would be entitled to ten percent of the sales price. This seemed to be a novel idea, and I talked with him about it for several minutes.

Years later, I sold one of my paintings to the Long Beach Museum of Art and decided to attach a similar label to the back before delivering it. After months passed without payment, I finally called the museum's director, who said the museum wouldn't pay unless I removed the label. I refused to comply, and more silent months passed. The next time I went to Kienholz's studio, I mentioned the stalemate. "Those sons of bitches!" he growled while grabbing his phone. He called his attorneys, telling them to represent me and, if necessary, litigate over the artists' rights issue. "Sue the bastards and send me the goddamn bill!" he said. It turned out to be one of the luckiest moments in my life. His law firm was Alexander, Inman, Kravitz, and Tanzer, located on Wilshire Boulevard in Beverly Hills, and they assigned me a newly minted, Harvard-educated attorney named Lowell Wedemeyer.

In 1973, we sued the city of Long Beach, which had jurisdiction over the museum. While awaiting trial, I began hearing from other artists who had not been paid by the museum for their paintings. This made me suspect the director could be pocketing the proceeds. My actions apparently shone an unexpected light on the issue, and after the trial, he was let go. But there was an unexpected downside to filing the suit. Some local art collectors and dealers let me know they were unhappy about the artists' rights idea. They were concerned it could complicate their ability to sell their art, adversely affecting its value. Raising the issue made me a troublemaker, which had a chilling effect on the marketability of my art.

When we got to trial, the judge and city attorney spent the first twenty minutes discussing their golf game while they kept us waiting. When they finished reminiscing, the judge turned in his seat to stare at me, remarking about my red hair and beard while the city attorney smirked. We argued the legalities, but the obviously biased judge ruled against us.

However, Lowell became my lifetime lawyer, friend, and true guardian angel. Kienholz's generosity had given me a connection to a law firm that understood art battles and was willing to take them on. These were the big guns who had represented Ed in 1966 when one of the Los Angeles County supervisors, Warren Dorn, threatened to cut off funding for the museum if it didn't remove his "offensive" sculpture *Back Seat Dodge* from an exhibition.

Back Seat Dodge was a 1938 Dodge sedan that Kienholz had shortened by removing a section from its middle and part of the engine compartment. The truncated Dodge was coated in blue flocking, putting it in the same sleazy oeuvre as a painting on velvet of a big-busted nude that might hang in a cheap bar. It sat with headlights on to suggest a night scene. When you opened the car's door, the interior light came on, so you would see a couple engaged in sex in the back seat. This made viewers into voyeurs caught between powerful tugs of curiosity and pulls of guilt about sneaking a peek, and it caused the timid to avert their gaze out of embarrassment.

The controversy over whether *Back Seat Dodge* should be shown was framed as a free speech issue in the media. The supervisors eventually reached a settlement with Kienholz and LACMA, who agreed to post a guard on stand-by to open the car door upon request. This compromise, overseen by the legal minds at Alexander, Inman, Kravitz, and Tanzer, was supposed to keep children innocent and old people from being offended. I visited the exhibition several times but found that having a guard witness my "voyeurism" made me uncomfortable. Was I feeling guilty? At least I had the opportunity to squirm.

Years later, my company, Cooke's Crating, crated and stored *Back Seat Dodge* for LACMA. Whenever I walked past the crate, I would stop and touch it out of remembrance for Ed and silently commune with a remarkable and important piece of art and free-speech history.

Though I lost my own Kienholz-inspired-and-financed suit, it was notable as it was the first time artists' rights to resale profits had been tested in the courts, and the files for the case earned a place in the archives of the Museum of Modern Art. Artists' rights briefly gained ground when the California Resale Royalty Act became law in 1977. But in 2018, the law was overturned by an appeals court that found it conflicted with copyright laws, effectively killing it. There's potentially good news on the horizon, though, in the form of NFTs. NFTs attach artworks to contracts kept in a digital ledger that can be programmed to pay the artist a royalty whenever the work is resold. That might finally help artists realize the long-held dream of sharing in the appreciating value of their work. I can just see Ed Kienholz minting up NFTs and handing them out like candy in trade for tools.

Marcia

Art was a passion and a family preoccupation for Marcia Weisman. While she collected modern pieces, including important post-war abstract paintings—her brother, Norton Simon, had amassed an encyclopedic collection of pre-war and Renaissance masterpieces that rivaled the best in the world, housing them in his namesake museum. Marcia had strong and confident tastes of her own, but occasionally, I got a glimpse of just how competitive she was with her brother.

I was installing an Andy Warhol painting in Marcia's living room when she took a call from a friend and learned that the French ambassador's wife wanted to visit the Norton Simon Museum but was turned away because the museum was closed that day. Marcia got the Frenchwoman on the phone and—after complaining that Norton should have opened up for someone "as highly placed as an ambassador's wife"—invited her over to see her "very important" collection. The woman arrived, probably expecting to see Old Masters, and seemed bewildered by the Clyfford Stills, Warhols, and other art she didn't understand.

I once heard it was actually Norton who helped Marcia gain the wherewithal to buy pieces like her briefly held Richard Serra. When she married Frederick Weisman, Norton introduced Fred to a Japanese auto manufacturer called Toyota, which was beginning to import small Japanese automobiles into the United States. With Norton's help, Fred landed a long-term franchise for the Mid-Atlantic states—receiving a percentage of the purchase price every time a Toyota sold in that region. Fred and Marcia invested their new wealth into contemporary art.

When Cart & Crate sent me to Marcia's, I could see she had a genuine love for art and a discerning eye. She could tell when a painting was an eighth of an inch too high on one side and demanded total perfection. Her wit was as sharp as her eye, and her tongue was even sharper. I once stopped by her house and found her standing outside berating the gardener because the lemon tree didn't have any lemons. She always greeted workers with a put-down. We'd show up in our Cart & Crate orange smocks, which felt demeaning enough as uniforms even before they turned pink with repeated washings, and Marcia couldn't resist a dig: "Here come those big strong men wearing those pretty little pink dresses!"

She could also be quite cavalier dealing with artists, even important ones, especially when it came to money. She took it for granted that they would put up with her out of fear of losing a sale, which is likely why she had so badly misjudged Richard Serra.

On one visit to her Beverly Hills home, I noticed a red, parabolic resin disk by DeWain Valentine lying flat on her dining room table. DeWain's disks are transparent and meant to stand upright so the light can pass through. Coincidentally, DeWain called a few minutes later, and I gathered from Marcia's responses that he was trying to sell her the sculpture. "Six thousand dollars is a lot of money, DeWain—for a salad bowl!"

I couldn't hear the reply, but Marcia went on, "It is a very pretty salad bowl, but I can buy a fabulous Baccarat salad bowl from Neiman Marcus for a lot less money." She listened for a few moments, "That's a little better, but it's still a lot of money, DeWain."

When I returned several weeks later, the "salad bowl" was still lying on the dining room table, but Marcia had a new idea. "Can you drill a hole in it and hang it on the wall?" she asked me. "It will look really wonderful hanging in my bathroom!" She was serious—until I told her a hole would ruin it.

I was with Alan McCollum when Marcia agreed to purchase his first painting for $1,200. Alan started working at Cart & Crate several months earlier, arriving at work each day in bell-bottoms, black and white tennis shoes, and a tie-dyed T-shirt. He was young and lanky and had a mop of long, brown shoulder-length curls that bounced in rhythm with his walk.

It may have been Frank Stella's *Union Pacific* paintings that inspired him to use Rit dye to tint white linen handkerchiefs he purchased at a thrift store a dark blue, and afterward, use bleach to add white stripes. Alan, who would later become an influential New York artist, didn't have the same art school pedigrees as many of his art handling co-workers—which was probably a good thing because his head wasn't full of art theory and limitations. He had a clean slate for creating art.

Alan kept several variations of his striped hankies in his pocket and would show them to collectors and gallery owners at every opportunity. He got them out while we were working at Marcia's house, and she liked them, so he gave her a couple. Soon after, she commissioned a thirty-six-by-sixty version for $1,200, a princely sum for minimum-wage workers like us. We were in awe of his good fortune and also slightly jealous. Several weeks later, Alan completed the painting, and the Cart & Crate dispatcher assigned a couple of us to accompany Alan as he delivered it. We had it in our truck and were preparing to depart when one of the office secretaries ran out to tell Alan that Marcia was on the phone and asking about her $1,000 painting. Allan went in to talk with her and returned to the truck. But just before we left, the same secretary ran out to tell us that Marcia called again to remind us to be very careful with her $800 painting.

As we carried the painting up her walkway, Marcia opened her front door for one more markdown. "Hello, boys!" she called. "Be very, very careful with my $600 painting!"

I glanced at Allan. He looked disappointed but didn't protest. We installed the painting, and Marcia stood admiring it as she handed Allen a check. "That's the best $500 painting I ever bought!" she exclaimed. Allan took the check without any comment but "Thanks"—which was smart because he soon sold more paintings to Marcia's friends, which launched his career as an artist.

Marcia owned a lot of art, but she could be careless about work she hadn't yet paid for, which was true for as long as I knew her. I was running my own business when the artist, John McCracken, asked me to pick up one of his sculptures from Marcia's home and deliver it to his studio. McCracken told me Marcia had been borrowing the sculpture to see if she liked it enough to purchase. After keeping it for nearly a year, she called him to complain that it was developing cracks in its corners. McCracken sculptures are refined minimalist cubes and planks, painted in layers of polished automotive paint over plywood interior cores. They definitely do not look good with cracks.

When I arrived with one of my employees, Marcia directed us to the backyard, where we found a bright yellow McCracken pillar, thirty inches square and sixty inches high. McCracken's resin work is intended to be displayed indoors and should never be exposed to the elements, but this one was baking in the sun. It rested directly on the lawn and had some scratches around the bottom where the gardener's weed trimmer had gotten too close. I could see vertical cracks running down the corner edges on all four sides.

We attempted to lift the pillar, but it wouldn't budge. This was unusual because McCracken's are hollow and don't weigh much. For a brief moment, we thought it had been bolted in place or filled with concrete. Together, we tried pushing against the top, and with effort, were able to tilt it. But when it fell back, loud sloshing sounds came from inside. It was full of water. I had seen this happen with outdoor bronze sculptures kept moist by lawn sprinklers. As the sculpture heated in the sun and cooled at night, a vacuum would form, gradually siphoning moisture inside through pinholes and small cracks. Over time, drops added up to gallons.

I called McCracken and asked him what we should do. "Drill a hole in the goddamn thing and drain it," he said, furious that the piece had been left outside. "Are you sure?" I asked.

"It's a piece of junk now, so don't worry about it," he said, hanging up.

I was reluctant to drill too large a hole, so we used a small bit, and a sparkling arc of water shot out. The yellow sculpture gave it a golden hue, and it reminded me of one of those Roman fountains decorated with slightly obscene peeing putti sculptures. We sat on the lawn for over an hour, watching it drain before we could load it on our truck.

McCracken was a good guy. He was one of the many Los Angeles artists I worked with and liked and whose art I admire. Some artists have a hard-edged personality that makes them difficult to approach, particularly when they think you're just a delivery boy. Some take out their frustrations with collectors or circumstances on you. But fortunately, there are also artists like McCracken, who are down-to-earth and approachable. I've enjoyed working not just with him but with Larry Bell, Ron Davis, Ed Moses, Judy Chicago, Bob Irwin, DeWain Valentine, John McLaughlin, Ron Davis, Betty Saar, Mark Bradford, and many others.

One of the kindest was Richard Diebenkorn. I got to know him when I was his studio assistant for several years after he hurt his back. That was a period when I was supplementing my art handling work with other art gigs. I stretched and primed Diebenkorn's *Ocean Park* series, mixed paints, cleaned brushes, and even cleaned the ashtray he kept on the table alongside his brushes. We would pack brown bag lunches and take turns bringing in bottles of California Cabernets—which we consumed on a saggy couch covered with a threadbare truck blanket and discussed the current painting hung on the wall in front of us. We talked art in general and often circled back to Matisse, who Diebenkorn greatly admired. Matisse books were scattered around, and Diebenkorn thumbtacked images of his work to the studio walls. I was still barely making minimum wage working for Cart & Crate, but I asked if I could have a painting in lieu of money. He let me sort through hundreds of drawings and paintings, giving me one I continue to cherish and have loaned to MOMA, LACMA, and the Royal Academy in London for shows.

Years later, at the opening of a big Diebenkorn retrospective at the Museum of Contemporary Art, I was walking around looking at the paintings when I saw him in a wheelchair talking to Eli Broad and several other VIPs, including the MOCA's director. He spotted me and began loudly calling my name, waving me over. He turned away from the others, and when they were out of earshot, he said he would rather talk to me than "a bunch of stuffed shirts."

I moved him to Healdsburg in 1986, and then, in March of 1993, his son, Christopher, called from San Francisco to ask if I would meet him at the studio in Santa Monica. When I got there, Christopher said that his dad was in the hospital and he needed my help inventorying the studio contents and moving the art into storage. I took this as a bad sign but decided not to intrude with questions. I began working through racks and shelves, identifying paintings while Christopher wrote down the information. I found Diebenkorn's first painting, numbered "1". It was a scene of the Berkeley tidal flats painted on an oil board. We were reverently looking at it—the painting that began a remarkable career—when the phone rang. It was someone letting Christopher know his dad had just passed away.

I got one last look at the studio several years ago when the San Francisco Museum of Modern Art had a Diebenkorn and Matisse painting exhibition and included photographs of the old Main Street space above Barrett's Hardware store. The old couch we shared was there, along with a small painting of Diebenkorn's favorite ashtray—the one I had kept clean. Such a small detail, but I missed him when I saw it.

A lowly assistant or art handler can be rich in ways a collector might never suspect. The intimacy we feel for the art we love and the artists we revere is one of the most rewarding parts of our profession. And that makes it easier to let the indignities, insults, and pettiness that come with this job roll off our backs—or at least it makes it easier for me on a good day.

On a bad day, I'd be back at Marcia's, wrestling with some impossible task. Like the time I was plunged into the turmoil of her whims when the Museum of Contemporary Art asked me to pick up her collection, which it had borrowed for its inaugural show, and reinstall it in her home. Marcia herself had hired me to take the art to the museum, and that job had gone off without a hitch. But putting it back was another matter, and things quickly got out of hand.

Marcia chose the placement of every piece around the house, and we spent two days hanging her paintings. But when we were ninety percent finished, she started changing her mind and instructing us to move them around. Why not take this chance to redecorate? In a commercial art gallery, where the walls are expansive, this wouldn't be a problem. But in a home where the walls are of varying sizes, it quickly became impossible. We'd install a large Warhol in a spot that had held two small paintings and then struggle to relocate the now-homeless canvases. Marcia insisted we hang every piece in her collection, and she was uncompromising about the spacing between paintings and their heights. Making things even tougher, she wouldn't take our advice and insisted on making every decision. A project that should have taken two days stretched to five, and since MOCA was paying, Marcia didn't seem to care.

On the fourth day, I left my installers in the early afternoon to purchase some hardware. When I returned, I found all four standing on the street, facing the house wide-eyed and shocked. Two of them had been working in Marcia's bedroom and bathroom when she barged past stark naked. "Don't mind me!" she called as she jumped in the shower. It took a lot of cajoling to get the guys back working in the house. I considered it a miracle that we ever finished, but when I invoiced MOCA, they were incredulous it had taken so long, and I had to fight to get paid. As usual, that wasn't Marcia's problem.

Nixon

I always enjoyed the freedom of driving around Los Angeles while delivering art. Every day brought new surprises and opportunities to see amazing pieces inside impressive homes and to meet influential people. It is astounding to see how much high-quality and rare artwork is hidden away in private collections throughout Southern California. We were often called to Bel Air, where some of the wealthiest individuals in the US harbor their troves in houses obscured by gates, hedges, and retaining walls that hold back steep hillsides and overgrown vegetation. The wealthiest of the wealthy live in estates in lower Bel Air that spill down to Sunset Boulevard, the enclave's lower edge. There is also an upper Bel Air along the mountain ridgelines, where homes destroyed by a brush fire in 1961 were rebuilt with smaller and less expensive housing than the mega-mansions below, though definitely not cheap.

In 1972, a fellow employee, Jim Dumont, and I delivered a painting to a residence in upper Bel Air. It was a beautiful spring day, and we were coming down through lower Bel Air to get back to Sunset. We had beards and long hair and looked like the other scruffy counterculture antiwar protesters and hippies who scared the hell out of the Republicans.

I was driving the decrepit, UPS-style step van, fondly named "Old Chevy." It was painted emergency-warning yellow and by any measure an ugly truck, which stood out wherever it went. The Old Chevy had a fiberglass body attached to a Chevrolet pickup truck frame, which made it lightweight, and with a small, straight-six engine, it was a quiet drive.

I was cruising in second gear so the engine compression would save the brakes and keep the truck from running away as we coasted rapidly downhill. Saving the brakes was critical because Cart & Crate didn't keep up with truck maintenance. And these brakes had failed me before. Several months earlier, as I headed down a steep grade toward Santa Monica Boulevard, I reached the intersection and tried to stop when the traffic light turned red. To my horror, the brake pedal sank to the floor, and the truck kept going. Cars braked and swerved to avoid me, angrily blowing their horns as I rolled downhill through the next major cross street, Melrose, before finally coasting to a stop. This incident was still fresh in my mind as I followed the twisty roads down through Bel Air.

Rounding a blind curve, we passed three men dressed in black suits and dark glasses. They were walking together on the right side of the road and looked surprised by our arrival. They instantly sprang into action as we sped by, jumping up and down and leaning toward our truck, wildly waving their arms. They were yelling at us, but I couldn't hear what they were saying over the road and engine noise as we shot by. I turned to Jim, "Who the hell are those assholes?"

I glanced in my right mirror and saw them running after the truck, ties flapping and arms still frantically waving. The sunglasses on one had gone askew, partially hanging off his face. I thought, "Screw them! Suits!" Who were they to criticize my driving?

As we rounded another curve, I suddenly saw two figures walking in the center of the road 150 feet ahead. I was stunned to realize that I was on a collision course with President Richard Nixon and Secretary of State Henry Kissinger. I momentarily froze. Part of my brain refused to believe that the president of the United States would be walking in the middle of a street in Los Angeles.

Both men were deeply engrossed in conversation and unaware of my oncoming truck. Kissinger was listening intently, walking with bowed head and hands clasped behind his back. He loped along in a measured, lumbering gate, the sauntering movements of a big trained bear. Nixon was on Kissinger's left. His steps were dance-like, short and quick as he moved sideways, looking at Kissinger, seemingly intent on making an important point and gesturing emphatically with his hands. Was he discussing the intransigence of the North Vietnamese? The need to carpet-bomb Laos? Watergate burglary? Jane Fonda?

Why is it that whenever an accident happens, before the screeching of tires and the crunching of metal and shattering glass, one hears the blasts of a car horn? Is the need to send a warning more important than braking or taking evasive action? Or is the horn-blowing a way of punishing the idiot responsible for causing the accident?

For some reason, and I still don't know why—although perhaps it was a hippie, screw-the-man reaction—I didn't touch the brakes. Instead, I leaned hard on the horn, which blared loudly, like a wounded Billy goat's bleating. Both men whirled to face us.

Nixon bolted left, scurrying across the road and pushing his back into the roadside bushes. Kissinger lumbered right, as quickly as his bulk would allow, before backing against the uphill retaining wall. I attempted to split the difference between them, but Kissinger's slower retreat forced me to veer closer to Nixon's side of the road. I'm sure he thought I was intentionally aiming at him because our truck missed him by only a few feet, passing so close I could have reached out and touched him. I locked eyes with the president of the United States, who was white-faced and frightened. It must have been unnerving for him to see a shaggy, bearded hippie careening past in a weird truck.

I have often wondered what could have happened if I had killed President Nixon and Secretary of State Kissinger that day. Of course, it would have been an accident. Would they have been at fault for jaywalking in the middle of the road? Would the Secret Service agents we passed have been blamed for dereliction of duty? Right! More likely, I would've ended up in federal prison for murder after the agents blamed me for not stopping at their command.

Poor decisions and small lapses in judgment can lead to momentous consequences. In mere seconds, I could have gone from obscurity to notoriety. And the course of history could have been changed. Peace with North Vietnam might have come sooner, saving the lives of many. Nixon would have avoided the humiliation of impeachment and resigning the presidency. And he would have died a martyr instead of a disgrace.

But I was a good driver with sharp reflexes, not trying to kill anyone. That day, there was no harm, no foul.

Stella

I was new to the Los Angeles art scene and naïve as hell when Cart & Crate sent two of us to pick up one of Frank Stella's *Union Pacific* series paintings from the Pasadena Art Museum in 1970. The museum had recently moved from a kitschy Chinese pagoda-themed building to an expensive modern space on Colorado Boulevard. It had a history of curating cutting-edge exhibitions, including Marcel Duchamp playing chess with a nude woman. Its acting director, near the end of his tenure, was the legendary John Coplans. John was the founder of Art Forum magazine and an influential art critic, artist, writer, and early promoter of Pop Art. We signed in with museum security near the loading dock. A guard escorted us upstairs to the hallway entrance to one of the galleries, then promptly left.

The gallery was unlit, and as my eyes adjusted, I saw Coplans sitting quietly on a bench in the center of the gallery. The only light came through the door of a neighboring gallery. As soon as we walked in, Coplans stood up, pointed at a large painting hanging in the gloom across from him, and left without saying a word. Obviously, he had been waiting for us to arrive. But his aloof behavior and abrupt departure seemed odd, as was the darkness of the gallery. Why weren't the lights on? I cautiously walked toward the painting. As I got closer, I began to notice the thick, sweet smell of paint thinner. I placed my nose within inches of the stripes and sniffed each one. The eighth stripe had the strongest scent. It also appeared darker than the others, though my eyes could have been playing tricks on me.

I walked back to the entrance and began feeling along the wall with the flat of my hand to find the light switches. I located a plate covering five switches, but flipping them back and forth didn't turn on the lights. So, I walked out to the reception desk. It was empty, which was strange since the museum was open to visitors. In fact, the whole museum seemed abandoned. I found a security guard in the basement. He had his jacket neatly folded over a chair and was holding a coffee cup when I walked in. He was on his break, he said, and begrudgingly agreed to turn on the lights when he was finished.

Ten minutes later, the gallery lit up, revealing that one of the painting's stripes had recently been painted over. Stella had used aluminum paint, so all of the other stripes oxidized as they cured and aged. But the new unoxidized stripe reflected light differently and stood out from the rest. The surface was tacky to my touch, and I took care not to leave a fingerprint behind.

We took the Stella after doing a condition report—noting the alterations on our paperwork—and I returned to the basement guard to have him sign on behalf of the museum. I never found out what happened when the painting was returned to its owner. Coplans left the museum in 1972 for a five-year run as Art Forum's editor in chief, and the museum itself changed hands in 1974 when it couldn't recover from a sea of construction debt. The city of Pasadena recruited Norton Simon, Marcia Weisman's super-rich collector brother, to bail it out in exchange for control of its permanent collection. He also received naming rights to the institution and new building, which became the Norton Simon Museum.

Sadly, Simon didn't believe any art created after World War II was worth collecting. So the post-war paintings that the museum had specialized in—pieces by artists like Stella and Kenneth Noland and Jules Olitski—largely remained hidden in the museum vault.

Simon

I had my first encounter with Norton Simon in the early 1970s when Cart & Crate received several ocean freight shipments of crated

Cambodian and Indian stone sculptures and temple friezes. We picked them up at the LA harbor and put them in our storage warehouse under Simon's name. Management told us to keep this quiet because there was a high likelihood the sculptures had been smuggled out of their countries of origin and were being stored until the coast was clear. After a year had passed, we delivered a portion of the crates to Simon's Malibu Colony residence and began unpacking and installing some extraordinary Asian sculptures. Simon told us where to place each piece and supervised everything we did. At noon, he invited us to have lunch. We were shown into a small dining room facing the ocean. The room was set up with three small round tables, each with white linen tablecloths and three chairs. Six movers stiffly sat around two tables, while Simon and his wife, actress Jennifer Jones, sat at the third, a few feet away. A butler, who seemed annoyed at having to wait on a bunch of scruffy hippies, served us meager portions of bland-tasting sandwiches on fine china. We ate in silence. When working for minimum wage, what do you say to one of the world's most powerful men and his Academy Award-winning wife?

It was Jones who piqued Norton Simon's interest in Indian art. She loved Indian culture, and they spent their honeymoon in 1971 traveling in the subcontinent, where Simon became interested in collecting Indian sculpture. Over the next two years, he spent nearly $16 million acquiring Indian and Cambodian antiquities. After collecting approximately seventy high-quality stone sculptures, Simon deviated by purchasing an exquisite tenth-century bronze, *Nataraja*, for around $1 million, from influential art dealer Ben Heller. Like Simon, Heller had a Midas touch. He made his fortune in real estate and art—collecting artists such as Jackson Pollock, Rothko, Kline, and others early in their careers—and then cashed in as their values skyrocketed. Heller became a close friend of Jackson Pollock and supported him financially by purchasing his paintings.

Heller's New York City apartment had room after room with floor-to-ceiling paintings, all of which were masterpiece caliber. Visible in one photo of his home is an Indian sculpture similar to the ones purchased by Simon. Whether this was a coincidence or the two had other dealings in Indian art is unknown. It was never clear how and where Norton Simon got the stone sculptures, and the provenance of many pieces was murky. However, he made no secret of his purchase of *Nataraja*—a dancing Hindu God of creation and destruction—and it soon became a legal lightning rod. When asked about the piece during an interview with a *New York Times* reporter, Simon said, "Hell yes, it was smuggled!" But he added that it wasn't illegal to own a smuggled piece as long as it was declared and cleared by Customs. He then told the reporter he didn't know if it had been stolen.

Simon was exceptionally shrewd, and I believe he was purposefully open about purchasing the sculpture because he intended to use it as a future bargaining chip. Almost immediately, the Indian government took the bait and began trying to get the sculpture returned. They petitioned the US State Department, asking the US ambassador, Daniel Patrick Moynihan, to India for help. When none of their entreaties to the US government worked, they sued Simon and Heller in the US courts. After the suit dragged on for several years, the court agreed to a one-year pause, allowing all parties to negotiate a settlement.

In 1976, the Indian government reached an agreement with Simon and Heller. Simon would be allowed to keep *Nataraja* for ten years and display it in his museum. The Indian government, for its part, gave the Simon Foundation immunity to buy any Indian art outside of India for one year. The Indian government was probably unaware of the extent of Simon's holdings, all of which were already outside of India. Though Simon agreed to return *Nataraja*, he legally kept title to everything else. He had spent one million dollars to gain legal ownership of sixteen million dollars' worth of Indian sculptures—a shrewd bargain.

Simon moved those pieces into his new museum along with a substantial collection of art, including Old Masters he had long promised to bequeath to the Los Angeles County Museum of Art. He had been storing this art there, letting the museum cover the cost of insurance and conservation expenses of the pieces it was sure to receive. His world-class collection was now displayed in a world-class museum. And to LACMA's chagrin, it was his, not theirs.

Many people buy art for prestige or as an investment. Others collect what a dealer or art consultant recommends. Simon, the hard-nosed businessman and industrialist was knowledgeable about art and art history and had a discerning eye for the finest paintings and sculpture. He bought for himself, and his collections are filled with masterpieces. When I went to the museum on days it was closed to the public—to pick up or deliver a painting or sculpture—I would often encounter him sitting alone in the galleries, intently studying one of his paintings. Whatever else he may have been, he was a man who truly loved art.

Greece

In the fall of 1973, I took a leave of absence from work to use a cheap ticket that TWA was selling for a forty-five-day excursion trip to London. My goal was to visit as many great European museums and see as much great art as possible—free from the burden of wrapping it, lifting it, or thinking about anything but its beauty. I took in the Elgin Marbles in London, rented a Mini Cooper, and drove around southern England. I visited Bath, Oxford, Salisbury Cathedral, and Stonehenge, and then traveled to Amsterdam to see Rembrandt's *Night*

Watch, drink Dutch beer, and eat raw herring from street vendors' carts. In Paris, I paid homage to the *Mona Lisa*—which then hung unguarded only a few feet away from an open window. In Venice, I visited the four magnificent war horses overlooking San Marcos square before moving on to Florence and the Uffizi, and then to Rome.

I walked to the Colosseum after the tourists had disappeared for the day, taking a decidedly non-tourist route through a small piazza where three prostitutes were warming themselves over a fire burning in a steel barrel. The flames sent eerie, yellow light flickering across the brick walls of adjacent buildings and illuminated the women's tawdry makeup—completing a scene that could have come directly out of a Fellini movie. The Colosseum was cloaked in darkness and closed off by a chain-link fence. But I squeezed through a small opening and carefully felt my way along the wall of a pitch-black tunnel, emerging onto the Colosseum's floor, which was illuminated by the blue light of a massive full moon. After standing in silent awe for a few minutes, I began hearing sounds, soft whispering, indistinct words, sighs. They floated directionless in the cold air. Ghosts?

I traveled on in subsequent days, taking a ferry from Brindisi, on the heel of the Italian boot, to Corfu, where peasant farmers with handlebar mustaches rolled out of the hills driving BMW motorcycles, shotguns slung over shoulders, wives and kids stuffed into sidecars. The outlines of German crosses were still visible on the gas tanks. I made my way to Athens, stopping at the Parthenon and other sites. On the morning of my flight home to Los Angeles, I walked through the streets toward Constitution Square in front of the parliament building to find a taxi to the airport. It was a beautiful day saturated with golden Mediterranean sunshine, and I was in good spirits. But my timing was terrible. As I rounded a corner into the square, I was immediately confronted by a dozen heavily armed men, plain-clothed but carrying military-issued assault guns. Two of them grabbed and shoved me against a wall, where over two dozen other men were dejectedly lined up as prisoners. Was this a firing squad? Half an hour later, we were marched single file under guard through Athens to the Syntagma metro station and loaded into a ramshackle train car that took us to the port city of Piraeus. We boarded a ferry bound for the port city of Crete, where I understood I was to be exiled for an unknown duration. Luckily, I found a youth hostel where I could stay.

I soon learned that the armed men were members of Greece's feared military police, the ESA, known for torturing and murdering many of their prisoners. I had inadvertently been caught in the midst of the overthrow of the junta ruling Greece, a bloodless coup led by a ruthless colonel named Dimitrios Ioannidis. A 5 p.m. curfew was announced, reinforced by a World War II tank that rumbled down the road at 4:50 p.m., with a threat to shoot anyone violating the new restrictions. I took advantage of my strangely extended stay by renting a moped. I rode over the mountains to explore, careful to give myself plenty of time to get back before curfew. Thanks to the coup, I had enough time to see the Minoan ruins of Knossos and other archaeological sites. After a week, curfew ended, and I left Greece for home.

Art treasures plus a brush with trauma—it was the art mover's equivalent of a busman's holiday.

Barbara

Shortly after I returned from Europe, Cart & Crate became an agent for Mayflower Transportation. This allowed them to use Mayflower's interstate operating license and establish an art shuttle service. Almost immediately, the Walker Art Center in Minneapolis contracted with us to help it assemble an exhibition of Native American artifacts. We were to pick them up from multiple museum collections around the United States and deliver them to the Walker. This was Cart & Crate's first out-of-state trucking job, and I was assigned to the road trip. My itinerary was handed to me in the form of a typed inventory list, including museum addresses and phone numbers of the registrars there. The list didn't have photographs, just descriptions, and some dimensions: "1850s Comanche Eagle Feather War Bonnet." In the era before the internet, computers, and even fax machines, most information was prepared on a typewriter with carbon paper duplicates, and arrived via US mail, followed up with a phone call.

For the trip, I'd be driving one of Cart & Crate's aging 24-foot box trucks—a cab-over dark green Ford with substantial mileage. The cargo box didn't have air ride or climate control, and the cab wasn't air-conditioned. The oil hadn't been changed in years, and whenever the engine began running roughly, I had to pull out the spark plugs to clean off their scaly deposits with sandpaper and adjust their gaps using a matchbook cover as a gauge. I'd use the same matchbook to calibrate the distributor points. In the interest of staying alive, I also regularly inspected and adjusted the brakes before driving each day, as well as religiously checking tire pressures, lights, and fluid levels.

The poor quality of art moving equipment in the early 1970s was largely a result of the chokehold the household van and storage industry held for decades over trucking permits issued by the Interstate Commerce Commission and state public utilities commissions. Trucking is the heart of any art moving business, and it was impossible to get state and federal operating licenses. For decades, the van and storage industry—Mayflower, United Van Lines, Allied Van Lines, etc.—controlled commercial truck licensing, so small businesses couldn't obtain or afford permits. That meant they didn't have access to lucrative long-distance jobs. When they finally edged into the long-haul business, they did it on the cheap at first, using local trucks like the one at Cart & Crate that I called The Slug. A potential death trap, it was pieced together from wrecked trucks. It had a rear chassis that was never bolted to the body, which meant it would swing and the truck would jump unpredictably and terrifyingly in traffic.

Affiliating with Mayflower let Cart & Crate truck shipments across state lines, opening the possibility for higher profits and more roadworthy trucks. But the rigid tariff system that controlled prices for transporting every possible commodity made life difficult for companies that specialized in moving art. Art was lumped under household tariffs, even though shoving a couch into a truck is clearly not the same as handling a Rodin sculpture. Regulations finally began to loosen later in the 1970s, giving independent companies room to compete. This was good news for galleries, collectors, and museums who had not always been well served by van and storage companies such as New York's massive Hahn Bros. and The Seven Santini Brothers. Art moving skills didn't matter much in heavily unionized New York City, but knowing someone who would help you get a union card did.

Deregulation would give rise to specialty art moving companies around the country—Hague, Atthowe, Terry Dowd, and my own Cooke's Crating—which quickly gained the trust and business of the art world when it became apparent that artists and those who appreciate art do a better job of moving it than guys whose strength is lugging refrigerators up flights of stairs into apartments.

Soon after some of my fellow drivers and I began making interstate deliveries for Cart & Crate under the Mayflower banner, we carefully studied the household tariffs and rules to find ways to increase revenue. Tariffs dictated the hourly rates that could be charged by the household goods industry, including four-hour minimum charges. Since we were being paid by commission, we needed to mine the tariffs for extra charges, such as deliveries involving stairs, which brought in extra money. That helped, but what ultimately made the business viable for us was something I did a few years later when I established Cooke's Crating and Fine Art Transportation. Cart & Crate didn't want my competition, and they threw barriers in my way, like filing a complaint with the California public utilities commission, which forced me to obtain state and federal household goods licenses. It was a lot of red tape, but I saw an opportunity. The Interstate Commerce Commission also issued licenses for general freight common carriers and had tariffs covering every imaginable product. I studied the tariff list carefully and realized there was one that covered the transport of art by a freight trucking company, and it was lower than the one charged by household movers. I set myself up as a freight hauler and undercut the prices of the household goods movers, giving me a competitive advantage.

My former employer filed another complaint about that with the California Public Utilities Commission. In response, I requested a hearing with the PUC. The Household Goods Carriers Association sent a representative to oppose me, but I pointed out that the art category in the general freight tariffs was already well established, while the household goods authority didn't specifically mention art. It only made sense, I said, that the freight tariffs should cover art moving. The PUC agreed.

But it took me a few years to carve out that spot for myself and other art movers. Until then, I served a long "apprenticeship" at Cart & Crate, making my first solo interstate trips and venturing into far-flung metro areas with irreplaceable loads, fielding every kind of hazard as I went.

For the Walker's Native American trip, I loaded my truck with cardboard boxes, tissue paper, brown newsprint paper, tape, and tools and drove East. The first stop would be the Heard Museum in Phoenix, followed by the Museum of Indian Arts in Santa Fe, the home of a private collector in Oklahoma, and the Field Museum in Chicago. Next was the Peabody in Salem, Massachusetts, and the Heye Institute, located in a rough part of Harlem—whose collections later became part of the Smithsonian's National Museum of the American Indian in Washington, D.C.

I was given access to the vaults of each institution to pack the objects and found stunning collections at each location. But I was most impressed with the Field's storage vaults, where drawer after drawer in the vast basement held dozens of similar artifacts. The sheer volume of Native American objects was astonishing.

Most of the artifacts I picked up fit comfortably inside my cartons. However, due to my limited supplies, I was forced to pack several larger items with portions sticking out the tops of cartons. One of these was a Comanche eagle feather war bonnet, which I carefully packed by securing the forehead leather strap and beaded portion to the carton bottom. I left the feathers sticking out the top to prevent anything from touching them, as they were extremely fragile.

I placed all of the packed cartons on the floor of my truck and braced them with quilted furniture blankets to keep them from moving. Each time I stopped my truck, I checked to make sure every piece was safe.

My last stop was the Harvard Peabody Museum in Cambridge, whose registrar had requested a "last on, first off" delivery service. I was excited to visit Harvard for the first time and called from a payphone the day before to let the registrar know when I was arriving. I was disappointed when she told me to meet her at a crating company located elsewhere in Boston because she was "having our objects packed and crated to military specifications!"

The next morning, I backed into the crating company's inside loading dock and found the registrar waiting. She wore an expensive-looking dress and heels, and she was not very friendly. Behind her stood two crates, each of them seven feet long, three feet wide, and four feet high. I rolled up the back door, preparing to load them, and she immediately walked into my truck. This was a breach of good manners, as my truck was also my home, and it was inconsiderate for her to enter it without asking me. She walked to the front and stood looking down at the packed cartons. "My God!" she said. For a foolish moment, I thought she was admiring my packing. "This is the worst packing job I have ever seen! You shouldn't be allowed to handle art. You need to be fired immediately." She walked over to a phone on the loading dock wall and called my employer, loudly demanding that my company fire me. I could tell from her body language that my boss wasn't agreeing. She next called the Walker Art Center, whose registrar, Gwen Lerner, I had been calling from each museum to report my progress. Gwen told her the museum was confident in my abilities and wouldn't interfere. I loaded the Peabody crates, tying them to the truck walls, and in stony silence, Barbara signed my paperwork.

When I arrived at the Walker, Gwen and several art handlers greeted me. I could tell they were apprehensive, and I was nervous too. We unpacked all of the objects I had worked on, placing them on tables for inspection. Everything was fine. We didn't unpack the Harvard crates, although I was curious to see what "military packing standards" looked like.

Seven months later, my fellow employee Paul Drake and I drove to the Walker to pick up the artifacts to return them to the lenders. This time we were driving a new tractor-trailer. Gwen greeted us warmly. She let us know that after all the ruckus Barbara had made about my packing, several of the Harvard Indian artifacts arrived damaged inside their crates—even though the charges for the packing and crating had exceeded those for all of the other lending institutions combined.

Our first return delivery was to Harvard, at the insistence of Barbara, who once more wanted to be first off the truck. I marveled at the Peabody's stately red brick structure, proudly situated on the campus of the oldest American university, as I waited apprehensively for Barbara. When she came out to our waiting truck, Paul asked her where we should unload the crates since the museum didn't appear to have a loading dock. She led us to one side of the building and pointed to a pair of doors angled against the wall. I had spent my early childhood in Toronto, Canada, and guessed that they belonged to a coal chute, used to slide sacks of coal down to the basement to feed furnaces. Sure enough, when we opened the double doors, a long metal chute sloped down to the basement floor, barely visible below. Barbara told us to use it to deliver her crates. We protested that they were too heavy for the two of us to control on the slippery incline, but she angrily demanded that we follow her orders. Paul asked if she could find some people to help, which only made her angrier.

"Do as I tell you! Unload my crates into the basement!" she bellowed.

We took the first crate, and holding on tightly, lowered it on the slide as far as we could reach before letting go. The crate shot downward into the gloom, hit the basement floor, and flipped upside down with a resounding thud. We turned toward Barbara, expecting her to change her mind for the second crate, but were met with a glare. She didn't flinch when the second crate crashed into the first with a crunch of splintering wood. We got a signature on the paperwork, and Barbara walked away on stiff legs.

Fortunately, as before, the rest of the stops were uneventful—no drama or damage.

The following year, I was driving the tractor-trailer solo and received instructions from my boss to swing down from New York City to pick up a small painting from the Philadelphia Museum of Art for delivery to the San Francisco Museum of Art. Philadelphia's new head registrar was Barbara, she added. I knew there would be trouble.

At nine in the morning, I arrived at PMA's loading dock, where one of the workers pointed to a painting leaning against a wall. He told me it was for my shipment but said I couldn't take it until the registrar came down to release it. I waited all day, sitting in my truck and looking over at the painting, which was often left unattended. Around 5 p.m., the dock worker walked over to inform me the dock was closing and that I'd have to return the next morning. I was being paid by commission, so I wasn't earning a dime while I waited, and my commission for the small painting had already been lowered when my boss gave the Philadelphia Museum a discounted price to gain their business.

I spent an uncomfortable night in my truck, parked across from the loading dock. When the dock opened the next morning, the painting was still sitting there, unattended. Finally, around three in the afternoon, Barbara walked out. She didn't greet me but instructed the dock person to hand the painting over. I was eager to get moving and quickly tied the artwork to the trailer's wall in the first open position, figuring I could reposition it once I got away from the museum.

Barbara once again walked uninvited into my truck and, using a tape measure, wrote down the distance from the rear door to the painting. "If this painting has moved one inch from this spot when it gets delivered to the museum in San Francisco, your company will never get another shipment from my museum," she said. She also wrote down the truck license plate number and told me she would send the information to SFMOMA.

When I got back to Los Angeles, I told my boss the painting needed to be delivered on the same truck and not moved. "Nonsense!" I was told. "What are you talking about? That's absurd—who in their right mind would make such a stupid demand." So the painting was delivered on a different truck, and Barbara exacted revenge by refusing to give Cart & Crate any future business.

We had no further contact. But years later, after I started my own business, I joined the newly formed registrars' committee of the American Association of Museums. Barbara, I was worried to see, was the committee's chairwoman. I was careful to watch my back.

New York

On my second art moving trip into New York City after the Walker's Native American project, I was solo driving Cart & Crate's semi-tractor trailer, extremely nervous about taking such a large vehicle into such a chaotic environment. I stopped outside the city at a Jersey truck stop to plan my route, determine truck-passable streets, and find the locations of galleries and museums where my art shipments were going. This was 1974, years before Google Maps and global positioning made life easy, and I was staring at a folded paper map from a gas station. Looking from map to address list, I carefully planned each day's schedule. I had been to the city in 1955 when I was a 10-year-old kid, but that wasn't going to help me maneuver a big truck through crowded streets. Driving into the city in the evening would let me avoid most traffic, and it seemed logical to head to lower Manhattan, where my first stop would be Hague, an art moving company at 420 West Broadway.

On a Sunday evening, I began driving in a light rain across the George Washington Bridge into the city. The red glow of a stoplight on the other side, combined with the haze of sodium vapor street lights, created an eerie yellow-blue aura that reflected off the wet street pavement and sidewalks.

I noticed a solitary figure, a woman, standing on the opposite corner. She was wearing a cheap, fake-leather jacket with a fake fur collar. Her hands jammed under her armpits for warmth. Puffs of vapor marked the rhythm of her breathing. I stared too long—a mistake. Looking up, she made eye contact and instantly became animated. "Hey, Baby! Baby! Want some action? Hey there, sailor, I'll show you a good time. How about it, sugar? Don't you want me?"

She left the curb, ran across the intersection, and jumped up onto the running board on the passenger side of my tractor. She hooked one arm around the mirror bracket while her free hand grabbed my door handle. I always kept the passenger door locked, so she couldn't climb in. But she wasn't about to give up and kept pleading, even as the light changed, and I began shifting through the progression of gears to gain speed. I glanced over at the passenger window. Seeing this, she began kissing the glass and making moaning sounds. Red lipstick smeared across the wet glass, and it started fogging up from her warm breath. Through it, she looked ghastly, a clown corpse trying to invade my space. "Get the hell off my truck! Get off! Get the fuck off!" I yelled at her.

She stubbornly hung on for blocks until a red light forced me to a stop. She jumped down and began walking away, then wheeled around to give me the finger. "Fuck you, you faggot!" she screamed. Welcome to New York City, I thought.

As I drove down the island, I noticed taxi cabs were beginning to surround my truck, and soon I was being escorted by a phalanx of eight or ten. We hurried down the island, me sounding the big diesel air horn and them joining in with a cacophony of blaring, bleating horns. Opposing traffic was jamming brakes and adding their horns to the racket. We drove without stopping until we got all the way down to Canal Street, where the cabs dispersed and I was on my own. Welcome to *lawless* New York City! My jitters had disappeared, and I had been initiated. I felt at home.

I found a wide area where the Holland Tunnel emptied into Manhattan. It was paved in cobblestones, indicating that it was one of the original streets. The city painted a large triangle on the pavement in the center to direct traffic around each side. It made a perfect parking spot from which streets radiated to access Soho or continue north up the island. It was also somewhat secure because my truck was exposed amid a constant traffic flow. I didn't think anyone would mess with it with so many people around. I nicknamed this area the "Holland Tunnel Triangle" and parked there every evening. Incidentally, seven years later, Richard Serra installed an enormous and controversial sculpture, "*TWU*," in that location.

After my first night in the triangle, I noticed a railroad car diner across the street and walked over to get breakfast. Behind the counter was a giant bear of a man in a white apron whose only job seemed to be talking to customers. His partner was a short, stocky guy who was ambidextrous and working at an incredible pace, filling coffee cups with one hand while cracking eggs on the griddle, flipping pancakes, and turning hash browns with the other.

"Coffee?" he greeted me.

"Yes," I replied.

"Regular coffee?" he asked, and again I said yes.

In a split second, he was filling my cup and pouring milk into it simultaneously.

"Stop! What are you doing to my coffee? I asked for regular coffee."

He gave me a sour look. "This *is* regular coffee."

"No, it isn't. Regular coffee is black."

He looked at me again and said, "You must be from California. In New York, this is regular coffee." He introduced himself as "Manny," and we were friendly afterwards. The exchange taught me another New York City lesson: have a beef, stand your ground, and afterwards have a good relationship with the other person.

Hague was an art moving company that belonged to two enterprising Dutchmen, Walter and Fritz. They owned the building at 420 West Broadway, and their art crating business occupied the first floor and basement while they leased space to André Emmerich,

Sonnabend, and Leo Castelli on the upper floors. All three were major, highly important galleries that showed the world's best artists and set artistic trends for decades. A visit to 420 took you to the center of the contemporary art universe.

The building bordered Little Italy, and a good Italian meal was only a short walk away. Little Italy was thick with attitude in those days. Coppola's movie "The Godfather" had recently reached theaters, and those of Italian heritage were seriously into playing the wise-guy parts. They wanted you to think they were all Mafiosi or connected to a Mafia guy or knew someone who knew someone who was connected. Who knows? Maybe they were.

Walter and Fritz worked a Starsky and Hutch routine on their employees, their clients, and just once on me. The first time I backed into their loading dock, some guy was standing there, yelling obscenities and telling me to "Take your stupid fucking ass back to California!" It looked like another example of that New York way of getting into a big row with someone and afterwards becoming best friends. So, I got out of the truck, started laughing at Fritz, and talked shit back. Soon Walter came out and apologized for Fritz's bad behavior, blaming it on his high-strung nature. Fritz turned on his heel, walked back into the crate shop, and began yelling at the employees.

Walter invited me into his office for a coffee and explained that Fritz often acted out, so I should not take him seriously. Good cop, crazy cop. In the course of our congenial conversation, Walter said he liked me and was going to do me a huge favor—and I should do what he asked without questioning it. He took me out the back door and pointed down the street. It was lined with brownstone houses, the style with half basements, so there was a half flight of steps going from the sidewalk up to the first-floor porch and half flight going to the level below the street. He pointed to a house where a diminutive elderly woman dressed in black was sitting in the sun crocheting.

"Go down there, take off your hat and be very polite," he instructed. "She doesn't speak English, but talk to her anyway."

This seemed ludicrous, but I did what he asked. I approached
the woman, took off my hat, and politely nodded my head. The old
crone beamed at the attention, flashing a gap-toothed smile, and for
ten minutes, we talked at each other without understanding a word.

I went back to Walter's office. "Good job," he said. "Now, I'm
going to do you another favor."

I was to go to a small Italian market several streets over and ask
for Tony, then hire him to work with me delivering my art shipments the next day. "Tell Tony you want him for a full day and pay
him $15 an hour," Walter said.

This was a very high hourly rate for the recession-torn 1970s, and
it was more than I was making. It was also coming out of my pocket.
But I did as I was told and went looking for Tony.

Tony was seventeen years old and had never been outside the
boundaries of Little Italy. I wondered how someone could grow up
in a city full of taxicabs, buses, and subways and never leave such
a small neighborhood. Was it a lack of curiosity? Or was venturing
out of your territory dangerous? When Tony learned that I was from
California, he told me it was the next state over from New Jersey,
and someday he was going there to see it. He had never ridden in a
tractor-trailer and was agog at the experience, particularly thrilled
that he was up high looking down at pedestrians and taxicabs.

When I returned to New York several weeks later, I asked Walter what the old lady and Tony business was all about. I figured he
and Fritz had played a trick on me and would laugh at my gullibil-
ity. But Walter was serious and told me that the old lady was "the
Don's" mother and Tony was his favorite nephew. I had paid respect
to them, and from then on, no one would mess with me or my truck.
I could never verify the truth of this assertion, but during the thirty
or so times I drove art in and out of New York, nothing bad ever

happened—except for one nasty row at the Hahn Brothers warehouse, where "the Don" may not have had jurisdiction.

In addition to owning 420 West Broadway, Walter and Fritz bought other SoHo buildings over the ensuing years, and eventually, they became wealthy and closed Hague. In 2005, Walter called to tell me he had a terminal illness and not long to live. He asked if I would do him the favor of storing his art collection for five years. I owed him for my intro to New York, and I was happy to. He gave me contact information for his son, a doctor in Toronto, and told me to send the art to him when the five years were up. He shipped the collection to me from New York, and I assumed he intended to get the art out of his estate or away from some other encumbrance. I honored his wishes but never found out the whole story.

As for Fritz, he became a clothing model, and I would often recognize him in catalogues. Even as he grew older, he continued to model as a silver-haired, distinguished older man. I recently saw him in a catalog for *L.L. Bean*.

Pirate

By the end of 1973, Cart & Crate had opened a New York office above the Broome Street Bar, a neighborhood watering hole for SoHo artists and actors. If you sat in the farthest corner of the bar, near the windows looking out on the street, the underside of the stairway leading to the office was directly overhead. Occasionally a speck of dust would be dislodged by someone running up the stairs and float down into my beer.

The second floor was essentially an open loft divided into two areas by a windowless plywood wall with a door in its center that, in New York fashion, was secured by multiple locks. The fortified area behind it was occupied by "Jack," a young, somewhat arrogant guy who always wore a red sash around his waist. I nicknamed him "Jack the Pirate" because of the sash, which I thought was an odd wardrobe choice. But Jack was no stranger than the other denizens of the Broome Street Bar. "Mr. Peepers" and his girlfriend, for instance, were both in their early 20s, but Peepers always dyed his hair gray and was made up to look old. He wore old-fashioned clothing—sweaters with elbow patches and wire-rimmed glasses. His girlfriend dressed up as a virginal college coed, and they would sit for hours on barstools staring into each other's eyes and talking quietly. I would jealously watch them as I sipped a beer and ate my hamburger. She was gorgeous, and I couldn't figure out the kinkiness involved. Was she attracted to older men?

Cart & Crate's office, at the front of the loft, had three desks with phones and IBM Selectric typewriters. Behind the desks to the side was a small room where Janice, the office manager, lived. Janice found the Broome Street location as a sublet and set up the offices. She also hired a young woman named Karla to answer phones and promote art shipments for our semi-truck to deliver throughout the United States. I had a secret crush on Janice, who was smart and beautiful, with that secret sauce ingredient. She had grown up on a ranch in Wyoming and left to start a new life in New York City. Fearlessness and self-assurance are strong aphrodisiacs, and when she suggested I start an art moving business in New York City, I was tempted.

More than just an office, the Cart & Crate space was supposed to give our drivers a place to crash and shower in New York. A shower stall—just three walls, six-and-a-half-feet tall, and a shower curtain—sat in the center of the room, where there must've been an existing drain pipe. It was odd, but we'd take what we could get. We could be on the road for up to a week before arriving in the city, and we needed a place to clean up and have a quiet night's sleep. Staying in the semi-tractor's sleeper bed was dangerous, and the potential of being attacked while parked on the street overnight was always on our minds. We constantly kept one ear open for the sounds of someone breaking into the truck. We also froze in the wintertime. We didn't want to keep the engine running to power the heater because it would use too much fuel, and refueling cost time and money. The closest places to replenish empty tanks were across the river in New Jersey, a stressful drive across the George Washington Bridge. We frequently spent three or four days in Manhattan, making the rounds of museums and galleries to pick up and drop off art before heading back to Los Angeles, and conserving our fuel would mean fewer runs to Jersey.

The new set-up sounded great. But when we walked into the Broome Street offices for the first time, Janice told us that Jack wouldn't allow us to stay there. We decided we needed to hate the selfish creep.

On a cold fall day, I arrived from Los Angeles around 10 a.m., and after parking the truck, I walked up the stairs to the Cart & Crate office. The door was unlocked, and the office was abandoned. Thinking that Janice and Karla must have stepped out for breakfast, I sat down to wait. About an hour later, the phone rang, and I answered, "Hello, this is Cart & Crate."

"Who is this?" a nervous-sounding voice asked.

"Bryan Cooke," I replied. "One of the drivers."

"This is Jack," the voice said. "You gotta help me! Please help me! I've been arrested for dealing. Go into my room and look in the closet. There's ten thousand dollars in my suit jacket pocket. Please take the money and hire an attorney to bail me out. Please!"

I heard a voice in the background saying, "Time's up, buddy," and the phone went dead.

I sat there for a long while, looking at Jack's door, fighting temptation. How easy would it be to break through all those locks? What had the sonofabitch done for me and my fellow drivers except keep us from getting a hot shower and a good night's sleep? Ten grand was a lot of money when we were lucky to carn $12 an hour. Larcenous thoughts rattled around in my brain. New York state had recently passed draconian drug laws with sentences of more than twenty years for first offenses if you were a dealer. If I took the money, there was nothing Jack could do about it. But the money wasn't mine, and it was wrong to take it—even if it was earned illegally. As I thought about it, it seemed likely that the cops overheard Jack's side of the conversation or bugged the jailhouse phones. I also figured that Janice and Karla left in a hurry because they received word of Jack's arrest, and knowing he was a dealer, decided to leave before the cops showed up. Or before some Mafia types came for Jack's drug stash. I decided it would be prudent to wait downstairs in the bar.

I ordered a hamburger and a dark beer and took them to my favorite spot—in the corner, under the stairs. Sitting there with my back to the wall, I had an unobstructed view of who came into the bar and could also watch the street.

I was only halfway through the burger and still on my first beer when three black-and-green NYC squad cars rolled up. They were typical New York cop cars covered in grime and a patina of scratches and dents. And they weren't running the sirens, which likely meant they wanted to tamp down public attention.

Six cops dressed in brass-button uniform coats hopped out. They were all overweight, with tough-looking demeanors and greasy hair sticking out from under their caps. They congregated at the trunk of one car and extracted a battering ram and a pair of shotguns, then headed to the loft, thumping loudly over my head. The stairs vibrated from the stress of big boots and big bellies, and I put a hand over my beer to keep out the falling dust and flakes of paint. The bar could have dated back to the Revolutionary War, so the paint was probably lead.

A brief silence upstairs was followed by loud crashing and splintering sounds. A few more minutes passed before the thundering sound of boots came back down the stairs. The six cops emerged into the street. After putting the ram and shotguns into the trunk and slamming it closed, they stood watching as the one with sergeant's stripes began dividing a wad of cash into seven piles on top of the trunk. Since there were only six cops, I figured the seventh pile was for the lieutenant back at the station. After equally dividing the money, the sergeant held up the extra bill leftover. Although I couldn't hear what was said, I could see the other cops motioning him to keep it. He stuffed it, along with his share of cash, into a pocket and put the extra pile into another pocket. The cops jumped into their cars and drove off.

I walked upstairs to assess the damage. Jack's door was hanging off its hinges, and his loft had been turned upside down. All of the clothes from the closet were tossed on the floor with pockets turned or ripped out. The mattresses were cut open, as were upholstered chairs, and an upended couch revealed a wooden box screwed into the underside. The box had been smashed open, and several empty metal canisters lay next to it, along with their lids. Evidently, the cops had found Jack's drug stash and taken it. Would it be used as evidence? Recreation? Or sold on the streets? I never found out, and I never saw Jack again.

Winsor

In 1974, Paul Drake and I picked up a Jackie Winsor sculpture, *Double Bound Circle*, from an exhibition in Chicago with instructions to return it to her Bowery studio in New York. Jackie used materials like bricks, rope, and burnt wood to make minimalist forms. For *Double*

Bound Circle, she wove a five-inch diameter hemp rope—a ship's hawser used to secure ocean liners to docks—into a circle that was twenty-four inches wide and five feet in diameter. I marveled at how she'd been able to manipulate and weave the stiff, heavy rope into a shape resembling a cake donut the size of a large truck tire.

Paul and I made regular art deliveries in and out of SoHo to artists who were moving there to take advantage of cheap rents on huge spaces once used for manufacturing and the garment trade, which were ideal for studios. In those years, the area was quiet and gritty. The only semblance of civilization consisted of a couple of bars where the locals hung out, plus some small businesses on Broome and Spring streets. There wasn't yet a chain store or boutique in sight.

In the 1960s and '70s, artists began painting huge canvases, and Lebrun Brothers invented stretcher bars that could break down to enable huge paintings to be rolled. But even those rolled paintings were so long you needed elevators to move them to ground level. The industrial-size freight elevators in many of the SoHo buildings made that easier, but the nearby Bowery was more rundown—and while lofts were cheaper—many of them were walk-ups. Paul and I knew this and surmised that we might need to carry Jackie's 500-pound flexible mass up flights of stairs, meaning we would need additional help. We both worked for commissions and received a percentage of every delivery we made, but we also paid all expenses we incurred, so we tried to avoid extra hiring if we could help it.

After leaving Chicago, we called Jackie from a payphone and learned that indeed, there was no elevator, and we'd be lugging her piece to the fourth floor.

"But don't worry," she assured us. "The stairs are wide, and you shouldn't have any trouble getting the sculpture up to my studio. After all, it only took a couple of art handlers to get it downstairs without straining."

We pointed out that they had gravity in their favor going down the stairs and firmly said she needed to provide a couple of strong men to help us. After some back-and-forth, she reluctantly agreed.

It was dark outside her building when we arrived. The streets were slick with black ice and snow, and the curb gutters were full of frozen dog shit. The sidewalks were grimy, and a few streaks of poop were left by some unfortunate individual who failed to obey the New York mantra of walking with eyes cast down. At least the cold rendered the dog poop harmless until the spring thaw.

Shivering in white clouds of breath, we walked to the double doors at the entrance to Jackie's building and peered through the grimy panes. Our breath fogged the glass, but we could make out a small lobby and a wide wooden staircase leading up. There were landings on every floor, each with a doorway on the left side and a single, low-watt incandescent bulb providing the only light. The stairs seemed to rise forever, and moving 500 pounds by hand up that mountain was going to be a challenge. We hoped Windsor hired some very large guys to assist us.

We banged loudly, trying to get someone's attention, and after three or four minutes, an upstairs door opened, and a flood of light illuminated the top landing. Jackie Winsor emerged. She walked down accompanied by a scrawny young man she introduced to us as "Joey." He appeared to be only nineteen or twenty years old, with arms covered in tattoos that stood out on his pale skin, which had a corpse-like hue in the dim hallway light. He offered me a weak, moist hand. My first thought was he must be a friend who was hanging out with Jackie. No way could this kid possibly be any help. Surely the real muscle had yet to arrive.

Paul and I looked at each other apprehensively and asked when the helpers were arriving. Jackie fidgeted. She hadn't been able to find anyone, she confessed, but she and Joey could do it!

"Joey is very strong," she said, "and so am I."

Paul and I exchanged looks. We needed to get the sculpture off of our truck because we knew if we waited another day, Jackie might disappear. Artists worked on their own timetables and were often oblivious to the time of day. It wasn't easy to connect with someone who worked all night and slept all day. And if drugs and booze were involved, an artist could disappear for days. We didn't know Jackie, but we knew the pattern. If we missed our window for delivery, we would have to take the sculpture back to Los Angeles and try another time. We needed to deliver now. No delivery, no pay.

We went back to the truck and climbed inside the trailer to discuss what we should do. We decided the two of us could roll the sculpture off the back of the truck and into the lobby to the foot of the stairs. If push came to shove, and we could not move it up the stairs, we would leave it in the lobby. Since the lobby door locked, it would be safe from vandalism. Theft was entirely out of the question. Who would steal five hundred pounds of rope? But then we worried. This was New York, after all, where anything could and would be stolen. Five hundred pounds of rope, though? We proceeded with Plan A.

Ignoring the sidewalk filth, we maneuvered the sculpture through the doors, rolled it inside, and balanced it upright against the first step. I looked at my gloves and decided I'd have to throw them away when we finished.

All four of us grabbed the donut low to lift it. Paul and I got it off the ground, but the other two couldn't budge it. Carrying it wasn't going to work. We decided to try rolling it up the stairs. We experimented with positioning the sculpture so Paul and I could bend our knees and place our shoulders on each side under the curve. By straightening our legs and shoving upwards, we determined we had the strength to roll it up—one step at a time. But as soon as we let go to reposition our legs and shoulders, the sculpture rolled back down. The trick was to find a way to keep it from rolling back each time we let go.

We discussed a new plan with Jackie. Paul and I would muscle the sculpture up the incline one step at a time, and if Jackie and Joey could hold it in place, we could get back under the curve and leverage it onto another stair.

"We'll do all the heavy work lifting it," we told Jackie. "You and Joey can help us by grabbing it and holding on to keep it from rolling back downstairs."

Stair by stair, we grunted and strained until we reached the first landing. After resting a few minutes to catch our breath, we repeated our way to the second landing, the old wooden stairs creaking and groaning under the weight. The stairwell was unheated, but Paul and I were soaked with sweat. It was agonizing work—the same motion and physical exertion as pushing a football lineman's training sled. Sisyphus and his stupid boulder had nothing on us!

We began the final flight of stairs feeling exhausted but optimistic we would make it. Joey was holding onto my side of the sculpture, and my face was inches from his hands. I noticed his arms began to tremble, and I focused on his tattoos. For the first time, I saw the chicken tracks of multiple needle punctures. Joey was a junkie. A young, addicted, lost soul. Junkies often used tattoos to disguise their needle marks. I looked up at his pale face, which was contorted in agony. Beads of sweat glistened on his eyebrows. I bent down to prepare for the next heave, and looking through the donut hole, I caught Paul's eye and motioned my head in Joey's direction. We heaved up another step, and Paul glanced over. Jackie was looking anxiously at Joey too.

Just a few steps from the top, we repositioned ourselves for the final push. My legs were shaking from the exertion, and my shoulders ached from the pressure of lifting and chafing against the rough, coarse rope. But by sheer determination and grit, we could make it. We only had a few more steps to go. Suddenly Joey let out a shrill scream and started wailing, "I can't do it! I can't do it! I can't do it anymore!" He let go of the sculpture and collapsed to the floor. Curled into a fetal position, his hands between his knees, he began shaking and sobbing uncontrollably. It was unnerving. A moment later, Jackie also let go and stepped back.

We desperately tried to reposition our shoulders under the curve for a final heave onto the landing, but the sculpture kept rolling back against us. Our energy was fading, and we were desperate: "God-dammit, Jackie! Grab the fucking thing!" Paul yelled at her. But she stood immobilized, holding her hands at chest level, palms facing outward in a sign of surrender. We were stuck between the proverbial rock and a hard place.

Paul and I looked at each other and silently reached a decision. Counting out loud in unison to three, we stepped aside. *Double Bound Circle* began rolling downstairs, picking up speed as it went. The stairs shook with a deep rumbling sound, adding extra drama. When it reached the first landing below us, it was still rolling in contact with the stairs. By the next landing, it gained enough speed to partially vault over that landing, and when it reached the lobby, it was airborne. It crashed through the double doors and shot across Bowery Avenue, narrowly missing a passing taxi before colliding with a parked car and falling on its side, spinning in diminishing parabolic circles and coming to rest in the middle of the street.

Jackie looked stunned. Paul, who was always fast on his feet, didn't hesitate a moment. He handed her our bill of lading and a pen. "Sign here for the delivery, please!" She did, and we left. The "donut" now resides in the permanent collections of the High Museum in Atlanta, Georgia. And it still looks great, none the worse for wear.

Hahn

On a late Tuesday morning, several months after the Winsor delivery, I called the Hahn Brothers warehouse to ask if I could come by the next day to pick up a large Dubuffet painting for the Walker Art Center in Minneapolis. The Dubuffet was one of the dimensional bas-relief works he carved from foam and painted. It wasn't overly heavy, but it was nearly eight feet tall and sixteen feet long—too large for me to safely handle alone.

Hahn's warehouse manager, Sam, was not in an accommodating mood. He couldn't have the painting ready for release until Thursday morning, he said, so I would need to spend an additional day in New York. And he wouldn't let his warehouse workers help me load it into my truck, even if I paid them. This was unusually unfriendly because truckers and warehousemen routinely assisted each other. I would now have to find temporary help with the skills to safely handle the art. Not knowing where else to go, I decided to hire Hague Art Transporters to assist. The hourly charges for two art handlers were going to put a considerable dent in what I was being paid to truck the painting to Minneapolis. But I didn't have any other choice, and it would only take a couple of hours at most to load my truck.

On Thursday morning, my hired hands and I arrived at the Hahn Brothers loading dock. Sam was seated inside at a desk behind a chest-high wooden counter. A closed access gate on the counter kept him safely apart from arriving truckers, and a large freight elevator to the right ferried goods into the warehouse.

I introduced myself to Sam, who gruffly told me the painting wasn't ready yet and we would need to wait. At noon the dock closed for lunch, and we were told to leave and return at 1 p.m. By 3 p.m., I was becoming anxiety-ridden and asked again when we could have the painting. "You need to wait," Sam said. "We are very busy right now." I thought this was odd because no one had used the freight elevator all day, but we waited until 5 p.m. when the warehouse closed. Sam told us to return the next morning, and when we did, he put us through another round of the waiting game. By mid-afternoon, I knew I'd be paying my entire commission for the delivery to the Hague guys for this wait. I tried to stay calm, but rage was bubbling inside. Finally, at 4 p.m., the elevator door opened, and I saw the Dubuffet sitting inside, but the car was gone before anyone unloaded it. Sam's back was toward the elevator wall, so he didn't know I had seen the painting. Without looking up, he began tidying the papers on his desk and told us we would need to return on Monday to get the painting.

I went nuts. I began climbing over the counter to get at him, screaming that I was going to kick his ass. The two Hague guys rushed over to pull me away, and when things calmed down, Sam finally released the painting, and we loaded my truck.

I was so stressed that I decided to go to a movie in Times Square and try to relax before leaving the city. When the movie ended at 10 p.m., I walked toward my truck. As I got closer, I noticed it appeared to be leaning oddly toward the sidewalk. I was fifty feet away when I saw that the tires along the curb were all flat, and a guy dressed in a trench coat and brimmed hat was leaning against it, holding a stiletto in his right hand. He was casually cleaning his fingernails, waiting for me to return, likely intending to stick me with the blade. I stopped to assess what to do and saw the glint of his eyes looking at me from under the hat's brim. It was like a scene from a "B" rated film noir. Did New York thugs really dress that way? The situation seemed ludicrous, almost laughable, but the hood—though he was small and scrawny—was armed, and I wasn't, so I had to take him seriously. By luck, there was an enclosed telephone booth a few feet away. I jumped inside and closed the door, so if I needed to, I could keep him out by pushing against it. I fed some dimes in the phone and called the police. The dispatcher, sounding incredulous, asked if I was injured. I told him I was trapped in the phone booth, and the thug was waiting outside with a knife. He laughed and said all of his patrol cars were busy. After that, I was listening to a dial tone. Apparently, he thought I was a crank caller.

Mr. Trench Coat was now standing a few feet closer to my booth, trying to decide what he should do next. I pretended to still be talking with the police, excitedly gesturing toward him and looking at nearby addresses to inform the cops of my location. The bluff must have worked because he put the knife in a pocket and walked away rapidly. Once he was out of sight, I assessed the damaged tires. Each had a ¾ inch slice in the sidewalls and was totally flat. It was late Friday evening, and unlikely a tire repair service would come out that late, so I locked the truck's doors and went to sleep.

When I awoke on Saturday morning, Times Square was getting busy. I used the book in the phone booth to begin calling truck tire repair services, all of them near the truck stops in New Jersey. No one was willing to come into Manhattan—"too dangerous over there"—and I was becoming desperate when I noticed a small ad for a tire shop in Midtown. The guy answering the phone had a thick Italian accent and seemed to have difficulty understanding me.

"What's that you say? You tires cut? No shit! Who cut you tires?"

He finally agreed to come to Times Square—"Just as soon I can get my truck started!"—and hung up. I waited for more than an hour and had almost given up when a decrepit old Chevy panel truck drove up. It was painted dark green and black, colors that seemed popular in the '40s and '50s. The truck's brakes squealed to a stop, and its engine valves loudly clattered under the hood. An older man with a crew cut and three or four days' worth of unshaved gray stubble on his face climbed out. He was wearing grease-stained coveralls, and his fingernails were black.

"My name's Tony," he said. "You got a big problem here, kid! What we going to do? How you get yourself in this fix?"

He stood looking glumly at the slits while shaking his head disapprovingly, and I worried he was going to leave without helping. Instead, he opened the double doors on the rear of his truck, revealing an enormous air compressor that filled the interior. It appeared to be of World War II vintage and was streaked with rust, dirt, grease, and pigeon poop—and powered by a rubber belt from a small gasoline engine. He opened a dented toolbox, removed some tire patches, walked over, and glued them over the holes in my tires. I knew about tire repairs from my gas station days and wondered how this was going to work. Truck tires have tubes inside, and patching the outside wouldn't stop the tubes from leaking. But Tony wasn't done. He climbed into his truck and wrapped a cord around the gas engine flywheel. There wasn't enough overhead clearance to let him stand, and he was hunched over inside as he began yanking the cord. Nothing happened, so he re-wound and yanked again. He continued this time after time, cursing in Italian and yelling at the equipment. Finally, almost reluctantly, the gas engine sparked to life, shaking violently as it ran.

Tony made an adjustment to the carburetor, and the engine leveled off and began filling the tank with compressed air. Tony unfurled a long hose from the compressor and started filling my tires. The filled tires hissed as air escaped. He then made another round before stuffing the hose into his truck and slamming the doors shut. The compressor was still running inside. "Follow me!" he yelled, and I scrambled to start my truck. His driver's side window was partly open, and a cloud of blue smoke poured out as he drove away and disappeared into traffic. For a while, I could see the blue smoke rising from the traffic up ahead and followed it until my tires lost too much air and was forced to stop. Twenty minutes later, he drove back to find me. "Why you stop?" he yelled. The compressor was still going, and when he opened the rear doors, a pungent cloud of blue smoke poured out. He refilled the tires, and I again followed him through traffic. We stopped in front of a small warehouse tire shop on a narrow residential street where cars were parked on both sides, leaving barely enough room for two vehicles going in opposite directions to squeeze past each other. Tony ordered me to park my truck in the street, even though it was sure to block traffic. I asked if this was okay.

"It's no problem!" he assured me. "Never traffic on this street."

There were two chairs on the sidewalk in front of the tire shop, and he walked over and sat down in one, jamming two fingers in his mouth to produce an ear-piercing whistle. The garage's overhead door began grinding and squeaking as it slowly rose, and a second man, similar in appearance to Tony, walked out. He was pulling a greasy, steel-wheeled automobile jack and started jacking up each of my truck's axles. When each was high enough, he placed a concrete block under it. Soon all of the axles were up on blocks, and all of the wheels were suspended a few inches above the pavement. The man walked over and sat down in the second chair. As he did, Tony returned to the truck and removed the first tire with a wrench. He took it into the shop, where he patched the inner tube and filled the tire with air, then brought it back and reattached it to the truck. He sat down again, and the second man got up to work on the next tire.

"Why aren't you both working on the repairs at the same time?" I asked Tony.

"Because my brother is a lazy shit, and this way, I make sure that he does his fair share of the work!"

His brother, leaning over to remove a tire, yelled back, "Don't believe him. He's a big liar and will sit around on his fat ass doing nothing if he gets a chance!"

It was another one of those crazy accommodations New Yorkers make to avoid killing each other.

While they worked, I walked up the street and pondered how long these brothers had been joined at the hip, running the tire shop under their insane rules. Had they acted this way since they were kids? Walking along, I noticed a red light on a building at the corner of the intersection up ahead—a firehouse. Walking in the other direction, I saw a blue light on the other corner—a police station. My truck, sitting primly on concrete blocks in the middle of the street, was bookended by emergency vehicles. As if on cue, alarms went off, and fire trucks rolled out of the station and headed down the street toward us. They arrived in a din of sirens and flashing red lights that came to a stop behind my truck. Firemen jumped out and began milling around, yelling at Tony to get it out of the street. Tony and his brother yelled back. In typical New York fashion, where emergency vehicles go, taxis follow, and the street behind the fire trucks soon filled with cabs, most of them leaning on their horns. The racket was deafening. I heard more sirens coming from the opposite direction, and three cop cars rolled up, also trailed by taxi cabs. The cops jumped out and began yelling at Tony and his brother, who, in return, were making hand gestures as they shouted back.

After several minutes of chaos, everyone finally calmed down. The cops and firemen stood glaring at Tony and his brother, who, hands-on-hips defiantly glared back. The cops walked up to the fire station at the end of the street and began directing taxis to back out and free the fire trucks. This took twenty minutes, and I hoped that someone's house hadn't burned down by then. Finally, with the street cleared and repairs completed on the tires, I headed to Minneapolis to deliver the Dubuffet.

It was only when I arrived at the Walker I discovered, much to my chagrin, the painting had a damaged corner that I hadn't noticed during the confrontation at the warehouse. I also realized Sam, the warehouse manager, had been intentionally stalling me, hoping I would give up and leave without the painting so he would have time to make repairs and hide the damage. By losing my temper, I'd gotten the painting released. But I didn't condition report the Dubuffet—a rookie move—and Sam's problem conveniently became mine. I made sure I didn't get sucked into an emotional reaction that way again. It was bad for me, bad for the art, bad for my clients.

Kathy

New York long hauls were definitely no place for amateur drivers, but that didn't keep my boss from sticking me with one. She met Kathy, a big-boned woman who wore her pants like a man, at one of the Wednesday night women's liberation meetings she hosted at Cart & Crate. Kathy convinced my boss she knew how to drive a tractor-trailer, and without checking her experience or testing her capabilities, the boss assigned her to be our first female mover and my co-driver.

By the time we finished loading our trailer with the art going to New York, it was early evening. Not knowing how good a driver Kathy was, I took the night shift, and after driving eight hours, I woke her at daybreak. We stopped in a Union 76 truck stop near Phoenix, Arizona. Being August, it was already over 90 degrees outside when I crawled exhausted into the truck's sleeper, and Kathy climbed into the driver's seat.

I woke up in an oven, soaking in sweat, disoriented, and dying of thirst. The engine was off, all of the windows rolled up, and the enclosed cab was sweltering. When I put on my glasses, the first thing that came into focus was Kathy zipping up her pants as she climbed out of a nearby truck. She turned, looked up smiling, and waved at the truck driver, whose head and shirtless shoulders were peering out from his truck's sleeper bunk. He was smiling back. She never left the truck stop. We had been parked for hours, and I knew then it was going to be a long trip to New York.

I continued to do the night-shift driving, which was tiring and very boring because there was so little to see as we passed through the dark countryside. I constantly struggled to stay awake. If I was lucky, the radio would pick up Wolfman Jack, the legendary DJ, and I'd distract myself listening to the teenage girls calling from all over mid-America to make song requests and dedications.

"Wolfman, please play a song for my boyfriend, Billy Bob. I love him soooooooo much!"

"Darlin' sweet girl, where ya callin' from?" Wolfman would reply in his deep, raspy voice. "Which Bobby Darin song do you want to hear for your true love Billy Bob?" Their voices would drift in and out as if spanning a great distance or coming from outer space—the sounds emphasizing the vast emptiness of the countryside. Where the broadcasts originated was a mystery, although it was rumored they came from an illegal radio station in Mexico, near the US border. A Mexican location would allow Wolfman's pirate radio transmitter to exceed the FCC mandated wattages, which limited the reach of legitimate, federally licensed broadcasters. I didn't care if he was broadcasting from Mars or Maine, because all the other Midwest radio stations were dominated by preachers whose "hallelujahs" and "praise the lords," along with the ubiquitous "send money to help Jesus" were stultifying—only adding to the misery of the endless drive. Wolfman was a welcome, friendly voice in vast swaths of the midlands.

A day after Phoenix, we were in the cornfields of Iowa. I was finishing another night shift, and it was Kathy's turn to drive when a small truck stop came into view. I hadn't eaten in hours, so I pulled into the parking lot.

Kathy and I went into the small café and sat down in a booth with a pink Formica tabletop and shiny, red tuck-and-rolled vinyl upholstery. We were the only customers. Our waitress, a pretty teenage girl wearing a prim pink apron, walked over and handed us menus and cups of coffee, then stood on Kathy's side of the table, waiting patiently to take our orders. She likely chose that spot because she noticed I was having a hard time keeping my eyes off of her large, classically shaped breasts. Kathy, being female, must've seemed like a safer bet. But then she opened her mouth.

Moving her head close to the waitress's bosom and slowly casting her eyes up and down, Kathy uncorked a breathless come-on voice and said, "Girl! You got an unbelievable set of knockers on you!" A momentary expression of disbelief and shock crossed the waitress's face before it crumbled and she ran sobbing hysterically into the kitchen. Kathy sat watching her go with a satisfied smirk. The kitchen door closed, and there were a few moments of quiet before it flew open with a loud crash and an angry behemoth charged toward our table. He wore a greasy apron and had blond hair with a tight crew cut. His shoulders were covered in tattoos, and his face, so red it matched the upholstery, was contorted in rage as he rushed up to Kathy, brandishing a meat cleaver.

"Now she's going to get it for running her smart-ass mouth," I thought.

He focused on Kathy, and for a moment, his face showed confusion and uncertainty as he realized he was confronting a woman. A woman wouldn't have commented on his waitress's breasts, so it had to be me!

He swung his bulk around the end of the table, reached over, grabbed my lapel with a beefy hand, and yanked me straight up. My legs jammed under the table edge and against the seat. I couldn't move—I was helpless as a rag doll. He held the meat cleaver's cutting edge within an inch of my nose and brought his face in close. Stale cigarettes, onions, and bad breath washed over my face as he yelled, "Who the hell you think you are talking to my waitress that way! I ought to cut you from one end to the other, you dirty sono-fabitch!"

"Leave him alone, you big bully," Kathy said, calmly looking up. "You're bigger than him. Leave him alone! You should be ashamed of yourself, you bully!"

The cook forcefully released me and sent me sprawling across the booth seat, my head narrowly missing the wall. "Get the hell out of my place, and don't ever come back here!" he thundered.

We scrambled out. So much for eating.

Kathy drove, and I tried to sleep. Was it the hunger pangs, jangled nerves from the assault, or Kathy's driving keeping me awake?

Several days later, when we entered New York City, Kathy was at the wheel again. We were immediately pulled into a familiar tango with Manhattan's notorious taxi drivers, who are always looking for an advantage in traffic. They are prone to passing on the right, even if it means cutting across a sidewalk to get in front. They're a hazard if you don't know how to handle them. From the high vantage point of a semi-tractor, it is difficult to see another vehicle when its nose is partly stuck in front of the right-side front fender. So, the unwritten rule—understood by truckers and taxi drivers alike—is truckers should yield to let the faster taxi forge ahead. Being that this was Kathy's first trip into the city, she was oblivious, so I focused my attention on warning her each time a taxi began maneuvering in front.

As we proceeded down a street, I noticed a couple of men running on the sidewalk on Kathy's side. They were keeping pace with our truck and soon joined by several others. They were all pointing and shouting: "Look, it's a woman driving a truck! There's a woman driving that truck!" Their numbers grew, and soon a phalanx of laughing, pointing, excited guys were keeping pace alongside. I realized that in New York, where unions and mob bosses controlled the trucking venues, drivers were always men. It was another unwritten rule, and the sight of Kathy driving was so unusual it was causing a big stir.

Kathy began smiling and waving back, nodding her head toward them to acknowledge the attention. She was the star of the parade. Then bam! She ran into a taxi that had cut in front. The driver angrily climbed out, and Kathy and I jumped down to assess the damage. The driver yelled until she sassed him back, and he realized he was dealing with a woman. Not knowing what to do, he turned his wrath on me. I kept insisting I wasn't the driver and wasn't responsible for his damage. The taxi's passenger climbed out, carrying a brown leather briefcase, and when the driver saw his fare walking down the street, he gave up and sped off. Kathy hit another cab that afternoon, so I took over driving.

We made deliveries in the city for three days, with a final stop at the Met, where we loaded a dozen crated Old Master paintings belonging to Norton Simon and destined for the Los Angeles County Museum of Art. By the time we finished, it was around 3 p.m., a good time to leave Manhattan before traffic got too congested at rush hour, but Kathy pleaded for some time to spend in SoHo. With misgivings, I agreed, but told her to be back at the truck by 6 p.m. because we had a tight schedule and needed to start driving west.

At 7 p.m., I was still waiting by the truck. By 8 p.m., I began to worry something bad had happened, so I went looking for her. It was approaching 9 p.m. when I found her standing on top of a bar counter, beer in hand, as she extolled a large crowd with stories of her trucking exploits. The crowd was wildly cheering and applauding, and Kathy was glowing from the attention and adulation as I walked up to tell her I was leaving. If she didn't come immediately, I yelled up at her, I'd go without her. The crowd began booing as I ushered her out the door.

Tired, angry, and not thinking clearly, I decided she should take the night shift for a change. I gave her directions on how to leave the city and connect to the I-40 going west, crawled into the bunk, pulled the curtains, and went to sleep.

The urgent warning sounds of a blaring air horn startled me awake. I could hear the hiss of airbrakes and the sounds of a rapidly approaching truck skidding on wet pavement. Our truck rocked violently from air pressure as another truck passed by us within inches, its tires pelting our side with spray. We were stopped dead, and I could hear Kathy sobbing from the driver's seat on the other side of the sleeper curtains. What was happening? What was she crying about?

I opened the sleeper's side air vent, an opening measuring twelve by four inches, and looked outside. We were stopped on a freeway in the slow lane, and it was raining heavily. I could see a metal guardrail dividing our side from the lanes going the opposite direction. Several oncoming cars rushed by in those nearby lanes, the glare of their headlights reflecting on the falling raindrops. I was about to tell Kathy that stopping on the freeway was dangerous and ask if we had broken down. But suddenly, she shifted into first gear and began moving across the neighboring lanes. I saw she was starting to make a U-turn through an opening in the center divider—an opening that was very small. Perhaps a state patrol car or emergency vehicle could maneuver through, but it looked impossible for the bulk of our semi-truck. Kathy picked up speed, and I realized it was too late to stop her. If I yelled and startled or confused her, we could end up stopped across all lanes and blocking the entire freeway. She was wearing a seatbelt and might survive, but I was high up in the sleeper and would most likely die if we were hit by an oncoming truck. Semi-tractors look formidable, but lightweight construction makes them big tin cans on wheels. If a car came along, the driver would end up decapitated under our trailer, but another truck would smash us to pieces, leaving Old Master crates and parts of my body scattered along the freeway. I had no choice but to pray she could get through before the drivers of a truck or car realized too late that they couldn't avoid the collision and crashed into us.

She drove the cab through the opening, pulling across the opposite traffic lanes, and I watched through the narrow vent to see if the trailer following behind was going to make it. The trailer's tires hit the guardrail, briefly caught against it, and then bounced off and scraped through the opening. Kathy straightened out the truck and began picking up speed, driving in the opposite direction. I climbed out of the sleeper into the passenger seat and didn't say anything until we stopped at a rest area an hour later.

Kathy told me she thought she had gotten onto the New Jersey Turnpike by mistake and that we were headed in the wrong direction. She saw the emergency opening and stopped in the slow lane, waiting for a clearing in traffic to make the U-turn. She was crying when I woke, she said, because of the angry, blasting truck horns and the frustration of driving nearly fifty miles in what she thought was the wrong direction.

I took over the driving, and when we arrived at the exit toll booth, I handed our ticket to the attendant. As he started to calculate the toll, he looked confused. He grabbed the phone to make a call, and a minute later, two men walked quickly over from a small office on the side of the toll plaza. They pushed inside the tollbooth to be out of the rain and looked at the ticket, conferring and gesturing with upturned palms. Finally, the one who appeared to be in charge leaned out and asked me how we had gotten there. I was worried we would be fined or arrested for the U-turn and decided to play dumb, saying we had driven, and if the ticket was wrong, well heck, it was given to us that way. The three went back to conferring, again gesturing their frustration.

Only two of the booths were open, probably because of the late hour, and in my side mirror, I could see traffic beginning to back up behind us. The supervisor made a phone call and, several minutes later, a state patrol car arrived with flashing blue emergency lights. Two troopers got out, their wide-brimmed hats wrapped in plastic against the weather. They joined the other three in the tollbooth, all packed in tightly to get out of the rain. It was now pouring. The patrol officers looked at the ticket, and I could hear them discussing which traffic codes had been violated and what they'd cite if they issued a traffic ticket. The arguing in the booth was increasingly interrupted by the cacophony of blaring horns from frustrated drivers, who by now were backed up behind us until the line disappeared in the distance. Finally, the toll supervisor decided that the best way to settle the matter would be to charge us tolls for traveling both directions. I made Kathy empty her wallet, but she was short, so I used my money to cover the rest. Luckily, we had enough between us to leave without ending up in a New Jersey jail. The supervisor handed me the receipt, gave me a hard look, and said, "Don't you ever pull a bullshit stunt like this again. Get out of here." I drove away, followed for a few minutes by the patrol car, its flashing blue lights bouncing off our mirrors in a kaleidoscope of reflections inside the cab. That was my only trip with Kathy. She left Cart & Crate shortly after, and I heard she became a screenwriter.

Black Truck

Of all the hazards on the road, the ones we had to be on constant guard against—especially in a place like New York—were the clueless errors of drivers like Kathy or companies like the Black Truck. The Black Truck was an art shuttle business owned by "Jim," who drove a black Iveco Magirus diesel, a twenty-four-foot straight truck. In the days before refrigeration became standard for maintaining moderate temperatures inside the cargo boxes of trucks, black was the worst color to paint a truck. The art transported inside was at least ten degrees hotter than a white truck during summer interstate driving, albeit a little warmer in the winter if the sun was out.

Jim drove his truck back and forth between Los Angeles and New York City, stopping in other cities along the way, picking up and dropping off art. He was a hard worker and began to build a large clientele of galleries and auction houses. Jim stopped by my warehouse every couple of weeks to pick up art we had crated for clients, and although I liked him, I would never give him one of our shipments because he had a quirk that scared me. When Jim came into our offices with paperwork in hand, he always left his truck in the street with the engine running. When I asked him about it, he told me that all truckers left their trucks running while using the bathroom or eating meals. But he missed an important caveat. The truckers who left their engines idling were doing it to keep their bunks cool in the summer or warm in the winter because they had partners asleep in the cabs who needed comfortable conditions. Jim's truck was a twenty-four-foot bobtail without a sleeper—so he had no reason for leaving his truck full of valuable art on the street with a running engine and keys in the ignition. I figured if he kept doing it, it would only be a matter of time before something bad happened. And because I didn't want it to happen while he was at our warehouse, I instructed my warehouse manager to station an employee next to his truck whenever he arrived.

When Jim's business grew enough, he hired another driver for alternating trips. This gave him time off to recuperate from the punishing routine of driving 500 or 600 miles per day. It worked well for several months until the relief driver and the Black Truck disappeared. The truck was gone for several weeks until a sheriff in Tucson, Arizona, traced it using Jim's vehicle registration documents. Jim flew in to recover the vehicle from an impound lot, where it had been towed for violating local street parking signs. The female driver had found love in a local bar and run off into the setting sun. Jim was relieved to find nothing missing, and although his deliveries were very late and clients upset, he managed to smooth things over and continue building his clientele. He should have learned a valuable lesson but continued playing trucker with the idling engine.

Things finally went to hell one day when Jim was in New York City. His truck was packed with art sold at a Sotheby's painting auction, a crated Louise Nevelson sculpture exhibition, and dozens of other art shipments destined for collectors, galleries, and museums across the US.

It was late afternoon when Jim parked in front of a SoHo gallery and ran upstairs to pick up one last painting before leaving town. He left the engine idling as usual, and when he returned five minutes later, the Black Truck was gone.

The police were called, and because the case involved interstate theft, the FBI was brought in as well. The owners of the missing art notified their insurance companies, and weeks passed without any resolution until one day, a postcard arrived at one of the insurance offices. It was a ransom note, its message pieced together from letters cut out of magazines. The insurance company had millions at stake and found itself caught in a quandary: play footsie with the criminals to get the art back, or tip off the FBI and risk losing everything? They did the expedient thing and paid the crooks through a wire transfer sent to a numbered overseas account. Several days later, another postcard arrived, providing an address, where they found an abandoned warehouse with the missing art inside.

The extortion scheme continued for months, making its way through individual galleries, insurance companies, and anyone else unlucky enough to have consigned valuable art to the Black Truck. Eventually, enough art was recovered that most parties were willing to risk losing what remained and reported everything to the FBI, who was not pleased to learn that their investigation had been undermined. But the FBI was duty-bound to capture criminals and decided to set a trap when the next postcard arrived. The hijackers laid low for several months, but finally, a card arrived at the first insurance company, listing an address out on Long Island. Insurance company investigators, along with the FBI, drove to a remote area and located the address—an abandoned farm overgrown by shrubs and tangled weeds. They drove down a dirt track, found the ramshackle barn, and opened the creaky doors. Inside, they saw the Black Truck. Its rear doors were open, and after climbing inside, they found the rest of the stolen art. Jim gave up his business and went to work for an art moving company in the Bay Area.

Five years later, at a meeting of the American Association of Museums in Philadelphia, I sat in on a session about museum security and art theft. Among the presenters was Bill Smith, a highly respected insurance adjuster specializing in art. A tough-as-nails ex-Marine with a tightly trimmed crew cut and a thick neck, Bill announced he was going to use the saga of the Black Truck as an example of how lax security had resulted in substantial losses for the insurance industry. Jim was sitting several chairs away from me, and as Smith explained the events surrounding the hijacking, Jim's face turned ashen, and he headed for the exit. I never saw him again.

Hustler

On one of my early solo trips from Los Angeles to New York, I swung into New Orleans and made a stop in the French Quarter for a pickup at Larry Flynt's Hustler Club. Standing on the sidewalk outside the main entrance was a group of men, holding bottles of beer, talking, and squabbling loudly. Over their heads, a balcony extended the length of the building, providing shade from the hot afternoon sun. Looking up at it, I envisioned buxom and scantily clad beauties standing there during Mardi Gras, tossing beads and medallions to the cheering crowd below. These thoughts were made more poignant by my long, lonely hours of driving.

Hustler magazine had borrowed a dozen paintings by an artist named "Lilly" to photograph for a feature story, and I was to return them to Lilly's Tribeca studio. I had missed seeing the photos in print, being a Playboy magazine man, myself. Hustler always had a sleazy, unsavory aura, and at least Playboy offered a façade of intellectual content, which gave cover to justify its purchase. Highbrow porno or prurient porno? In the 1970s, this was every man's existential question.

So I was taken aback when I saw Lilly's paintings in person. They depicted naked women, as I expected, but these women had physiques like the ones done by Michelangelo—which is to say they were essentially men with boobs. Lilly could've ripped them off the Sistine Chapel ceilings and attached them to her four-foot-square canvases. I guessed she might be a big woman, or butch, or a man in drag, which could explain the preponderance of heavy-set, muscular women in the work.

I finished loading my truck and went looking for the club manager, who signed my paperwork and then said, "Before you leave, the boss wants to talk to you. Follow me." It was not a request. We walked through the club, past scantily clad dancers and a busy bar, stopping at a closed door in the back. The manager knocked, and a voice from inside said, "Come in." The manager held the door for me and stepping inside, I saw Larry Flynt sitting behind an expansive desk. He looked young and fit—the assassination attempt that would put him in a wheelchair was still a year away. The office walls were covered with framed images of women in various stages of undress, and to avoid being distracted, I kept my attention tightly focused on him as he spoke.

"What's your name, kid?" he asked. "I understand you're delivering the paintings to my good friend Lilly in New York and want to make certain you are careful with them." He slid a $50 bill across the desk. "Take this, and be sure you take extra good care of Lilly."

Arriving several days later at Lilly's studio, I was surprised to find she was a young, petite woman dressed in modest business attire. She wore a navy-blue skirt with matching jacket, a white blouse, pantyhose, and flats. With her dark-rimmed spectacles and her black hair tied back in a ponytail, she was, in every respect, a model for a Sally Secretary. This was not what I expected, given her connection to Hustler, and after noticing her nice figure, I wondered if she was being featured in the issue along with her paintings.

She greeted me coolly and instructed me to take her paintings up the stairs and arrange them against the studio's walls. I could only carry one at a time, which meant twelve trips. By the second trip, she disappeared, remaining out of sight. I was just leaning the last painting against a far wall when I heard the entrance door slam shut and was startled by a loud explosion in my right ear. I turned to see Lilly standing fifteen feet away, holding a bullwhip. She wore a snug black leather outfit pulled so tightly up to her crotch that not much was left to the imagination. Stiletto-heeled boots ended several inches above her knees, and a black leather executioner's hood with eye holes covered her head. Sally Secretary had a hidden life. She expertly swung the bullwhip several more times, its tip cracking within inches of my shoulders. I could feel the wind generated against my cheeks and desperately looked toward the door, which had four locks of varying types. I would likely be cut to shreds before figuring them out.

"Let's party!" she yelled. "Let's get it on!"

I backed around the room, trying to keep myself out of the whip's range, but she stayed in the center, moving to cut me off. Was this foreplay? How much pain would I need to endure before enjoying her pleasure? I didn't know the rules of this game and began talking fast.

"Listen, lady, I don't want to do this! I'm not the masochistic type. You need to stop before something really bad happens and someone gets hurt."

She stopped, looking disappointed. "But don't you want to have some fun? We could have a really good time together."

"I'm sorry, Lilly," I said, "but I have a lot of work to do and need to get going."

Lilly rolled up the whip and hung it on the back of a chair, and just like that, Sally Secretary reappeared. "Thanks for taking good care of my paintings," she said curtly.

I had her sign the paperwork and fled.

Peter Yarrow

The plots and characters in a single trip could take me from the salacious to the sublime. After the Hustler delivery, I swung over to a Manhattan storage warehouse to pick up art and antique furniture belonging to Peter Yarrow, of the folk singing group "Peter, Paul and Mary," which had recently broken up. He was moving to California, and the goods were destined for his Malibu Colony home. Peter showed up in the afternoon, just as I finished loading, and asked if I wanted to go clubbing. He was looking at female singers for his new band, and we were treated like royalty in every club. The next day, he asked me to drive him to Woodstock to pick up an antique table from his agent, Albert Grossman. Yarrow was in a reflective mood as we traveled and described being set up by the police during the chaotic 1968 Chicago Democratic Convention, where he was involved with the anti-Vietnam war protests, and spent time in jail.

At last, we reached Grossman's, an eighteenth-century stone farmhouse set on what had once been tillable farmland, but had long since reverted to woodlands covered in maple and oak trees. The house was filled with beautiful antiques, and gold and platinum records hung on all the walls. Janice Joplin, one of his clients, had recently passed away, and her famous psychedelic Porsche was parked in the driveway. I went outside to sit in the driver's seat and commune for a while with Janice, remembering her amazing voice and the pleasure her songs gave to the world. For all the jerks and crazy stress we dealt with, there were private moments like this to find balance and make the long drives and hours a little easier.

I tried to recreate the experience a few decades later when I happened to pass the Porsche in the lobby of the Grammy Museum in LA, where an exhibition label said it was on loan from Albert Grossman. I asked the registrar I'd come to visit if I could sit in it again, but I was on the other side of the rope this time. The answer was no.

A Servant Must Never Forget His Place

Winnetka

WHEN COLLECTORS PAY for services, some of them believe they've purchased the right to treat those they've hired in demeaning and degrading ways. They think that because they are rich, influential, and successful, their desires are all-important—and the wellbeing of those who try to satisfy them isn't their concern. One of the worst of this ilk, a man who took great pleasure in humiliating the little guy, was a wealthy Chicago art collector named Morton.

When we arrived at the ornate gates of his estate in suburban Winnetka, Illinois, there was a pair of tire tracks heading down the long driveway and disappearing into a thick veil of falling snow. The day was windless, and the flakes fell straight down, obscuring anything beyond a few hundred feet. The tire tracks had begun to fill, indicating they had been there for a while. This was not good because we'd been instructed to arrive punctually at 8 a.m., and we were already fifteen minutes late.

We had received the assignment just the day before when we stopped in a Skelly truck stop and checked in with our LA office from

Dallas. Skelly truck stops were small, often dingy operations in the South and Southwest. The advent of the Interstate highway system had isolated many of them along the older highways. They'd been hurt by competition from large, modern operations with restaurants and stores, showers, and most importantly, spacious paved parking lots. But whenever we were in a hurry, we stopped at a Skelly because they were often empty, which allowed us to get back on the highway quickly. That meant we were poised to go when our dispatcher told us to contact the Sotheby's New York offices and ask for Wesley.

I met Wesley several months earlier when I delivered a group of Dutch Old Master paintings to the Sotheby's New York loading dock. They hung in a Frank Lloyd Wright Prairie house in a Chicago suburb and were to be auctioned as part of the owner's estate, who had died several months earlier. When I arrived to pick them up, the house had been emptied of everything but the paintings, which were still hanging on the walls. Though the house was an important architectural monument, the rooms were gloomy, and the paintings—darkened from years of yellowing varnish and soot—made the place feel even more depressing.

As I walked around carefully lifting the paintings off their hooks, I noticed one hanging above an ornate brass heating vent. That got my attention because the vent looked older than the house, and I wondered if Frank Lloyd Wright had actually approved it in his design plans. Wright designed all of the fixtures and furniture in his homes, and with his massive ego, I imagined he would have had a tantrum if he had seen this ugly grate.

The painting above it depicted a harbor view, with some ships at anchor and others in full sail headed to open sea. It had a gilded frame, and when I removed it, a dingy outline remained on the wall, indicating it had not been moved in decades. As I did with the others, I tightly wrapped it in plastic for protection during transit, then tied it off against the wall of my truck.

When I arrived in New York several days later, Wesley came out to receive the shipment. He gave me a friendly welcome and a handshake. And although he was dressed in a suit and tie, he didn't hesitate to start grabbing paintings, placing them on a cart as I handed them out the back door of my truck. I liked him for this because suit and tie-wearing men generally considered themselves too important for manual labor.

I handed him one of the paintings without looking at it, so I didn't know what to think when he asked: "Where's the painting?"

"I just handed it to you," I replied.

"Yes," he said. "But where is the *painting*?"

Looking up at what he was holding, I was shocked to see an empty frame, still wrapped in plastic. This was both frightening and perplexing. My first thought was that the painting had been stolen. But how could a thief have gained access into my locked truck? And why take time and effort to remove the artwork from its frame and rewrap the plastic? Had I failed to notice the painting was missing when I'd wrapped it in Chicago?

I took the frame and examined it closely. My heart sank. There wasn't a trace of the painting. Then, on an impulse, I turned it upside down, and dust and paint chips began cascading inside the plastic covering. It was as if I'd shaken a snow globe and unleashed a swirl of flakes to envelop a jolly old Saint Nick. I suddenly remembered that this was the painting hanging over the ugly heating grate. Years of dry, heated furnace air had blown up from the floor and baked the paint and canvas, making it brittle, and apparently, road vibrations during the drive to New York caused the whole thing to completely disintegrate. Wesley stood quietly for a minute as he pondered what to do. Then, without saying anything, he signed our paperwork and took all of the paintings—including the empty frame—inside. He had let me off the hook, and I felt I owed him a debt of gratitude.

That debt came due during our call from Dallas. Wesley told me a man named Morton was consigning an important group of contemporary paintings and sculptures to the auction house, and we were to pick them up from his summer home in Winnetka—a wealthy suburb 16 miles north of Chicago on the shores of Lake Michigan. Sotheby's had spent months persuading Morton to go with them, as this would be an essential part of their spring auction. Wesley explained that Morton was driving out from Chicago at eight the next morning to open the house, and he had told Wesley that if we were late, he would take his collection to Christie's instead. Wesley sounded worried and asked if we would be able to make it by Morton's deadline. Morton was a difficult man, he added, and we'd need to be extremely polite and agree to do whatever he asked.

I said it might be tight, but I thought we'd make it. As for being polite, I didn't expect that to be a problem.

It's a long drive from Dallas to Chicago—970 miles on I-30. But we couldn't take I-30 because it went through Missouri, and in the 1970s, trucks couldn't travel through Missouri without first purchasing a permit. This permit had to be ordered by phone during business hours from the state capitol in Jefferson City—forty-eight hours in advance. It was then nine in the morning, and we had twenty-three hours to get to Chicago, not enough time to wait for the permit. We'd have to avoid Missouri by taking secondary highways north, which would slow our progress. We headed north from Dallas, taking turns driving and sleeping, only stopping once for fuel and a quick meal.

Three hundred miles south of Chicago, it began to rain, and as we drove farther north, the rain turned to sleet, which then turned to snow. The highway became icy and dangerous, and soon we were joined by snowplows with sand sprinklers. Night fell, and visibility was marginal, with falling snow obscuring both our headlights and the stripes on the road. We needed to stop for fuel and food, but the fear of being late kept us moving. After enduring this marathon, it was a miracle we'd arrived. We were tired and starving, but we were only fifteen minutes late.

We drove through the gates of the estate and down a long driveway. A large, sandstone-colored mansion began to materialize from behind the falling snow, and as we got closer, Morton's black Lincoln town car came into view. Its headlights were off, but the steam rising from exhaust pipes indicated the engine was idling.

We jumped down from our truck as a chauffeur opened the Lincoln's rear door, and Morton stepped out. He was dressed in an expensive wool overcoat over an equally expensive suit and tie. Without as much as a hello, he went on the attack: "You're late!" he yelled. "Sotheby's *guaranteed* me you would be on time. This is outrageous! You can thank your lucky stars that I didn't leave. Just a few more minutes and I would have gone, and you two imbeciles and Sotheby's would have been out of luck. My time is extremely valuable, and I do *not* appreciate having it wasted. I am going to lodge a complaint with Sotheby's!"

We started to apologize, but he cut us off. "Never mind! You're wasting even more valuable time with your excuses, and you need to get to work."

He marched up the steps, his overshoes squeaking in the fresh snow as he strode across a broad stone porch to an ornately carved wood and glass entryway door. He unlocked it and ushered us into a large foyer. At its rear, grand stone staircases with elaborate black and gold balustrade railings curved up each side, ending at a second-floor balcony. High on the wall to the right was a large Picasso painting of a woman, likely a portrait of one of his mistresses. Important nineteenth and twentieth-century masterpieces were hanging everywhere. Morton may have been a jerk, but he had a stunning collection. He walked ahead of us through large rooms—a study, library, and living room—pointing at the paintings and sculptures he wanted to send to Sotheby's. Some were very large pieces. A multi-part Marisol assemblage of a family walking a dog filled the center of one room. A Frank Stella *Protractor* painting and an enormous Rauschenberg hung in another. Dismantling and wrapping this art would take all day, and we started right in, working nonstop. We were interrupted several times by the arrival of trucks delivering crated paintings, which Morton demanded we unload. Though our job was to pack, he insisted we open the incoming crates so he could look at the contents, which he then had us carry through the three or four college-size art galleries that were attached to the house and extended in a chain along one side of his property. These rooms appeared to have been constructed at different times to accommodate his growing art collection. They were stuffed with paintings, hung salon-style, one on top of the other, with some attached to the ceilings. Each gallery had its own storage rooms, and these, too, were overflowing, making it difficult to find spaces for the new arrivals. The noticeable thing about his collection was that the quality of the paintings got worse the farther into the gallery labyrinth you walked. The house was filled with masterpieces, but most of the galleries contained schlock and amateur, student-level paintings. I wondered if he had some kind of compulsion to hoard art. An off-kilter personality could explain the poor way he treated us.

At a quarter to five, Morton walked into the room where we were working, looking at his watch. The delays and interruptions meant we still had several paintings left to wrap and load, and it had been twenty-three hours since we had last eaten. I stopped looking out the windows at the falling snow because its motion made me dizzy.

"I am leaving now," Morton said, ushering us outside into the cold and locking the front door. "If you had arrived on time you would have finished! I'll be back tomorrow at eight." I replied that we would be back then as well. "Oh!" he said, "you two aren't leaving. I can't have my valuable art being driven around all night."

This announcement came as a shock. There wasn't any place for miles we could walk to eat or stay, so I asked if we could stay in the house.

"Of course not!" he snapped. "Why would you think you can stay in my home? I'm not running a hotel."

He jumped into the limo, which drove out through the snow, and we watched as his driver got out and chained the gates closed. We were trapped. Normally, we would have idled the truck's diesel engine all night to stay warm and sleep, but because of the rush to get to Winnetka, we were low on fuel and couldn't take a chance on running out. Diesel engines have injectors spraying mists of fuel into their piston cylinders, and the compression of air and fuel causes the mist to explode, generating power. If the engine runs out of fuel, you can't just fill 'er up and go. A mechanic has to remove each injector and prime it with fuel before reinserting it into the engine's cylinder head, a time-consuming and costly procedure.

We sat shivering in the truck cab for several hours, killing time before going to sleep. I let Jim take the sleeper. He had a sleeping bag and would stay warm. Jim had a wife and a baby at home, and it would be a greater tragedy if he froze to death than I. As the single guy, I'd take my chances and rough it. I crawled into the trailer through the rear doors and tied them shut inside. I made a mattress using furniture blanket pads and wormed fully clothed under another pile of pads. It was difficult to sleep with my stomach growling and the cold penetrating my body, but gradually the truck pads helped warm me, and eventually, I drifted off.

An incessant pounding on the trailer's side woke me, and I crawled from under the cozy pads into the cold and untied the doors. Morton stood there in the falling snow. "Time to get to work!" We went back into the house to pack the remaining paintings, and around 10:30 a.m. we finished and presented our bill of lading and inventory for his signatures.

"Oh, you're not done yet," he said. "I have another painting I've decided you need to take." He pointed up the grand staircase to a Ben Nicholson painting in a wide, heavy frame that hung on the curve of the wall. It measured four feet by six feet high, and like the wall, its canvas curved. Perhaps it had been painted by the artist as a commission, or maybe someone had re-stretched a flat painting to make it fit the space. I walked up the stairs to figure out how we would get it down safely. By standing on my toes on the upward side of the stairs and reaching up, I could lift it high enough on my fingertips to unhook it from the hangers. Jim, however, was too short to reach it. Attempting to lower it would be sketchy because if we weren't able to control it, there was a danger it could topple over and be damaged.

I continued up the stairs to the balcony directly above the painting and found I could easily lean over through the railing and hold the top of the picture frame against the wall. With two people lifting below and one person holding it at the top, we could safely get it down. I was relieved. One last hurdle, and we'd be able to eat. By this time, we had gone thirty-eight hours without food, and I could visualize the hot, delicious meal waiting.

I explained my plan for removing the Nicholson to Morton and asked if his chauffeur could help us for a moment by holding the top of the painting. He exploded in anger. "What was Sotheby's thinking? Why would they send such unprepared idiots to handle my art?" He stomped off into the study to call New York, and I could hear him loudly complaining about our incompetence and unwillingness to work. He demanded Sotheby's send someone immediately to help get the painting down. There were pauses in the conversation as Sotheby's responded. Morton came back into the atrium with a look of satisfaction.

"They're sending a man out from New York. You better hope he gets here before five, or you two are staying another night!"

I couldn't take it anymore and said we desperately needed to eat something. I thought he might send his chauffeur to get some food while we were waiting, but instead, he marched us through the house into a small, dated-looking kitchen that was likely in the servant's quarters.

He opened the refrigerator, which was almost empty, and began pulling out the few items inside, perfunctorily thumping them down on a small table. There was a half-empty quart of milk that turned out to be curdled, a partial loaf of stiff, stale bread, a shriveled apple, and a small piece of orange cheese covered in blue mold.

He left the room, and I cut the apple in half, giving a portion to Jim. I was scraping the mold off the cheese when a young man with snow on his jacket and stocking cap burst into the room. He looked at both of us and the food and started yelling, "That's my food! Who said you could take my food? Give it back! Give it back!"

He barged between us and began grabbing the rotten groceries off the table with one hand and nestling them against his body on top of his other arm. He tossed everything back into the fridge. "Get the hell out of my kitchen!" he demanded.

I was now convinced that Jim and I were trapped inside a horrible nightmare. Morton had given us his caretaker's food, and the caretaker, who had been gone the entire time we were working in the house, had returned just as we were finally beginning to eat.

After this latest humiliation, we were feeling very gloomy. Hours passed as we sat on the atrium stairs and waited. I began to wonder if we would survive another night without eating. How could people go weeks without food when we were this messed up in only a couple of days?

Morton came out of his office. I felt my heart sink when I saw he was wearing his coat. Morton looked at his watch. "4:45," he said. "You have fifteen minutes before I leave. You better hope the guy from Sotheby's shows up."

I walked over to a window and looked down the driveway. If I concentrated on the distant gates, I could fight off the dizziness caused by the moving snow.

Minutes passed. Suddenly I saw pair of headlights rushing down the drive toward us. A yellow taxi pulled up and Wesley jumped out and ran up the porch steps. He was in a suit and tie but didn't have an overcoat, so I guessed he had rushed out of his office to get here. Without looking at us, or Morton, Wesley continued up the curved stairs, held the top of the painting so we could get it down, and immediately jumped back into the cab and left. With a moment's notice, he had gotten from New York City to the airport, caught a flight to Chicago and a taxi to Winnetka, and then—after spending less than a minute helping us finish the job—headed back to New York City.

Finally, our paperwork was signed, but as we prepared to leave, Morton, who was standing next to the limousine, called us over. "Boys," he said, "I have a painting I would like you to deliver to my penthouse in the Sears Tower tomorrow morning at eight sharp. You have worked hard, and I am going to take care of you and make it worth your while." He reached into the back seat and handed me a small painting. This change of attitude was surprising, and I was suspicious and on guard. He could easily take the painting himself. But our instructions were to comply with his wishes, and reluctantly we accepted it from him.

We arrived outside the Sears Tower on time the next morning. The signs read "No Parking," but we figured it wouldn't take long to make the delivery, and we left the truck. The first set of elevators went up to the tower's midsection. We then walked over to a second set of elevators that led us to Morton's penthouse, where he ushered us inside. The view was fantastic, but I had spasms of vertigo looking out, which was only magnified by the slight movement of the building buffeted by strong winds. Morton began instructing us to move furniture and hang other art in addition to the small painting. We were once again kidnapped, this time into rearranging his apartment.

After several hours, he seemed satisfied and escorted us to the door. "Oh," he said, "I almost forgot. You boys wait outside, and I will get something for you." He closed the door and left us waiting in the hallway for five minutes. Suddenly his maid opened the door. "Hold out your hands, please," she said. When we did, she handed each of us an apple and slammed the door closed. There was a ticket on our windshield when we finally got back to the truck. Our humiliation was complete, or so we thought.

Chicago

Pulling away from the Sears Tower, I stopped at a red light. Glancing left, I noticed a group of around twenty roughly dressed men hunched under the leaden sky—hands pushed into pockets or under armpits in an attempt to ward off the cold. They stood on the sidewalk evenly spaced in a line, waiting for a charity kitchen to open. Each was absorbed in his own thoughts, with eyes cast down on the shoes of the man ahead, perhaps a strategy to avoid talking or coming into conflict with their neighbors. Remembering how it felt to go several days without eating, I felt empathy for them. For me, it had been only a temporary imposition, but for them, a meal in a warm place meant survival, a respite from struggling on the streets. I thought of the contrasts and the way a fabulously wealthy man had badly mistreated a pair of hard-working stiffs like Jim and me. We were barely making a living, and he had millions. But here, only a few blocks from his Sears Tower penthouse were these penniless guys living hard on the streets of Chicago in the middle of the winter. How had they ended up this way? Alcohol or drugs? Bad luck?

One of them must have sensed my stare because he glanced up at me. It took a moment for his eyes to focus, and when they did, his face contorted into a mask of outrage. He yelled out in a voice thick with anguish and indignation, "Look! Look at the dirty hippie driving the truck! That stinking hippie is working when we aren't! How the hell does that bastard have a job while we starve?"

The other heads jerked up, their eyes staring at me. Faces became twisted with anger, and voices began shouting. Men who, moments earlier, had seemed to be defeated human shells suddenly coalesced into a mob and surged forward to the edge of the sidewalk. Their hands clenched into fists, and their arms began furiously thrusting toward me. Another voice yelled, "Let's get that cocksucker! Let's teach the muthafucker a lesson!" They stooped down, picked chunks of ice out of the gutter, and surged into the street to hurl them at me. As the ice crashed against the cab of my truck, they began chanting in unison: "Cocksucker! Cocksucker! Cocksucker!" The men I had felt sympathy for were attempting to kill me, with the perceived unfairness and injustice of their lives boiling over. They were the victims. It was someone else's fault. It was always someone else's fault. The hippie truck driver had stolen employment that was rightfully theirs, and now they had a scapegoat for their rage. The traffic light was still red, but I had to move. If a piece of ice or chunk of pavement broke through the window, they could get into the truck to pull Jim and me into the street.

I engaged the clutch and drove through the intersection, shifting gears to gain speed down the street. Glancing into the mirrors, I could see most were returning to the sidewalk, but one was still running in pursuit. Tears were running down his cheeks as he futilely threw one last chunk of ice that landed harmlessly in the street behind my truck.

South

Driving trucks throughout the United States carried certain risks, particularly if you stood out from regular truck drivers. When the movie *Easy Rider* came out, it reinforced the idea that being different in the South could get you harmed or even killed. Being a California hippie—a skinny, art-loving, college-educated, white guy with a beard and long hair—made me a target. Not just of hard-luck Chicago toughs but also cops and highway patrolmen in the more conservative states. I made a particular effort to avoid driving through the Deep South, which had been fighting a losing battle against integration and equal rights, and where there was a lot of pent-up anger, fear, and bitterness. I'd tasted it as a child, and I knew even then that Southern hospitality was just a self-aggrandizing myth.

In 1955, when I was ten years old, my parents emigrated from Toronto, Canada, to California, taking a month-long road trip through the region. I was deeply affected by seeing the abject poverty of the Black communities there. When we got to Little Rock, Arkansas, we went for a stroll in a city park to stretch our legs. The park had beautiful trees and flowers and paved walkways, but suddenly, we found ourselves in a rundown section with dirt paths, no flowers, and plenty of weeds. Rounding a corner, we bumped into a young Black couple with a small child who looked startled to see us and ran away in a panic. A short time later, a white policeman arrived and told us we were in the "Negro park" and had to leave. I never forgot the inequity I saw in that park and how we scared the young couple and their child. What hit me the hardest was whenever we came near, not a single black man, woman, or child would make eye contact—it was too risky. A couple of decades later, *Easy Rider* shed light on the disturbing fact that crossing barriers or being different in the South was dangerous and sometimes deadly.

I couldn't steer around that part of the country forever, though, and eventually, I had to deliver a painting near Montgomery, Alabama. Afterward, I stopped at a big Union 76 truck stop for fuel and lunch. The restaurant was large, with a counter that held more than forty seats, and there were twenty or more booths, nearly all of them filled with overweight, crew cut-sporting truckers. Truckers, in general, tend to get fat—a result of long hours in the driver's seat combined with the greasy, starchy food they eat for comfort. Southern fare seemed particularly unhealthy, with everything deep-fried, smothered with white chicken gravy, and accompanied by hominy grits. I found a seat at the counter and patiently waited while a petite blonde waitress with a sing-song accent flirted with truckers. She seemed to be forgetting me, and after fifteen minutes, I flagged her down and said, "Excuse me, ma'am, could I order some food, please?"

She turned to face me, rose on her toes with hands-on-hips, and jutted her jaw forward. "We don't serve no white niggers in this here restaurant!" she said in a loud, indignant voice. The truckers burst out in disdainful hooting and hollering laughter. It was humiliating, and I realized this kind of group psychology was how lynching happened. If I showed fear and walked out, it could spark an attack. I waited until they all went back to eating and talking before making my way out the door.

The next evening, after picking up an exhibition from the High Museum in Atlanta, I stopped at a small truck stop outside of town. It was warm, and I stood near the restrooms next to fuel pumps talking to a young truck driver. A *Dukes of Hazzard* Dodge Charger with big fins and a spoiler drove up, and a teenage girl jumped out and ran into the restroom. Two guys in their twenties waited in the car for a while and finally, realizing they were being ditched, drove off.

The girl stuck her head out the door and asked my trucker acquaintance if they had left. They began talking, and he put his hands behind his back and removed a wedding ring, sticking it in his hip pocket. After a few minutes, they walked over to his truck and climbed into the sleeper. While this was happening, a short, middle-aged guy was standing near me, pumping gas into his pickup truck. He wore gray pants with piping outlining the pockets, an ironed white shirt, and a gray Stetson hat. He also had a pearl-handled revolver sticking out his back pocket. Stupidly I said, "That's a nice-looking pistol you have, sir. What caliber is it?'

He whirled around, pulled out the pistol, and jammed the barrel against my forehead. "You got a problem with my nigger-shooter, boy?" Previous experiences with guns pointed at me taught me that it's better to stay calm in the face of a bullying threat because it denies the antagonist of what he most wants—to gain power by intimidating a victim. I looked him in the eye as he told me he was a sheriff and had shot more than one "thieving nigger." When he saw that he wasn't impressing me, he lowered the gun. He glanced over at the truck my acquaintance and the teenager had disappeared into. "I see what is happening over there," he said, "but I'm feeling mellow this evening, and I'm just going to look the other way." I was relieved when he got into the pickup and drove off.

Wolf

Humans weren't the only threats that lurked out on the open highways. During my last few months at Cart & Crate, I was assigned to drive a tractor-trailer from Los Angeles to Kalispell, Montana. I was to pick up a valuable load of finished and polished lodge-pole pine logs for a furniture manufacturer in West LA who was using the poles to make western ranch-style furniture. This trip was a welcome respite from driving back and forth to New York across the same network of interstate highways. I had made that trip so many times I'd memorized every pothole and crack in the pavement.

As I studied my map book to find the best routes, I noticed the Little Bighorn battle monument in southern Montana. I decided it wouldn't be too much of a detour to stop there on my trip north, even though I'd be taking secondary roads, which would be more direct than the freeway. I had always wanted to see it.

I drove out of Los Angeles, and by the second day, the desert fell behind, and rolling ranch lands began, outlined by miles of barbed wire fencing. Soon I left the interstate, continuing north on roads that were usually only two lanes, with an occasional single-lane bridge over creeks. The route was lightly traveled, and only occasionally did an oncoming vehicle—usually a rancher's pickup truck—drive past, slowing down against the oncoming bulk of my truck.

As the sun was beginning to set, I looked for a place to park for the night. It had been a clear, Indian summer October day, and I pulled off onto a gravel lot near a small clapboard building with fading white paint. It had once been a gas station with a single pump, the kind topped by a glass cylinder with lines and numbers showing the gallons of gasoline pumped by hand from storage tanks into the glass. The design, which let customers see the amount being purchased before it drained into the car by gravity, was from a time when money was scarce, and people wanted to know they were getting what they paid for. I jumped down from my truck and walked over to give it a closer look. Amazingly, the pump and glass globe were still intact. Here, local ranchers had a sense of respect for the property belonging to others, and artifacts like this lasted for decades. In a city like Los Angeles, it would have long since been vandalized or stolen.

The station's windows were boarded and the door secured by a rusty padlock. Who had made their living there? What had happened to them? Had the Great Depression forced them out of business? Or had the interstate construction in the early 1960s diverted their customers? The sky was clear, and a warm, caressing breeze whispered from the northwest. I was in my shirtsleeves, standing mesmerized as the sun began setting in a pale turquoise sky, painting the horizon in brilliant orange, yellow, and red streaks. Bright pinpoints of light started popping out as the sky grew darker, and soon the entire sky was covered in a twinkling sea of stars. Thirty minutes later, an enormous full moon rose from the hills to the east. I was at peace, tired from a long drive, and I climbed into my truck's bunk, lying on top of my sleeping bag and falling into a deep sleep.

I awoke blue and shivering in the morning, my breath hanging in thick clouds. The view outside the truck's windows was distorted and blurry, and I thought something had gone horribly wrong with my eyesight until I realized the windows were covered with ice. The warm evening wind had been a chinook preceding a cold storm. Rain had fallen, turning to ice and snow as the temperatures plummeted. Not anticipating cold weather, I'd brought only a light jacket, and it didn't do much to warm me up when I put it on.

A half-inch of ice entombed the truck, and I couldn't open the doors or roll down the windows—a problem of some urgency because I had to pee. Starting the diesel engine would warm the truck and melt or loosen the ice, but when I tried, it turned over but wouldn't start. This was typical of diesel engines, which don't have spark plugs and rely on cylinder compression to heat and fire fuel. Likely the fuel had also thickened from the cold. Truck drivers often leave their engines idling when parked in the winter to keep that from happening, but my fuel reserves were low because fuel stops had been scarce along the back roads. I hadn't wanted to risk draining my tanks any further since I didn't know where the next truck stop would be.

I stopped cranking the engine for fear of draining the battery and remembered there was a can of "Quick Start" ether in the truck.

Sprayed into an engine's air intake, it would ignite in the cylinders and help get the engine started. But that operation required two people, one to spray and the other to turn over the engine.

I banged my fist on the driver's side window and finally dislodged enough ice to roll the window down, a mistake because the blowing air made me even colder, and I began shivering uncontrollably. Leaning out the window and banging my fist around the door handle eventually loosened the ice enough to let me get out, and I stepped down into six inches of snow. The soles of my Red Wing boots left crisp waffle patterns as I walked behind the closed-up station—though the privacy was unnecessary since there was no one around for miles. I took a long pee and thought over the situation. The sky was clear under a rising sun, and the snow covering the road was undisturbed, indicating very little traffic came through this area. I was on my own to thaw out the engine.

The air intake was between the back of the cab and the front of the trailer. It was a tube, twelve inches in diameter, that ran from the engine compartment and extended straight up to nearly the top of the trailer, which was thirteen feet off the ground. I would need to reach that high to spray the Quick Start into the intake. I tried different ways of getting closer to the intake's opening and finally reached it by climbing up into the door opening and standing with my left foot on top of the seatback while grabbing the top of the door opening with my left hand. By cantilevering my body across the cab roof, I could stretch my right hand toward the intake opening. I took the pressurized can of Quick Start, leaned across, sprayed the opening, then ducked back inside as fast as I could to crank the engine. Nothing. I tried this again and again, listening as the battery began to weaken. My stomach was in knots, my limbs trembling from the exertion. But finally, very unevenly, the engine started to run. The cab shook and vibrated as I kept pumping the pedal and urging it on. "Come on! Come on! Goddamn it!"

Eventually, the engine heated up enough to run smoothly, and I drove back onto the road heading north. Several hours later, the ranchlands narrowed into a long, meandering valley bordered by low hills on each side. The road was twenty feet above the valley floor and followed the contours of a long hill, possibly a glacial moraine. Below me, at the foot of the slope, a stock fence paralleled the road, enclosing the valley to prevent cattle from wandering. It was made of split rail posts, with barbed wire strung between. Across the valley, groves of willow trees marked the course of a stream hidden from view. As the sun rose in the sky, its pale light illuminated golden stalks of grass that pushed through the snow, which sparkled with flashes of blue and yellow.

The magic abruptly ended as a truck loaded with oil-drilling pipe suddenly emerged from a side road, turning ahead of me and raising a cloud of snow as it did. I followed glumly, staying several hundred feet behind. After a mile, I glanced up and noticed a large white dog cresting the hill ahead. It was jumping through chest-high snow and heading down toward our road. The wind direction and the snow might have muffled our engine noises because the dog seemed oblivious to the danger of the approaching trucks. It reached the road just ahead of the lead truck, and I was shocked to see a puff of black smoke emerge from the truck's stacks as it accelerated in a deliberate attempt to run the dog over. The dog suddenly realized the danger and frantically scrambled to get out of the way, its feet slipping for traction on the icy pavement. It fell on its chest and desperately struggled up. The truck missed it by inches as the dog fell off the road's edge and tumbled head over heels down the embankment, where it landed entangled in the barbwire fence. It was lying there, legs up in the air and tail flopped to one side, as I drew alongside and stopped to look down. The animal locked eyes with mine, looking up with an expression of hurt feelings and embarrassment. With a jolt, I realized I was looking into the yellow eyes of a huge, male white wolf. For a moment, there was a connection between us, and we communicated:

"Why did you try to hurt me?"

"I didn't—it wasn't me."

Our unspoken communication must have reassured him that I wasn't posing a threat, and after a few moments, he looked away and began untangling himself from the wire. He stood up, shaking the snow off his thick fur in that rolling head-to-tail motion dogs use to dry themselves when wet. As the particles flew into the bright sunshine, they enveloped his white body inside a rainbow halo, which gave the wolf such a mystical, otherworldly appearance that I wondered if I was dreaming. He turned away and stepped daintily through strands of barbed wire, regally trotting across the field toward the river, head and tail proudly held high, dignity restored.

That evening, as the sun was setting, I arrived at the Little Bighorn monument that marked the site where Custer met his fate. It was closed and surrounded by a high, wrought iron fence with stone pilasters and a large, ornate entry gate with a padlock. Behind the fence, small, stone grave markers poked out of the snow. I had previously read these were placed where each soldier's body was found—and I hadn't driven all this way to look at them from a distance. With difficulty, I scaled the fence and climbed down inside. The parking lot was empty, there was no one around for miles, and with the temperature well below freezing, a fall and injury could be fatal, so I was taking a big risk scaling the slippery fence.

My boots crunched and squeaked as I walked through the grave markers where Custer's troops were buried. His body was later exhumed and interred in Arlington National Cemetery. The fool who led his men to their deaths was given a hero's burial posthumously. But he was the one who should have been left here, and all of his troopers taken to Arlington. The hillside gently dropped toward the Little Bighorn River in the valley below, and behind the hills on the far side of the ravine, a giant full moon began to rise. As it broke into the sky, a wolf began howling, its cry rising into a crescendo, echoing off the surrounding hills and prickling my hair. I listened with a shiver. Wolves were supposed to be extinct below the Canadian border, yet I had witnessed evidence of two wolves in one day. Perhaps it was a sign.

Saves and Near Misses: Staying Alive in the Art Biz

Larry Bell

NOT TOO LONG AFTER my wolf encounter, an inebriated forklift driver and a big pile of broken glass got me started in my own business. I returned from New York to the Cart & Crate warehouse in the evening and saw a fellow employee, Eddie, struggling to dump the contents of three fifty-five-gallon barrels from the loading dock into the trash dumpster below. I ran over to help him, and hundreds of jagged glass shards crashed, ringing against the empty dumpster's steel floor. This was no ordinary glass. The shards had a distinctive reflective coating. "Wow!" I told Eddie. "Those look like pieces of Larry Bell's glass."

They were, Eddie replied. That morning, the forklift driver came to work drunk and backed into Bell's storage vault, destroying the sculptures inside. But the news wasn't all bad, he said. Bell was paying Cart & Crate for insurance, so at least he would be compensated.

We emptied two more barrels, and I sadly looked down at what could've been a year's artistic output, now in shambles. And this wasn't the first time. A year earlier, I witnessed a damaged Lee Mullican painting being thrown into the same dumpster. And several years before that, I was taking apart a painting crate I'd pulled out of the dumpster after work to salvage the plywood. When I pulled out the cardboard lining from the inside of the crate, I was surprised to find a Frank Stella painting underneath—a piece belonging to a collector named Robert Rowan. I found a place to hide it until the company opened in the morning, but when I told my boss, she ostracized me for scavenging in the company dumpster.

A month or so after I helped dump the glass, I was sent across town to Larry Bell's studio in Venice to pick up some art. I liked Larry, who affectionately called us art handlers "schleppers" and always treated us with friendly respect. As he signed the paperwork, I expressed my sympathy for the damage to his work, assuming he must've been informed. But to my surprise, he didn't know. This set off a fateful chain of events, the first of which was that I got fired and had a month's pay withheld from my final check for my New York shuttle deliveries.

I spent several months unemployed, trying to figure out what to do with my life. By very good luck, I happened to be home in my storefront studio on Pico Boulevard when Mike Dotzenrod, a friend from the Walker Art Center in Minneapolis, called. Mike was a preparator I befriended while making deliveries to the Walker—one of the nation's best contemporary art museums, and an institution with high standards and an excellent staff. Whenever I showed up, the team would invite me to dinner or barhopping and put me up for the night at one of their homes. So, when Mike said he'd be in LA on business, I readily invited him to stay with me.

He arrived from LAX by taxi, and I bought us pizza and beer, then gave him my bed to sleep in while I bunked on the floor. The next morning, he asked me to drive him over to an artist's studio in Venice. On the trip over, Mike told me he left the Walker to join Richard Koshalek, the new director of the Fort Worth Museum of Contemporary Art. Richard had previously been a curator at the Walker and later became the director of the MOCA Los Angeles. To my surprise, when we arrived in Venice, he directed me to Larry Bell's studio. Larry was standing across the room wearing his trademark black fedora and had a big cigar in the corner of his mouth. As he came over to greet us, he looked at me and told Mike, "That's Bryan Cooke! He's a good guy, and I want him to handle and crate my exhibition." It was a moment that set my life on an entirely new course.

Bell was at a stage in his career where his work was monumental, and his reputation was on the rise. He began as a painter but soon started working with glass. His early pieces were minimalist glass cubes given reflective coatings in a small vacuum chamber. These reflective coatings were once used by NASA on masks worn by the astronauts who landed on the moon. Larry later scaled up, working with large sheets of glass coated in an enormous vacuum chamber he'd designed and fabricated—one large enough to let Larry, who was over six feet tall, walk inside without stooping over. He placed a pristine sheet of glass inside and pumped out all the air to achieve a nearly perfect vacuum. Then, a powerful electric current was run through an electrode in the chamber that was attached to a small piece of gold or silver foil. The current vaporized the metal, causing atoms to stick to the glass and gradually coat it. The longer the vaporizing continued, the denser the coating. By carefully manipulating this process, Larry could give a transparent glass sheet varying degrees of transparency or reflectivity. The process was similar to applying paint with a spray gun, except on the glass, the metal coatings were permanent.

Larry would combine the glass sheets by joining them at right angles using silicone to make them free-standing. As you walked around these works, they would magically change—first reflecting your image, then becoming transparent. His newest work was a room-sized sculpture titled *The Iceberg and Its Shadow*. It comprised forty-five pieces of 3/8-inch thick glass, some measuring 100 inches high by sixty inches wide. The genius of the *Iceberg* was that it could be put together in infinite combinations. All components were interchangeable and could be configured to fit any space—square or rectangular—but fully assembled, its footprint was sixty-five by thirty feet.

At Mike and Larry's urging, Fort Worth Museum agreed to hire me to pack the fragile behemoth. I had a table saw in my studio and told Mike we could construct five or six crates each evening and deliver and pack them during the day. I ordered lumber, and we set into this routine fueled by beer and pizza, pounding boards together in the evening and handling the glass sheets stone sober each day. We moved the glass with the same tools and methods used by glaziers, the people who install window glass, lifting each sheet with suction cups and lowering it into a crate we lined with fiberboard to cushion the edges. The fiberboard completely covered the front and back of each sheet inside a crate, evenly "clamping" the sheet to hold it rigid. It was excruciatingly stressful to lift and carry the heavy glass sheets, which had beveled edges and corners that could chip at the slightest contact with a foreign object. Glass is strongest straight up and down, so awkward as it was, we had to carry the sheets vertically.

Mike and I were holding clamps on each end of the largest sheets, carrying them parallel to a wall that separated Larry's studio from his neighbor's, when suddenly the glass exploded in our hands. Shards of glass shrapnel flew everywhere. We were stunned, but at least we weren't blinded. There was a ball-peen hammer lying on the floor between us, and after a few moments of bewilderment, we noticed a hole in the wall.

The neighboring studio was owned by movie producer and actor Tony Bill, who had recently produced *The Sting*—the hit caper movie starring Robert Redford and Paul Newman. Tony was renovating a vintage Duesenberg and had a young mechanic named Cody working on it full-time. Cody had a temper, and nearly every day, we would hear his muffled yelling and cursing on the other side of Larry's wall. It turned out that as we were passing by, he had hit his thumb with the hammer and, in a fit of anger, hurled it against the wall. It neatly traveled through the wood studs and plaster on both sides and destroyed the glass sheet we were carrying.

While we worked packing the *Iceberg*, a steady stream of visitors kept stopping by the studio, most of them female art collectors. Larry was handsome with an enormous, outgoing personality, and it was obvious women were smitten with him. He generously used that influence to give me the toe-hold that let me start my own business, introducing me to every one of the women who came in as I worked—telling them they should use my services for their art collections.

After two weeks of hard work, we finished crating the forty-five glass elements of the *Iceberg* along with some additional spare sheets, and the museum hired me to drive them out to Fort Worth. With Mike riding shotgun, we arrived and completed the delivery.

To celebrate, we jumped into his rusty 1960s pickup truck, stopped at a drive-through beer store just off a Dallas-Fort Worth turnpike off-ramp, and ordered a six-pack of Pearl beer from the window. Drive-through liquor stores were unique to Texas—a perk never to be found in California.

We drove around for a while quaffing the beer and decided to go back for seconds—this time a different Texas brew, Lone Star. I noticed the sky was darkening ominously, and there was a smell of rain and ozone in the air. Mike was out-consuming me three to one and had just cracked open his fifth beer when there was a terrific flash of lightning followed by an enormous, tooth-rattling thunder-clap. Rain poured down, mixed with hail. Without warning, Mike let out a "Yeeeeeeeeeehaaah!" rebel yell, swung the pickup out of the driveway, and goosed it, heading up the turnpike off-ramp and going the wrong way onto the freeway. He pushed the accelerator to the floor, and the truck shook from exertion. His pickup had seatbelts but no shoulder belt and a steel dashboard. He continued yelling as we picked up speed, still going the wrong way into limited visibility. Hail bounced off the windshield, and thunder crashed continually overhead. Blue-yellow lightning flashes eerily lit the sheets of rain as oncoming cars frantically swerved out of our way, horns blaring, headlights flashing past. I sat motionless, waiting to die. Suddenly Mike slammed on the brakes, and the pickup spun around and around, by luck ending up facing back the way we had come. We exited using the same off-ramp we'd driven up. All of the beer cans had fallen on the floor and rolled under the seat by the time we got off the freeway. Mike looked over at the empty carton. "Hey, we're out of beer!" he yelled. He drove back to the window and ordered another six-pack. When I asked him the next day what had possessed him to drive the wrong direction on the freeway, he looked at me like I was crazy. He didn't remember a thing, but since I made it out alive, I'll never forget it. In retrospect, it feels like some kind of christening.

Espanola

My next big job was driving Larry's huge vacuum chamber to his studio in Taos, New Mexico. The chamber was so enormous it required a double-drop frame—a trailer that lets the load rest low to the ground in a "well" between the front and back axles—to keep it at legal height. It stuck out from the sides of the trailer but was just inside legal width. I rented the trailer from a private party and the tractor from a truck rental company and loaded the chamber using a giant forklift, securing it with chain binders to the trailer. I dummied up a bill of lading and hoped it would pass scrutiny because I didn't have legal permits for the states I was passing through.

The first obstacle was a California truck scale, which I approached with a certain trepidation. A red light came on, and the loudspeaker ordered me to bring my papers inside, where three uniformed highway patrolmen were sitting behind desks looking at me. I didn't notice they had propped the door open by jamming a doormat under it, and my foot caught on a raised fold, sending me sprawling face-first to the floor. The patrolmen jumped to help me up, apologizing profusely and asking if I was okay. In the confusion, they only glanced at my paperwork before telling me I could leave. I think they were embarrassed. I made it through Arizona unscathed and arrived at another truck scale as I entered New Mexico on I-40 near Gallup. I knew from previous trips that the Navajo or Hopi officers in charge could sometimes be sticklers for papers and permits. From talking to other truckers, I also learned they could be bribed, especially with "pussy books." Anticipating this, I purchased the latest edition of Playboy in Los Angeles and had it conspicuously under my arm as I walked into their small office. There were two men on duty, and both focused their eyes on the magazine. "Is that a new pussy book?" one asked.

I hesitated before responding. "Yes, it is. Would you like it?"

Indeed, they would. They took it, stamping my papers without a glance, and were completely engrossed in the magazine as I took off.

It was early morning, and I figured I'd make it to Taos in the afternoon. I knew I'd pass through Espanola, a small, nondescript farming community in a river valley halfway between Santa Fe and Taos that lacked the "lodgepole and adobe" historic charm of both those towns. I wasn't worried because the small truck scale there had always been closed on my previous trips. This time, however, it was open. Through the window, I could see an officious character sitting behind a desk, gesturing at me to come inside the small shack. I walked in, and he gave me a steely eye. "What you hauling, Bubba? Don't look nowhere legal to me. You look like the kind that would be pulling a fast one. Probably stole the goddam thing. Lemme see your papers!"

I handed them over, relieved that they had been officially "processed" by the Navajos. When he saw the stamp, he was incredulous.

"What the hell! Those stupid Indians have their heads up their asses. I just know something ain't right, and you're staying here until I get to the bottom of it!"

He called the state permit office in Santa Fe, the state capital, and began loudly complaining about those stupid Navajos letting a truck with stolen goods into the state. He demanded a background check, but after the reference to "stupid Navajos," I didn't think I'd have to worry about that. At least half the government workforce in the New Mexico capital was either Navajo or Hopi, and it was likely the person on the other end of the call hadn't taken kindly to his slurs. Whoever it was kept him waiting for an answer, which kept my truck blocking the scale, and as the afternoon dragged on, it gave him an excuse to avoid the work of checking on all the other trucks passing by. He called the capital again, launching into another diatribe about stupid Indians and demanding a response. After hanging up, he looked at me and said, "Back when I was on the Long Beach police force, we wouldn't have put up with this shit. These fucking Indians are just as bad as niggers! Niggers are all a bunch of thieves, and we made sure any that tried to come into our city learned a lesson."

When I heard this, the hair stood up on the back of my neck. A professor I had at USC, the artist Conner Everts, had been beaten nearly to death by a couple of cops in Long Beach—I saw pictures of the bruises covering his body. Yet the cops were acquitted when they were tried for assault, and when Federal civil rights charges were brought, they were acquitted again. Convicting cops of anything was virtually impossible. While the cases moved through the courts, Conner received death threats, and people tossed bricks through his windows at night. The guy running the truck scale seemed like someone who would've cheered them on, and as I listened to him talk, I decided to be very polite and remain quiet.

Around four-thirty, I caught him glancing up at a clock on the wall. He likely wasn't going to keep me past five, because he wouldn't be paid for overtime. I sat nervously hoping the phone wouldn't ring. At five o'clock he stood up. "Damn lucky for you. Get your skinny ass out of here and don't ever come back or I'll make you sorry you did."

I made it to Taos and delivered Larry's tank.

Nan

Work after the Taos delivery was sporadic. The United States was entering a recession at that point in the 1970s, and several Los Angeles galleries closed for good. My fledgling art moving business completely dried up when the remaining galleries shut down for the summer and clients left on vacations. To make ends meet, I did odd jobs, including house painting. By the time a woman named Nan contacted me saying she needed an assistant to help her prepare for a "big exhibition in New York," I was almost broke and badly needed work. I was happy to take the job.

The first thing I noticed about Nan was that she always wore two pairs of pantyhose, perhaps to hide her veined and rippled thighs. As she walked around, the outer layer of her stockings would start shifting out of position over the inner layer, and when it became too uncomfortable, she would hike up her dress and tug to twist the layers back into place. The sheen of Vaseline covered her face and the backs of her hands—her secret for keeping her skin young, she told me. Nan had entered the difficult stage of middle age, and this was all part of her battle to stay youthful and sexy.

She lived with her husband, a powerful Hollywood entertainment attorney, on the flats of Beverly Hills in a large, two-story mansion with a pool house and tennis court in the backyard. The pool house had been converted into Nan's studio, where she played at being an artist. She excitedly described what an important breakthrough it was for her to have a New York gallery showing her work—though I found out several weeks later it was actually a boutique gallery that charged artists a weekly fee to rent the space to exhibit their art.

Nan made art by heating clear acrylic sheets using an acetylene tank with a wide flame attachment. Her husband had warned her against breathing the plastic fumes, which were a known carcinogen. Nan told me this was why she needed me to assist her—not caring that she was asking me to sacrifice *my* lungs so she could spare her own. I would heat the plastic while she stayed well out of range until it began to warp and bubble. She would then rush up and attack it with a claw hammer, box-cutter, and electric drill. When the plastic began to cool, it became difficult to manipulate, so she would stand back and tell me where to apply more heat. Sometimes she wanted me to keep applying heat until the acrylic caught fire, the acrid black smoke curling up and burning my eyes until she rushed over with a bucket of water. I tried to stay upwind to avoid breathing the noxious-smelling fumes, taking a deep breath and holding it while the torch flame hissed in a blue and yellow tongue across the pristine surface. But I did have to breathe. When I got cancer later in life, I wondered if this had been the cause.

I arrived at ten each morning, coming from the alley through the back gate to the unlocked pool room. Nan told me to use the pool house phone to call the front house and let her know I had arrived.

She would answer promptly but often kept me waiting for fifteen to twenty minutes before strolling up the path onto the pool deck, carrying a cup of coffee. She never offered me one or apologized for the delay. Around three or three-thirty, she would go back to the house, ordering me to come inside for the next day's assignment after I'd cleaned things up. I would find her sitting on the living room couch with a glass of wine. "It's an Haut Brion," she would announce with authority, "an important first-growth French wine." Although she waved her glass in front of me, she never offered me any, probably thinking it would be wasted on a peasant worker. I had studied wine and knew about the "first growths" but kept that knowledge to myself to avoid upstaging and offending her ego.

Each Monday, Nan would send me to buy thick sheets of clear acrylic from a Plexiglas supplier in Paramount, a city on the opposite side of Los Angeles from Beverly Hills. The sheets were half an inch thick and up to six feet long by four feet wide. I would pick up two or three and tie them to my Volkswagen Beetle. When I got to the Beverly Hills house, I'd give her the sales receipt, and she would reimburse me with a check or cash, including my pay for working the previous week. Thick acrylic was expensive, and it took most of my savings each week to purchase the sheets. Although they were covered in protective film, I worried they would be damaged during my trips, and she wouldn't pay me.

At the end of the fifth week, Nan announced she and her husband had a big tax bill and were short of money, so they couldn't pay me until the end of the project. She told me not to worry, and as an assurance of payment, she was going to have me crate and ship her show to New York. I could've quit then, but I'd worked the previous week and worried that she wouldn't pay me for that if I left. I was halfway in the door and halfway out, and I just couldn't walk away. I foolishly figured that she needed me to pack and crate her work, which would give me the leverage to get paid before shipping it.

The next three weeks passed uneventfully until the final day. As usual, I called the main house and waited for Nan to arrive, but this time, when she walked up the path, a young man was with her. He was around seventeen or eighteen years old, and she introduced him as a neighbor stopping by to see her work. As we began discussing when I'd pick up all the art the next morning, she abruptly started berating me and accusing me of having done mediocre work. She said she was disappointed with my effort and obvious lack of skills. I realized she expected me to argue, but I knew if I did, I'd be giving her a reason to get rid of me without paying, so I said nothing. That ended the discussion, and she told me to come back the next day for the pick-up.

In the morning, I rented a truck with my diminished resources and parked it in the alley behind Nan's house. As usual, I entered through the back gate, but when I picked up the phone to call the house, I heard Nan talking with someone who sounded a lot like Jerry Solomon, a local art framer. My suspicions rose as he repeated dimensions that matched those of her art, but I felt guilty about eavesdropping, and instead of continuing to listen, I interrupted to announce my arrival. Nan told me to hang up and wait. Minutes passed, and anxious that something was wrong, I picked up the phone to call again. This time she was talking to a man with a deep gruff voice who sounded a lot like a cop. "Yes, Ma'am," he was saying before they both hung up. "We'll have someone over there right away."

A few minutes later, Nan came striding down from the house with the neighbor kid following close behind. With a big smile, she began profusely thanking me for all my efforts in assuring the success of the New York show.

"Bryan, I'm sorry about last night. I've been so nervous and stressed about my work, I must have come across the wrong way. I'm very relieved you are crating my work because I trust you to take the very best care of it and . . ." At that moment, there was a loud knock on the door, and two very big Beverly Hills policemen walked in, the older one carrying a billy club and holding it in an aggressive manner. "What seems to be the trouble here, ma'am?" he said. I knew I was in trouble.

Nan took a step back, rose up on her toes, and pointed her index finger at me dramatically. "Officer, he attacked me! He attacked me!" The kid standing behind her vigorously nodded up and down in agreement. I was stunned about being set up but remained calm. The younger cop seemed decent enough, so I looked him in the eye, holding my gaze without saying anything. After a few moments, he turned away and went outside with his partner, where they stood discussing the situation. They walked back in and handcuffed me, pushing me ahead of them and out the rear gate into the back alley. I thought they'd beat me up, but instead, they undid the cuffs: "We're letting you go with a strict warning. The homeowners in Beverly Hills don't want any trouble from weirdos like you. So, get into your truck, and we'll follow you to make certain you leave town. If we ever catch you back in Beverly Hills, we will bust you really good!"

Humiliated and broke, I drove out of 90210 with the cop car following closely behind.

The next day, I called Lowell Wedemeyer, the Beverly Hills lawyer who had represented me in my artists' rights suit, and described the situation. I asked if he knew Nan's husband, and fortunately, he did. Lowell couldn't do much about restoring my dignity, but took him just one phone call to sidestep Nan and get me paid.

Sorenson

Business picked up somewhat in the fall of '76, when Nicholas Wilder Gallery, one of the premier contemporary art galleries in Los

Angeles, started giving me lots of work. Like virtually all of the important LA art galleries in the 1960s and '70s, the gallery was on La Cienega Boulevard between Melrose and Santa Monica Boulevard. The Ferus Gallery, which had an enormous influence on the Los Angeles contemporary art scene and an early arrival on La Cienega, was still there in its new incarnation as the Irving Blum Gallery. Nick Wilder's place was only a few doors away, and another influential gallery, Felix Landau, had come into the neighborhood along with Eugenia Butler and Molly Barnes. All of them showed the avant-garde of the day, unlike the pseudo galleries in hotel lobbies or Beverly Hills that sold schlock to tourists and collectors with bad taste.

Wilder, whose stable included Ron Davis, Billy Al Bengston, and Robert Graham, was renowned for his discerning eye and talent for finding and promoting the careers of up-and-comers. One of those was Donald Sorenson, whom I met when Nick sent me to pick up paintings for a show. What was most noticeable whenever I visited Sorenson's studio were the piles of twisted and torn masking tape scattered across his floor. Strips of tape, their surfaces covered in a kaleidoscopic variety of colors, stuck to more torn strips and were wadded into softball-sized clumps. Sorenson was making hard-edge paintings, and the debris on the floor had been pulled off the face of canvases after he'd used them to map his bright, zig-zag layers. Many of his canvases were large, measuring six by ten feet, and they took a lot of tape.

Sorenson was finding success, but I wondered how a newcomer like him had gotten into Wilder Gallery when there were many other good, established artists who would have loved to exhibit there. It could well have been personal attraction—Sorenson was a handsome guy, and Nick was openly gay at a time when many hid their sexual preferences for fear of being demeaned or attacked. Barney's Beanery, with its infamous sign "FAGGOTS KEEP OUT!" was close by and perfectly indicative of the sentiment in the area. Whatever created the chemistry—looks or talent or both—Sorenson now had a gallery.

Wilder sold lots of art to wealthy collectors, but money seemed to fall out of his hands, in part because he had expensive personal tastes involving young men and cocaine. He always seemed to have difficulty paying his bills. He would complain that collectors were making down payments on art purchases and never paid the entire amount owed, but with Wilder, you could never tell. It may have been a façade to keep artists and vendors like me at arm's length to avoid paying us.

I was making a late delivery to the gallery one evening when Barbara Walters, the television personality, and her husband showed up. Nick asked me to stay to assist, so I waited while they negotiated a purchase and then went to the storeroom to retrieve a rolled Billy Al Bengston painting, which Nick asked me to unroll on the gallery floor. It was thirty feet long and painted with repeated irises—Bengston's *Dracula* motif—and Nick told Walters that the painting sold by the foot. If they chose an eight-foot section, they would have two paintings, he said. But if they added another foot, they could get three. He outlined the three with hand gestures, and they agreed to purchase nine feet. Nick went back to his desk to write up the purchase and get Walters's check, handing me scissors and leaving it to me to cut out the paintings. His hand gestures hadn't been very precise, so I had the uncomfortable task of judging where to cut without ruining the paintings. I went to work with the scissors, wasting as little canvas as possible, but I found the whole thing a bit crass—like cutting a wedge of cheese from a large round and charging by the pound.

Wilder would sometimes do "three-card monte" with artists. We would pick up a group of paintings from a studio and take them to his gallery. Then Nick would tell us to return one or two to the artist and bring three others back to the gallery, hanging some of them for the show and putting the remainder into the storeroom. A week later, he would take one off the wall and several out of storage and return them to the artist, telling us to pick up more at the studio. In the meantime, he'd sell paintings and replace them on the gallery walls with ones from the storeroom. Soon the artist would become confused about what he had given Nick. Wilder, for his part, claimed to have a photographic memory, which would have to serve as the ultimate arbiter because he never kept written records—something I suspected was to keep the tax collectors away.

Ron Davis, a brilliant artist who, at the time, was getting advances of $50,000 for paintings he had not yet made, purchased one of the first Apple computers and programmed it himself to keep track of his inventory and what he had given Wilder. Not coincidentally, Nick always paid him. The amazing thing was that no one ever seemed to get mad at Nick for his business practices. Some of us just worked around them. Knowing I probably wouldn't get paid, I decided to trade my services for paintings by artists I admired—a barter arrangement that enabled me to build a respectable collection over the years. Whenever my invoices piled up, I would visit the gallery, chat with Nick, and tell him I wanted to look in the backroom to see if there was something I liked. I wound up at Don Sorenson's studio because of one of those backroom visits. I'd seen a painting of his that I liked, but Nick claimed it had already been sold, so he suggested I talk to Don about a trade.

Standing in the midst of the masking tape debris in hopes of finding a painting to add to my collection, I spotted a small piece that held its own against the larger works, which got my attention. Often small paintings represent studies or fragments an artist uses to develop ideas for larger versions. While these can be interesting, they often lack the visual pop of a large painting an artist has devoted more time and energy to create. The one that caught my eye, however, was strong, and I really liked it. Don read my eagerness and stiffened his terms. We haggled for a while and finally agreed on how much work I'd need to do for him to earn the painting.

A year later, the contract was about to be completed with a painting I was returning to his studio, which we installed a few days earlier above the living room couch of a collector who lived in a large home in the Beverly Hills flats. The collector's interior decorator had pronounced it "hideous" because the colors clashed with her décor, and we'd been summoned to take it away. I contacted Don to make certain he would be at the studio when we arrived—and reminded him that this transaction completed our agreement and I would be picking up my painting.

My employee, Ralph, assisted as we backed our truck up to the small loading dock of an old brick building at the edge of central LA. It was six stories high, with a grimy façade and windows that hadn't been washed in years. The building had outlived its original manufacturing purposes and had been converted into artist studios. An ancient freight elevator opened directly onto the dock, and was perfumed with a distinctive, musty smell of old brick and dust. The elevator car was like a basket on a rope, with five-foot-high sides and an open-top so you could see all the way up the shaft to the ceiling. It had two wooden gates that pulled down to close its entrance, the inner one to protect occupants and cargo, and the outer one as a failsafe. Both had to be closed before the elevator would operate, which was supposed to prevent someone from falling into the shaft when the car started moving.

The grimy, oil-stained gates of this ancient contraption had shiny spots worn in by the generations of hands that had opened and closed them. And the floor was a rusted steel diamond plate, with the tops of the diamonds polished by boots and cargo. The car had an overhead steel yoke connected to its sides. Steel cables wrapped a pulley wheel in the center of the yoke and extended to the ceiling six floors above, where another, larger wheel and electric motor sat bolted to a massive girder at the top of the shaft. The winding of these cables raised and lowered the elevator, which was guided on channels attached to the shaft's walls.

Don arrived at the loading dock through a door from the adjacent stairwell and greeted us.

"So, you're going to take my painting?" he said. I could tell by the tone of his voice he was reluctant to give it up. "Yes," I replied, "that was the deal." I provided the agreed-upon services, and I had earned it.

We opened the gates and attempted to move the returned painting into the elevator, but it was too long to fit inside. Don suggested we feed it through the gates and turn it on end so it could stick up into the open space above the elevator. That worked, but with the painting angled up inside the car, only two of us could stand inside. Don said he would walk up the stairs and meet us on the fifth floor, where his studio was located.

We closed the elevator gates and pushed the button labeled five, and with a lurch, we headed up. Through the slats, I could see Don looking up at us with a smile as we passed through the second floor. He had been slipping glances at Ralph, a big guy with a mop of red hair, a red mustache, and a lot of girlfriends, and now he was almost overtly flirting. Just as he was about to disappear from sight, though, his expression abruptly changed to a look of shock, and he screamed. I looked at Ralph. What had happened? We couldn't see. As we continued upward, we could hear the pounding of Don's shoes echoing from the stairwell, accompanied by his desperate yells, but with the rumble of the elevator and thickness of the shaft walls, we couldn't make out what he was saying.

The fifth floor approached, and we prepared to stop—but the elevator kept going. I pushed the stop button. Nothing happened.

I pushed it again and looking up, I could see the ceiling was getting closer. Too close. I began frantically pushing all the buttons, trying to get the damn thing stopped. Nothing worked, and we continued inexorably upward. Ralph and I were trapped, jammed helplessly between the painting and the elevator walls.

The painting bumped against the concrete ceiling and, for a moment, shifted a few inches until the growing pressure locked it between the elevator floor and the ceiling. It began shuddering, and the wooden stretcher bars started to bow and distort. The painting was making human-like groaning sounds as the canvas tightened. Ralph and I turned our faces away, folding our arms around the backs of our heads to protect ourselves against the shrapnel we knew was about to fly. Moments later, there was an explosion of ripping canvas and the stretcher bars disintegrated into shards that ricocheted off our backs and the elevator walls.

The elevator bumped against the support beam and stopped several feet above the sixth floor. Moments later, Don arrived red-faced and out of breath. He was gasping and sputtering in outrage. "I was yelling at you to disconnect the wire when you reached my floor! Why didn't you listen to me?" He looked at the crumpled mess. "Oh shit! Shit! Shit! My greatest painting is ruined! Totally ruined by you idiots! You, you . . . morons!" I was incredulous. The painting was trash now, but we could've been *killed*.

Ralph asked what wire Don was talking about. Sorenson opened the elevator gates, crawled up to our level and reached behind the control panel to pull out a pair of wires whose stripped ends were loosely twisted around each other. "You just needed to disconnect these to stop the elevator. That's all you had to do!" The controls had been jury-rigged to keep the elevator operating, but Sorenson had been too distracted to tell us. Don died less than a decade later, at age thirty-six—part of a generation lost to AIDS. I never got my painting.

Elevator

Risk is a given when you're an art handler. We work on tall ladders, climb scaffolding, and lift heavy objects. And sometimes, we casually entertain dangerous possibilities because we're more focused on solving the problem at hand than considering the odds that we won't make it out alive.

That's what got me into trouble the day I delivered a seven by sixteen-foot Frank Stella to Security Pacific Bank in downtown Los Angeles. The bank had an extensive art collection that decorated its offices and main lobby. Its art consultant had purchased the piece for the plush reception area of its executive office suite, which was in the penthouse of a 55-story office tower at 333 South Hope. The building sits at the top of Bunker Hill, just down the street from the Museum of Contemporary Art, the Broad Museum, and the titanium curves of the Walt Disney Concert Hall. Security Pacific had made its own contribution to the neighborhood art scenery planting a huge orange Calder stabile from its collection on the plaza outside its front entrance.

The new Stella had been shipped to my warehouse from a New York gallery, and when we delivered it, it was immediately apparent it wasn't going to fit in the elevators. In many modern office towers, freight elevators are left off construction plans because building a large, separate elevator shaft with heavier machinery is so expensive. Occupants make do by pressing passenger elevators into freight service with protective quilts on walls and Masonite floor coverings—although they're stuck with limited space.

We tried carrying the Stella up the stairs, making it to the seventh floor by laboriously lifting the painting up, over, and around railings, but then the stairwell narrowed, and we couldn't continue. The art consultant was chagrined because the bank had paid a lot of money for the painting, and the executives would be unhappy if it couldn't be installed. Nevertheless, she told us to put it back in storage.

A week later, she called to say she had found a solution and asked me to meet her at the bank lobby. There, she introduced me to a representative of the Otis Elevator Company, who suggested we transport the painting on top of an elevator while an Otis technician controlled it from inside. The catch was that someone would need to stand on top to hold the painting, as there was no other way to secure it. The Otis man assured me it would be "perfectly safe, and the elevator will travel at a slow speed." The art consultant, with a wide smile on her face, concurred that this was a wonderful idea and suggested I be the one to ride with the painting. I knew it would be dangerous as hell, but on the other hand, I thought it could be a real adventure—so reluctantly, I agreed. We'd do it on a Sunday morning when the building was largely unoccupied and the elevators mostly unused.

On Sunday at 10 a.m., I showed up with one of my employees carting the Stella. We had wrapped it in plastic with the stretcher bars exposed on the reverse to give me a way to hold onto it as the elevator ascended. The Otis technician walked us over to a bank of four elevators and summoned the center one to the lobby. When it arrived, he pulled the emergency stop button, unscrewed the control panel cover, and installed a hand-held controller by connecting it to some wires. He tested it with a ride to the fifty-fifth floor. Returning a few minutes later, he explained that he would lower the cab with the doors open and stop it when the top was even with the lobby floor. I should step into the shaft and brace myself on the cab roof with the painting. "I won't be able to see you, so stamp your foot three times as a signal when you are ready, and I'll take you up," he said. He lowered the elevator, and I gingerly stepped onto the top of the cab, being careful not to trip on any of the raised framework elements—including cable attachments, tops of light fixtures, and wires that were partially sticking out. The steel yokes connecting the cables to the elevator cab further narrowed the flat portions, leaving little open floor space for me to stand.

My employee fed the Stella through the open doors and tilted it up the shaft so I could hold it upright. At sixteen feet, it towered above me and I began to have doubts. What if I couldn't maintain control of it and it got damaged? How safe was this ride, really? The cables suspending the cab were greasy, rising upward and disappearing into darkness. Focused on keeping the painting from touching any grease and trying to find secure footing, I didn't look around until the elevator began to ascend. I'd always thought elevators each rose inside a fully enclosed shaft. But my cab and the other three in the elevator bank shared the same space—they were set four feet from each other, riding on rails that stood out from the walls of the shaft. This system made sense for high-speed elevators because enclosed shafts would compress air as the cars rose or lowered, and the air resistance would reduce their efficiency. This open system allowed air to flow freely around each cab. But it also meant I was standing on top of a moving platform with my heels inches from a precipice that dropped hundreds of feet below—and I didn't have a safety harness or any place to grab hold. There was nothing to prevent me from falling to my death if I lost my balance.

The elevator was traveling at a moderate speed, but the large expanse of canvas was catching some of the breeze, making it difficult to control. Its top, sixteen feet up in the air, began waving around, and I struggled to maintain the ninety-degree angle. The more it tilted out of alignment, the more air pressure grabbed and pulled against the painting. Suddenly there was a loud "whumpff" as the elevator next to mine shot past at high speed. The blast of wind in its wake pushed the Stella like a sail, shoving me off balance and back toward the void. I saved my life by dropping to my knees and shouldering the painting inward.

After several heart-stopping minutes, I made it off the top of the cab, sweat-soaked and shaky, and crawled out to the top floor, where we installed the painting.

Years later, Bank of America absorbed Security Pacific, along with its art collections, and the Stella was among the pieces to be sent to their San Francisco headquarters. When their art mover, Scott Atthowe of Atthowe Art Transportation, asked me to help him remove the Stella, I told him my elevator story. He then decided it would be safer to un-stretch the painting and roll it on a Sonotube so we could carry it down the stairs.

We went in after 8 p.m. when the offices were empty, so we could use the Security Pacific boardroom to stage and roll the painting. We spent a couple of hours removing hundreds of staples, rolling the painting on the tube, and taking apart the stretcher bars so the components would fit inside. Once we were on the stairs, we had to hold the painting over the railings to get it around the stairwell corners as we descended—which was no easy task since the tube was so heavy. The stairs made four rotations per floor inside the stairwell, and the juggling was so physically exhausting that we were dehydrated and tired by the time we were only halfway down. We were also trapped inside the stairwell since the doors entering each level were locked from the inside. By luck, I noticed a door that was slightly ajar. Setting the tube down, we propped the door open with one of Scott's boots and walked into an office kitchen. We figured the office was part of the bank's operations, and they wouldn't mind if we grabbed a couple of Cokes and granola bars. We were happily chatting and enjoying our refreshments when a silver-haired man wearing a white shirt and tie walked in. Seeing two disheveled and sweaty characters, one missing a shoe, he became alarmed.

"What are you doing here? This is a law firm, and it is private property. You're trespassing!" He crouched down, taking an aggressive stance. "I know karate! Don't mess with me!"

He must have been working late alone in his office when he heard noises and went to investigate. I imagine he thought we were homeless street people. I felt terrible for the distress we were causing him, and we backed out the door explaining that we were working for the bank and meant him no harm. A few days later, the Bank America president called and chewed out Scott for having intruded into the offices of the bank's most important tenant, a major law firm. But we'd managed to get the job done, and the bank got their Stella intact.

Warhol

In addition to Nicholas Wilder, I was getting jobs in the early days from Ace Gallery, which then had a small space on Melrose with a top roster of artists. Douglas Chrismas, Ace's founder, had asked me to ship an Andy Warhol portrait painting of the Oglala Sioux activist Russell Means to André Emmerich Gallery in New York—and now Means stared at me as he leaned against a wall. His head was slightly turned, chin thrust forward in a confident pose, but his eyes gave no indication of what he was thinking.

His long hair was braided, and he wore a wide, beaded porcupine quill necklace—clothing similar to what his ancestors wore when they overran George Armstrong Custer at the Battle of the Little Bighorn.

I knew from my reading that Custer made captives of Sioux women for personal enjoyment, abuse that not only harmed the victims but was also humiliating to Native men and an affront to their manhood—as Custer meant it to be. He studied military history as a cadet at West Point and learned that throughout history, conquerors took the women of the defeated as a reward and to emphasize their dominance over the conquered men. His motivation for attacking the combined forces of Sioux and Cheyenne wasn't strategic, though, according to a recent book, *Death at the Little Bighorn* by Phillip Thomas Tucker, Custer just wanted to capture a Sioux woman he spotted during an earlier scouting mission. Things didn't go well for him, possibly because his pants got ahead of his brains.

Ultimately, though, the outcome was disastrous for the tribes. Russell Means couldn't undo that, but he wanted to raise the self-esteem of his people through action. He gained notoriety defending Native American rights by participating in the San Francisco Bay occupation of Alcatraz Prison. And later, he planned and led the armed takeover of the town of Wounded Knee, a potent symbol for the Sioux because it represented their own tragic last stand—the final crushing of their culture and souls. Some of the most beautiful native artifacts ever made were decorated for their Ghost Dance ceremonies, which expressed the messianic belief that such rituals would bring back buffalo and freedom to roam the plains unmolested. Fantasies often result in disillusionment, but Means knew the power of symbolism combined with activism, and he used it well.

I thought of this as he stared at me from one of seventeen portraits Warhol had painted of him in 1976—perhaps some kind of commentary on the US bicentennial. The canvas measured seventy by eighty-four inches, and I'd be crating and shipping it to Emmerich Gallery, back at 420 West Broadway in lower Manhattan. This was my second important art shipment, after Larry Bell, and I was enjoying having the Warhol in my small crating shop. Perhaps I was too proud of myself.

The painting reminded me of the mystical experiences I had a few years earlier driving through Wyoming and Montana, and I deluded myself into believing these gave me an understanding of the connections Native Americans had to the land they roamed. During the counterculture sixties and early seventies, it became fashionable to spin fantasies about "noble savages," when it was likely they had been more interested in securing their next meal than spending time communing with nature. I probably projected a few of those onto the painting, but it genuinely moved me.

I crated it and shipped it on a Flying Tigers Air Cargo flight, notifying Emmerich that it was on its way. Flying Tigers was perhaps the largest airfreight company in the world at the time, with a fleet of cargo planes including several Boeings 747s that circumnavigated the globe. Tigers ran one eastbound 747 cargo flight daily to New York City, which continued across the Atlantic to Europe. The second one went to Japan and onward through Asia. The westbound flights refueled in Anchorage, Alaska, before crossing the Pacific to Japan, a route that reduced the over-ocean distance traveled and avoided flying directly into westerly headwinds, saving fuel.

Flying Tigers was named for the legendary fighter pilot group that volunteered to assist the Chinese Nationalist Government in its fight against the invading Japanese, who were ruthlessly gobbling up large areas of China in 1940. The Chinese lacked a viable air force, and the Americans sent planes and pilots to help, though it would be another year before America entered World War II. The Tigers' pilots and ground crews resigned their US Army Air Force commissions and worked as civilians under the command of Gen. Claire Lee Chennault, who had already been in China for several years, advising the government. The group operated under their own rules instead of the more restrictive US military regulations. In many ways, their cowboy mentality had been the reason for their incredible success against Japanese planes and ground targets. The same mentality guided the airfreight company they later put together using war surplus cargo planes, and from what I could tell, they still operated with a "seat of your pants" approach. The key difference was that fighter pilots could bail out of their planes in an emergency, while cargo plane pilots had to ride theirs to the end.

Like everyone in my business, I became familiar with them because most airfreight companies didn't own airplanes, and shipments were subcontracted to passenger airlines or larger companies like Tigers. You could also send shipments directly with Tigers, which I often did. It was a Flying Tigers truck that came to my shop and loaded the Russell Means crate, taking it to the company's enormous warehouse at Los Angeles International Airport.

That should've been the end of the story, but a week later, the Emmerich Gallery registrar called to tell me the painting had not arrived as scheduled. Could I check on it? This was slightly worrisome, but I shook off my feelings of foreboding and called Tigers. The agent put me on hold for several minutes and came back saying that the painting had been delivered the previous day. Relieved, I called to tell the gallery to check again because there must've been a mistake on their end, but the registrar, miffed, denied having received it and hung up on me.

The next morning, I received another call from the gallery, this one more threatening in tone, saying that the painting definitely was not there and that I'd really need to do something about it. My stress level rising, I called Tigers, asked for a manager, and waited for twenty minutes until an officious voice got on the phone and condescendingly insisted that the painting was at the gallery in New York. I asked him for the name of the person who signed the delivery receipt, and after another twenty minutes was told that a "Mr. Shapiro" had signed. Emmerich, when I reported this, said no one by that name worked at the gallery. A follow-up call to Tigers to verify the delivery address got me the same results as before: they insisted they'd made the delivery and hung up.

The next morning, a New York attorney representing André Emmerich called. He had one of those deep, resonant voices that all high-priced lawyers seem to have and the demeanor of one who never loses. He told me I had forty-eight hours to deliver the painting or they were going to sue me.

After a sleepless night, I was working in my shop when I heard a diesel truck pull up out front and the hissing pop of air brakes being set. The engine remained idling, followed moments later by a whine of a lift gate. These sounds were punctuated by a loud "thunk!" as something hit the wall outside. I opened the front door and stuck my head out just in time to see a Flying Tigers truck speeding around the corner. On the sidewalk to my left, leaning against the wall, was my Andy Warhol crate, soaking wet. Water slowly trickled out underneath, forming a puddle on the sidewalk, and tire tracks crisscrossed its face. Whatever had driven over it caused the sides to collapse, deforming it into a parallelogram.

My heart pounded as I struggled to drag the waterlogged crate inside my shop and lean it against a wall. Electric screwdrivers hadn't yet been invented, and it took twenty frantic, wrist-aching minutes with a hand screwdriver to remove the lid. When I did, there was Russell Means, staring at me through a haze of condensation trapped under the plastic wrapping. I tore off the plastic and leaned the Warhol against the crate. By some miracle, the painting appeared to be undamaged. I walked eight feet back to take in the whole thing and was relieved to see the painting was none the worse for wear. It was okay!

But as I stepped closer to look carefully at the surface, I thought my vision was beginning to blur. I shook my head, trying to clear it. Something was wrong. I watched in horror as the paint began to slip, and with a soft hissing sound, slowly slid down the face of the canvas, leaving nothing but a raw, white, gesso surface. In just moments, Russell Means had disappeared into a pile of mushy paint flakes on the floor. In hindsight, I probably should have laid the painting flat. Perhaps the paint could have re-adhered to the gesso once it had dried. But it seems just as likely that it would have dried into a powder and blown away.

Emmerich's lawyer didn't sue me, but the gallery's insurance company went after Flying Tiger's liability insurance for negligence. In depositions over the ensuing months, Tigers admitted to losing track of the crate and trying to cover it up. It had been loaded onto their Japan-bound plane by mistake, and the error was noticed when the flight arrived in Anchorage for refueling. The crate was taken off the plane, set out on the tarmac for a later return to Los Angeles, and then forgotten. At some point, it fell or blew over and was buried by a snowstorm. Several vehicles drove over it, but nobody bothered to investigate what they had hit. Meanwhile, Flying Tigers headquarters was frantically attempting to track down the missing crate—while stalling me by lying about delivering it to Emmerich.

Tigers found the crate when the snow melted and flew it back to their Los Angeles warehouse, where managers saw the damage and panicked. They decided to send a Tigers vice president over to check out my location. He reported that my business was operating out of a storefront, which probably meant I was a nobody who had exaggerated the value of the painting. They decided to solve their problem by dumping the crate with me and denying they'd received it. Fortunately, I had the presence of mind to keep the shipping documents, and eventually, they were forced to pay for the painting. Somehow, I doubt that Means would've been surprised by his final fade to white.

Dresden

I had several other Flying Tigers misadventures over the years, including one that unfolded when I was hired to oversee the crates containing the *Splendor of Dresden* exhibition as they were loaded onto a Tigers 747 flight from Los Angeles to Europe. The exhibition, organized by the Dresden Museum in East Germany, featured 700 priceless paintings, sculptures, and porcelain and silver objects—all of which had miraculously survived the firebombing of Dresden during World War II and later escaped confiscation during the

Russian occupation. The exhibition had been at the Metropolitan Museum and the National Gallery, and ended in the summer of 1979 at the Palace of the Legion of Honor in San Francisco. Dave Epstein, who founded Masterpiece International and had worked for W.R. Keating—a large customs broker based in New York—asked me to truck the show to LAX accompanied by the Dresden Museum's director and his watcher. His watcher was a tough-looking East German Stasi character, who was obviously there to ensure the director wouldn't defect. After we safely warehoused the crates for the night, I invited the director home for dinner while ignoring his handler, who was very unhappy but unable to do anything about it. The director was well-read and erudite but sad about the bleak conditions in East Germany.

The next morning, we returned to LAX to watch the crates get packed onto pallets in the Flying Tiger's hangar. I managed to talk my way aboard the aircraft to see how they'd been loaded. I was alarmed to find that Tigers had put a twenty-four-foot steel turbine shaft into the same space and strapped it to three flat pallets. It was aimed directly at my Dresden crates, a potential spear of destruction. I checked the straps that were securing it and found they had come loose, so I grabbed one of the Tiger's loading guys to help me tighten them. We were still busily at work when the plane's engines fired up, and we started rolling away from the hanger for takeoff. The rest of the loaders had left the plane and closed its hatches without notifying us—just another example of Tiger's casual operating mentality. The poor guy who stayed to help me looked stricken, likely fearing for his job. I felt terrible, but we were protecting world heritage treasures, and if we got in hot water with the Tiger's brass or the FAA, so be it.

We began loudly yelling for help from the cargo hold, and suddenly the engines shut down, and the plane stopped moving. High above the cargo bay, the flight deck hatch opened, and a red-faced pilot appeared to chew us out. The airport had to bring out stairs mounted on a truck to get us off the plane, and the FAA investigated the incident. I never found out the fate of my cargo-handling partner, but the crates made it safely back to East Germany.

Disney

The Tiger's quick-and-dirty style left me with a personal mess when I used them to ship a rare collection of Disney animation cells, drawings, and other artwork for an exhibition at the Whitney. The museum's registrar, Nancy McGary, enlisted me to collect original cells and artwork from the Disney Studios archives in Burbank and several retired Disney animators. She cautioned that I'd need to be respectful and reassuring to the animators because they were very reluctant to loan their artwork to the exhibit, fearing that the Disney Corporation would seize it. At the time, Walt Disney had a strict policy preventing his artists and animators from keeping any of their art—going as far as subjecting them to searches when they left the studios at the end of their workdays to ensure they weren't sneaking anything out. For this reason, very little of the art from Disney classics, such as *Bambi*, *Snow White*, *Dumbo*, and *Mickey Mouse*, is in private hands. However, the animators had been able to smuggle out small quantities of their art, and the Whitney wanted to include it in the exhibition.

I went to the Disney studios in Burbank and helped an archivist rummage through flat files and boxes containing hundreds of original cells, most of which had been stuffed into their containers without interleafing or proper protection. This was not unusual because, until recently, most movie studios were cavalier about preserving their history and invested little time or thought in properly storing props, costumes, and other remnants of movie productions. That has changed as public interest in the history and legacy of the movies has grown, and many studios have recognized the importance of keeping and protecting movie memorabilia and establishing archives, museums, and staff to catalogue and care for the objects. But the shift came too late for the art I was gathering for the Whitney at Disney. Animation cells, the thin acetate sheets the animator paints on, are particularly fragile because the bond between acetate and paint is weak, and paint can easily crack or flake off. The acetate itself is easily creased and becomes brittle as it ages. It was tragic to see so much of the work damaged because these treasures had been treated like trash.

By contrast, the cells kept by the animators were in excellent condition, protected in frames behind Plexiglas. As I made the rounds to pick them up, each animator asked for my personal assurance the drawings would be returned to them after the show, and they wouldn't release their work to me until I promised I would. As Nancy warned me, all of them were paranoid that the Disney Company would take it back.

After packing all the art and some additional materials into eight small crates, the Whitney asked me to courier the shipment to New York. I booked the shipment and myself on the Tigers' eastbound 747 freighter, an overnight flight to Kennedy Airport, but naively, I didn't realize that riding as a courier meant fending for myself. I sat in the pilot's cabin on a seat directly behind the crew and learned then that, of course, there wouldn't be food service. The three-person crew had bags of McDonald's hamburgers and fries, but I flew on an empty stomach. The sun was rising when the flight touched down and taxied to Tigers' hanger, and the crew walked off the plane, leaving me behind to find my way. It wasn't easy. Tigers had just merged with Eastern Airlines and was in a state of personnel chaos. The freight handlers were on strike, and only one freight door was open, with a line of waiting trucks that stretched for blocks while sullen freight handlers stood around doing nothing but cursing and sulking.

It took nearly six hours for the truck Tigers assigned to my delivery to arrive at the dock. It was a decrepit pile of wheezing junk, driven by a rumpled older man. When he rolled the door up, I was shocked to see the floor covered with rollers and that there were no logistics posts for tying off loads. This type of truck is routinely used to transport aluminum containers, "igloos," between airfreight terminals or out to aircraft, and the floor-mounted rollers are there for sliding the igloos on and off. I could either make this truck work or wait another six hours, I began hunting for ways to keep my fragile Disney crates from crashing around loose in the back. I pulled cardboard boxes, pallets, and debris out of nearby dumpsters and used the whole mess to jam the crates against the truck's front wall so they wouldn't budge.

When I was finally convinced they'd be safe, the driver climbed into his side of the cab, and I climbed into mine—where I almost fell through to the road. The floor had rusted out, leaving jagged, rusty, man-eating teeth around the edge of a large hole. The driver not only hadn't warned me before he pulled out, he hadn't even waited for me to fasten my seat belt, which I soon discovered was broken. I wedged myself against the seat back by shoving my feet into the dashboard and watched as the concrete expressway shot past underneath while I struggled to stay balanced as the cab constantly bounced and shook. The truck's suspension was shot, and hitting some of the bigger potholes lifted me off the seat. I fought to stay upright and adhere my ass to the vinyl seat as my shoes slipped off the metal dashboard. It was an exhausting and frightening trip.

Somehow, the cargo and I arrived intact, but the Whitney staff stared in shock when they saw the disheveled driver and me and then watched me pull their crates from a trash heap. I knew I'd be forgiven. I'd done right by the Whitney and Disney—and the animators most of all.

Pig

I got a break that helped my fledgling business gain the trust of museums when Dr. Armand Hammer became a client of Cooke's Crating. The unlikely chain of events that led to my hiring by the man I'd last seen when I wrestled a painting away from him at the USC art galleries involved a pig, a Rembrandt, a strip club, and a couple of cops—my side of the art world in a nutshell.

The saga began when the Jewish Defense League tied a pig to Hammer's front porch, something that jokingly became known in LA Police Department circles as the "Porch Pooping Pig" case. The JDL was pissed at Hammer because of his long association with the Russian Communist leadership. Hammer had traveled to Russia in the famine years after the revolution and worked out a deal to trade US grain for furs and hides. The goodwill he earned led him to meet and develop friendships with Vladimir Lenin—and later Joseph Stalin—resulting in arrangements with the government that allowed him to take large quantities of Czarist art and jewelry out of the country. He would scoop it up cheaply in Russia, and later sell it through department stores and his gallery in New York City. His connections and friendly relations with the Russians continued through subsequent regimes.

Anyone who befriended Lenin had great cachet in the eyes of the Soviets but was highly suspicious in the eyes of the Americans. Some in America believed Hammer was a Russian spy, and some American Jews were certain he was a traitor—especially when he refused to support efforts to rescue fellow Jews from the Soviet Union. This made him a target of the JDL.

Its activists found a giant pig, and for a week, they fed it beans and other gas-provoking food. After dosing it with laxatives, they took it to Hammer's home under cover of darkness, leaving it tied to the front porch with a warning note posted on the door. The pig liberally defecated, leaving large and stinky deposits on the doormat, and then, as pigs are wont to do, it wallowed in the mess, spreading it all over. Hammer construed the note and action as a threat, so he called the Los Angeles Police Department and asked for protection.

Because of Hammer's importance, the LAPD assigned two detectives to shadow him, with instructions to make sure nothing happened to the doctor. One of those cops was a guy I nicknamed "Big Jim" when I met him. He was over six feet tall with messy brown hair and always wore a disheveled and wrinkled brown suit. The ill-fitting suit jacket appeared to be one size too large, but the extra size may have been intentional to make it easier to retrieve his shoulder gun. Cops are paranoid, I've observed, and never like to be slow on the draw.

Big Jim had cobra eyes, hooded and full of warning not to get too close, not to provoke him. And to be very careful what you said to him and how you presented it. He was approaching retirement, and after many years with the LAPD, he had seen too much sorrow and witnessed despair, death, and the bottom of life. Cops swam in the cesspools of humanity, and a lot of them carried the stink with them. As I spent more time around him, I could see that Big Jim was full of nitroglycerin, and one wrong move would cause an explosion. When one of my employees once offended him with a wisecrack, Big Jim laid into him with a verbal tirade so full of vitriol I was concerned he was going to physically assault the man.

Big Jim and his partner started hanging around Hammer's outer office in the late afternoons, waiting to escort him home or to some event. But whenever my work brought me into the office, I got the sense that their real motive for waiting around inside was to access the free coffee while making time with the secretaries, who began bringing donuts and home-baked cookies to work.

One day the two cops learned from Hammer's curator that a large shipment of his art collection would be arriving at Los Angeles Airport around ten that evening. The curator proudly boasted that the shipment contained a Rembrandt, a Van Gogh, and many other masterpieces. This intrigued the cops, so after getting Hammer safely home, they decided to go to the airport on their own time and watch over the artwork. Perhaps they were also hoping the JDL would show up and provide some action to relieve the boredom of their Hammer guard duty.

Big Jim's story of what happened next is a favorite of mine, in part because it's so colorful, but mostly because of the way it tipped fate in my direction. He and his partner parked their unmarked sedan in a discreet location with a clear line of sight to the airfreight loading docks. After waiting for nearly forty-five minutes, they saw a Cart & Crate truck back into one of the docks. Two bearded, long-haired guys climbed out of the cab and went inside to hand their paperwork to the night manager. A few minutes later, several forklifts appeared, carrying aircraft aluminum freight cans that they deposited near the truck doors. The two drivers began carefully lifting crates, painted light blue, out of the containers and loaded them into the truck. They worked deliberately and tied each crate to the inside truck walls. Big Jim was impressed by the care shown, particularly since it was being done by hippies. Big Jim often said that the only decent hippie was a hippie in jail. But these guys appeared to be professional, and his attitude began to soften.

Once the truck was loaded and paperwork signed, the shipment headed out of the airport and turned east on Century Boulevard toward the 405 freeway, with Big Jim and his partner trailing behind. Just before the truck reached the freeway, its brake lights came on, and it made an abrupt left turn into the parking lot of the Pussycat strip club. Signs on the sides of the building promised gorgeous topless go-go dancers.

The two drivers left their vehicle and went inside. Big Jim and his partner stayed outside, keeping an eye on the truck and growing increasingly angry as the minutes went by.

Finally, Big Jim went into the club and watched as the drivers ordered beers and stuffed dollar bills into the G-string of a topless dancer performing on top of the bar in high heels. As she gyrated to the music, she pulled aside her minimal covering and urged the patrons to "feed my slot boys! Feed my slot!" The dancer had large breasts, each with a metal ashtray taped just above the nipple, and when she gyrated to the music, the ashtrays banged together, keeping time. If Big Jim had been off duty, he might have been impressed and even stuffed large denomination bills into the "slot" in hopes of seeing action at the end of the dancer's shift. But now, he was furious that these two jerks were preventing him from going home and getting some sleep. Perhaps he was also concerned that the truck loaded with millions of dollars of valuable art was sitting unattended in the parking lot of a cheap honky-tonk bar. Looking back, I wonder what Rembrandt would have thought had he known that 400 years in the future, the painting of his beloved son Titus would be left in the back of a truck at a topless bar. Perhaps some form of Amsterdam's red-light district was in operation back then, and he wouldn't have cared.

Finally, the two paid their bill and staggered outside, laughing and joking. They jumped into the truck cab and headed east, passing under the freeway and weaving on surface streets up and over the oil dome, through Baldwin Hills, across Stocker, and down Fairfax until they arrived at the LA County Museum of Art and delivered Hammer's treasures.

The next morning, the detectives called Hammer's curator and told her about the topless bar episode. They were careful to leave out the more prurient details but gave her enough information to scare her. She immediately told Dr. Hammer, who angrily called LACMA's director to complain. Hammer had promised to leave his collection to the museum when he died. In anticipation of his gifts, the museum not only named one of its buildings after him but also stored the Hammer collection without charge and provided other free services, including conservation work and insurance.

The alarmed director called the museum registrar, Pat Nuart, into his office to talk about what they should do. Pat was a beautiful blond woman with a brilliant sense of humor and a completely unflappable demeanor. She was also smart and fast on her feet. She knew of me from my Cart & Crate days and from seeing me at American Association of Museums meetings, where she was involved in the registrars' committee. Fortuitously, the two of us had recently become reacquainted when I made a delivery to the museum. Pat told the director that Cooke's Crating was the best company to handle Hammer's art collection going forward, a big leap of faith on her part because she didn't know me that well. Her recommendation would give my new business a certain credibility in the museum world, and I thanked her for her generosity when she called to tell me about this development.

About six months later, I was asked to personally oversee the delivery of *Titus* to *The Tonight Show*. I accompanied a couple of my drivers as we picked up the crate from LACMA and drove it to Johnny Carson's studios for the show's taping in front of a live audience. I worried a little that Hammer would see me and remember the way I'd kicked him out of the USC Fisher Galleries when he attempted to cart off a painting—but I tried to push that thought aside.

We arrived with *Titus* inside its crate and were told to wait in the holding area outside the stage. Ten minutes later, Hammer walked in and was met by the stage manager and one of Carson's assistants, who discussed his cues and the questions Carson would be asking him about the painting. Then they turned to us, and the stage manager told us to open the crate and prepare to carry the painting onto the stage and place it on an easel next to Carson's desk. As he waited, Hammer looked at us for the first time and focused on me. I saw a question beginning to form in his face, but at that moment, the comedian George Burns appeared, carrying his trademark cigar, and sauntered up to Hammer. The two shook hands and fell into conversation as they headed to the green room.

Titus and I crossed paths again a few years later when I was asked to pack the painting and ship it to Europe. The crate was over-height and couldn't fit in the below-deck aluminum "Igloo" containers used to ship freight in the belly of passenger planes. It would need to go out on a cargo plane, and I booked it on American Airlines. Freight being sent on cargo planes were grouped and stacked on flat aluminum pallets, with the highest objects in the center to match the inside curvature of the aircraft. The loaded pallets were then covered in plastic or tarps secured by cargo nets clipped onto the pallet edges. I didn't want to ship the Rembrandt crate exposed in that manner, so I requested an exclusively covered container, which American Airlines promised would be waiting at their airfreight warehouse near LAX.

When I arrived with *Titus*, I discovered that the container was used to transport racehorses—and that a recent occupant left a fresh pile of dung on the floor. I rummaged through American Air's dumpsters, looking for discarded cardboard cartons, using one to scoop out most of the poop and covering the floor with the rest. We secured the painting inside using the same harness restraints that keep horses from falling during flights, and Hammer's Rembrandt arrived safely in Europe.

As it turned out, I wound up having a longer relationship with Hammer than LACMA did. After a falling out with the museum over how his collection would be displayed, he moved his art to a high-rise office building in Irvine, California, for storage. The location proved difficult to service because it was so far from Hammer's offices at the Occidental Petroleum Building in Westwood near the UCLA campus, so when Hammer later acquired an entire floor of the building, he relocated the collection there. While this was conveniently close, it also caused many logistical problems. For one, art had to be delivered using a freight elevator that rose from the sidewalk on the corner of Wilshire Boulevard and Gayley Avenue, a bustling intersection with heavy automobile and pedestrian traffic. Even more challenging, there wasn't truck parking in the area, and the closest parking meters were half a block away in either direction. Our workaround was to schedule deliveries after midnight when traffic was light and pedestrians few. We would park our truck as close to the corner as possible, and roll crated paintings on dollies one at a time down the sidewalk to the corner. The freight elevator would rise out of the sidewalk, and we'd place one or two crates inside, then send the car back down to the parking garage, where art handlers walked down automobile ramps to meet it. Next, the crates had to be rolled across the garage so they could make the final leg of their trip on a passenger elevator. Each of these steps took time, and whenever a substantial portion of the collections traveled, the process took many hours. Through all this, Big Jim was working protection for Hammer and the art, so we spoke often. It's difficult to get close to cops, who are generally wary and guarded with the public. Big Jim never talked about his personal life or became more than circumspect about his police career. But he did talk about retiring and his dream of moving up to Idaho and raising trophy sheep, even though he didn't have a farming background.

Eventually, he did retire, and several years passed when I didn't hear from him. This was not unusual because we were on polite terms but not friends. Then, much to my surprise, I got a large manila envelope from him with a return address in Idaho. It contained an eight by ten glossy color photograph of Big Jim holding a large ram by the horns. He had his arms wrapped around the ram's front legs and under the spiraled horns, pinning the animal on its back, immobilized. Oddly, the camera was aimed up between the ram's rear legs and looked across its belly toward Big Jim, who was cheek to cheek with the ram's face. The bulging Beelzebub eyes of the ram stared directly into the lens. Big Jim's eyes did too, and I noticed that while there was a big smile across Big Jim's face, there was something else in his eyes—and something quite unsettling in the photo. The ram was fully aroused, and his large balls flopped to one side of his stomach, the closeness of the camera angle accentuating their size. This picture was truly bizarre—Picasso would have loved it. I sent a polite thank you note to Big Jim congratulating him on his magnificent ram and wishing him well with his farming enterprise.

I never heard back.

Deng Xiaoping

Lela phoned late in the afternoon from the Hammer Foundation. It was the spring of 1982 and Lela was the collections registrar. She sounded nervous, which I attributed to stress caused by Hammer's sometimes rushed demands. The foundation had a director and three or four employees who maintained Hammer's collection of paintings, Daumier drawings, and the Da Vinci Codex—a book of Leonardo's drawings that was the doctor's most prized acquisition. It seemed to me there were too many staff members for the size of the collection, but Hammer frequently loaned portions of it to museums around the world. He also used it for business and political purposes, which probably justified the expense.

Stress was the norm for the foundation employees, who were in constant fear of losing their jobs. Hammer had a mercurial temperament and was known for firing people when they made mistakes or couldn't meet his demands. I witnessed this firsthand several years earlier when his curator Olga asked us to pack and crate a painting. She made her request late in the afternoon, with orders to deliver the crate to Hammer's jet the next morning at seven. We worked past midnight crating the painting and went home for a few hours of sleep before driving it to LAX.

Hammer's jet, a converted Boeing passenger plane with long-distance capability, was outfitted with an office, bedroom, galley, and other amenities to make Hammer's frequent overseas business trips comfortable—including a mural by the artist Joe Goode on the jet's ceiling. We arrived a few minutes late, and the jet's engines were already in a high pitch, warming up for takeoff. Olga stood, hands-on-hips and agitated in the jet's doorway at the top of the stairs. "Hurry up! Hurry! Hurry!" she yelled at us. "You're late! You're causing a flight delay! Hurry!"

We grabbed the crate from our truck. It was heavy and awkward, and after running with it 150 feet across the tarmac to the foot of the stairs, we were gasping for breath. We adjusted the position of our hands on the crate and staggered up the stairs, groaning under the weight. Clunk! The crate wouldn't fit through the door opening. We stood stunned and momentarily confused by this unexpected development. Olga's face turned ashen, and she looked like she was going to faint. "Oh, God! Take it away," she told us. Then, with a look of total defeat and despair, she turned back inside. The stairs retracted, and we watched as the jet taxied away from us toward a runway.

I later learned that Hammer had berated poor Olga for her failure to get his painting on the jet. She was trapped with him during the long trip across the Pacific, and he not only fired her when they arrived, but he also left her stranded without money or a return ticket. So, when Lela called and asked me to send two of my employees and a truck to the foundation, I attributed the stress in her voice to the pressure of another make-or-break task. We were to pick up a small painting measuring thirty by forty inches and then follow her precise set of instructions. "Deliver it to Newell Color Lab in Hollywood," Lela said. "Please wait while they photograph the painting and then

deliver it to the doctor's jet at eight tomorrow morning. The painting is by a Chinese artist working in New York and is a gift from Dr.
Hammer to Chinese Premier Deng Xiaoping. Dr. Hammer is flying to
China to open a huge coal mining project. So, it is extremely important you make certain the painting gets safely to his plane in time."

Lela's stress became my stress, and my guts tightened from the responsibility. I decided to personally pick up the painting at the foundation's Westwood headquarters to make sure it got to the plane on
time. My stalwart employee Rita Gomez, who later became a lead
preparator at the Getty Museum, agreed to stay late to help me.

Driving a step van, we arrived at the foundation offices around
5:30 a.m. and rode the elevator up to the seventh floor. There was
no one at the reception desk, but Lela and another employee came
to meet us and ushered us into a back room where portions of the
collections were stored on shelves and racks. Oddly, Lela didn't
seem very happy to see me. In fact, she was curt and stiff. I had
known her for years and regarded her as a friend, so her terse demeanor was puzzling.

A Bill Zamprelli crate lay horizontally on the floor with its lid off
to reveal the painting, wrapped in brown paper. Zamprelli, based
in New York City, was one of the pioneers of the art moving industry and always constructed crates for Hammer, who was willing
to pay the extra costs to have them shipped empty to Los Angeles.
Zamprelli crates were immediately recognizable from the light blue
paint used to coat them. Bill designed his crates so the paintings
were packed facing up. As an art handler, this bothered me because
whenever the crate lid was being removed or put back in place, the
painting was vulnerable. What if the lid slipped and a corner fell
into the crate? The set-up posed risks for canvases with large surface areas or those not properly keyed (tightened). They could sag
against the stretcher bars and become creased. But Hammer preferred Zamprelli, regardless.

Lela asked us to lift the painting out of the crate. When we removed it, we saw that the paper covering was heavily taped. I pulled our bill of lading out of my shirt pocket and said we'd need to unwrap the painting to do a condition report.

"You don't have time for that," Lela said heatedly. "Newell is waiting late tonight specifically to photograph this painting, so you need to hurry!" I tried to insist, but since she was adamant we leave right away, I marked the paperwork *"received packed by owner, condition unknown"* and had her sign it. Handing her a copy, I asked about taking the crate. "Oh, I'm sorry, but the crate needs to stay here," she said. "You can deliver the painting tomorrow to the doctor's jet wrapped in cardboard."

Rita and I drove the painting to Newell and left it for the lab to photograph while we got some dinner. When we returned, I could see it sitting on an easel inside the glass-enclosed photography studio, with bright lights illuminating it and a camera on a tripod set up in front. My heart sank. Even from our distance, I could clearly see there was a hole in the painting. "You've damaged the painting!" I started shouting. "This is an extremely important painting, and you've damaged it!"

The manager defensively rushed over. "We didn't damage it. We received it this way. Look!" He held up the wrapping materials to show they were clean. "We have Polaroids taken when we unwrapped it that show the damage." We looked at the photos, and all of them showed the round hole near the center of the painting. It was about the diameter of a quarter.

I walked into the studio for a closer look. The hole was perfectly round on the surface, and torn, jagged flaps of canvas had been shoved inward by whatever had pushed against the painting's face. I was beginning to feel sick. "You must have damaged it after you unwrapped it," I insisted.

The manager was joined by the photographer, and both insisted that the hole was there when they unwrapped the painting. I had home numbers for Lela and several other foundation employees, including the director, and I asked to use a phone. Not a single person answered when I called.

I didn't know what we should do. It was late, Rita needed to get home, and I was really feeling the pressure. Something bad was going to happen. But just then, an artist I knew, Doug Shields, walked up. It was one of those moments in life when good luck pushes bad luck aside. Doug said he was working evenings at Newell and had his VW bus in the parking lot. "I have my paintbox in my bus, and I'll lend it to you," he said. "Maybe you can use it to fix the painting?" His generous offer gave me sudden hope. I went with him to the bus, where he opened the side doors and pulled out a wooden paint box. Inside were dozens of tubes of oils and watercolors, as well as varnish, cobalt drier, brushes, and pallet knives. It was a complete artist's paint kit. He handed it to me, and I took it.

It was 10 p.m. by the time I dropped Rita off and got the painting to my home in Beachwood Canyon. I cleared off the dining room table, placed the painting face-up on top, and grabbed every available lamp in the house so I'd have as much light as possible.

I sat down and stared at the hole. It was beginning to take on enormous dimensions in my mind, a yawing wound in an otherwise pristine painting. Could I even fix it? Was it ethical to attempt it without permission? I tried calling the numbers again, but still, no one answered. Why weren't they picking up? I needed them to tell me what to do.

It was nearing 11 p.m., and the painting had to be on Hammer's plane in nine and a half hours. My stomach churned, and the fear of making a wrong decision was paralyzing. If I didn't deliver the painting at all, Hammer would be outraged. If I delivered it damaged, he would also be angry, and my friends at the foundation would lose their jobs. I definitely would lose his business and perhaps that of LACMA, among others. Would he sue me? What if Deng Xiaoping was insulted and canceled Hammer's big deal?

I wasn't a trained conservator. If I tried to fix the damage and failed, the attempt would be obvious and get me in deeper trouble. And it would make me look guilty of having damaged the painting and trying to cover it up.

Trying to calm myself, I looked at the hole again, and the torn canvas flaps inside. How could I quickly repair the canvas to give myself an even surface on which to apply touch-up paint? Suddenly, I had an idea: white glue. It was water-based and dried quickly, and it would bond the torn flaps together. It would also follow good restoration practice because it could be reversed. And I just happened to have a squeeze bottle on a shelf in my garage.

I took a bottle cap and placed it under the canvas, using it as a flat surface to push the flaps back together into a position even with the painted surface. There was still a slight indentation, but that could be filled in with paint once the canvas flaps were glued together. I rubbed the bottle cap with soap to prevent the white glue from sticking and placed the cap back under the canvas until I was satisfied with the alignment of the flaps and canvas surface. I diluted the glue and used a paintbrush to soak the flaps with it. A hairdryer sped up the drying times. Once the first application dried, I applied a second layer. In an hour, the hole was repaired and ready for painting. Luckily the artist had mottled his colors, making it easier for me to blend in my paint so it wouldn't show.

Oil paint would probably take too long to cure, so I chose Winsor and Newton gouache colors, mixing them on a dinner plate until I found a good color match. I began carefully painting, matching the artist's paint strokes and drying the results with the hair drier. My skills did not fail me under pressure.

The artist had varnished his painting and likely used a water-based varnish that would cure more quickly than oil-based. Luckily, Doug had a good quality polymer varnish in his kit and a large, soft brush I could use to apply it, which enabled me to blend it with the surrounding area.

When I finished, it was very hard to tell that the painting had been repaired. I was both relieved and proud of accomplishing a miracle. It was 3 a.m. when I loaded the artwork into the van and drove it to my warehouse in downtown Los Angeles. I put a backing on the painting to cover the repairs visible on the reverse side of the canvas and built a crate to pack it in.

It was nearly 8 a.m. when I finished and headed to the airport, and I pulled up just as Hammer's jet was starting to rev its engines. The crate fit neatly through the door, and Hammer left for China with his painting and meeting with the Chinese premier.

Although I was exhausted from stress and the full night of work, I knew I was too wound up to sleep, so I went into my office. Working at my desk, I began pondering whether or not to call the foundation to let them know about the damage to Hammer's painting. Would they be outraged I had repaired it? Perhaps the doctor would have hired a professional restorer to fix it and sent it to China later. My conscience was kicking me so relentlessly by mid-afternoon that I decided to call Lela.

"I have something to tell you about the painting," I began.

"Yes!" she blurted out too quickly.

"Newall damaged the painting," I said.

"Yes!?" Her voice went up an octave.

"But I repaired it and delivered it to the plane on time."

"Oh my God! You did!" she exclaimed. But it wasn't an accusation. There was audible relief in her voice. "We didn't know what to do!"

At that moment, I realized someone at the foundation damaged the painting and set me up to take the fall with the ruse of sending it to the color lab.

"Lisa's pen fell out of her pocket when she leaned over to lift the painting out of the crate, and the pen punctured the painting. We didn't know what to do," Lela blurted. Then she hung up. No apology. No thank you for all my effort. Cold!

Irving Blum

I repeatedly learned not to expect thanks or compassion from the people I worked for. That, I found, was too much to ask of some customers, who were often outsized personalities like Irving Blum—director of the legendary Ferus Gallery in Los Angeles, which showcased uniquely West Coast styles like Finish Fetish and Light and Space. It was also the first Los Angeles gallery to show Andy Warhol's soup cans.

I met Irving when he was operating the Irving Blum Gallery, which he started after Ferus's nine-year run. With a loud, booming baritone voice that emanated from deep within his chest, he reminded me of the fairy-tale troll who lived under a bridge and challenged any person wanting to cross with a "who dares to tread on my bridge?" Or the Cyclops, who roared out a challenge to Odysseus from deep inside his cave. Of course, those characters were ugly and mean-spirited, while Irving Blum was charming and handsome. Nevertheless, Irving had a voice that could be intimidating, commanding attention and obedience—and more than a touch of that troll-Cyclops sense of being king of his territory.

This came to the fore while I was hanging a large Robert Morris felt sculpture in Irving's LA gallery. The sculpture, made of inch-thick felt, and measuring ten feet long by five feet high, was heavy and awkward. It had two or three cuts running horizontally across the middle, spaced twelve inches apart, and was to be hung on two large nails hammered into the wall studs. These were placed at distances pre-determined by Morris so the felt could sag down and outward, causing the cuts to open and expose the wall behind. We only had one ladder with us and needed a second, so Irving opened a closet and told me to use his stepladder, which I couldn't help but notice was beat up and worn.

We positioned the ladders facing each other at the outer edges of the felt and, with great difficulty, lifted the piece from the floor. By leaning away from each other, we could pull and stretch the felt enough to hook it over the nails as we walked up the ladders. My partner, John, got his side hooked on, and just as I managed to get my end over the nail, my ladder abruptly folded in half and collapsed. I fell backward, plummeting five feet down and slamming my back onto the floor hard enough to knock the wind out of me. If I hadn't learned judo and gone into a protective position, I'm not sure where I'd be now.

Irving shouted out a loud, booming, "Jeeeeeeeeeezsusssss!" then went silent for a few moments as I lay on my back, determining if I'd been hurt. Then his voice boomed out again: "Well, don't just lie there, get back to work!"

Ad Reinhardt

Several years after Irving closed his Los Angeles gallery, he called me from Blum Helman Gallery in New York City. I instantly recognized his voice. He wanted me to pick up a painting by Ad Reinhardt in Beverly Hills and ship it to him. "Be sure you thoroughly condition report it," he instructed as he hung up the phone.

Ad Reinhardt paintings are scary to handle because they are virtually impossible to restore once damaged. Even an inadvertent fingerprint will ruin a painting, and Ad's technique of subtly applying paint has remained something of a mystery. Most painting restorers don't have a clue how to make undetected restorations.

The painting was owned by an elderly couple living in the Beverly Hills flats, north of Santa Monica Boulevard, and the husband met us at the front door. He wore thick glasses and was bald on top, attempting to compensate by growing unkempt hair that stuck out over his ears and the frame of his glasses. He was fat and short, probably five feet at most. While his owlish eyes suspiciously looked us over, his wife appeared from the kitchen. She, too, was portly, just as wide as she was tall, and wore a kitchen apron over her muumuu.

The Reinhardt hanging on their dining room wall was a beautiful painting and appeared to be in excellent condition, with dark, silky colors that seemed to glow with mysterious energy. Remembering Irving's condition report instructions, we began inspecting it closely from twelve inches away, noting every flyspeck and dust particle. The subtlety of the hues meant there were no visual reference points, making it difficult to relocate our position on the painting if we looked away. It soon became hard to remember which areas we had already examined, and our eyes were aching with the effort. This process took time, but after only a few minutes, the old man became impatient.

"What the hell are you boys doing!" he demanded.

"We're condition reporting the painting, sir," I replied politely.

"There's nothing wrong with our painting," he snorted.

"Well, sir," I pointed out, "there is a flyspeck, and over here is some dust."

He pushed next to me to take a look, mumbled something under his breath, and stomped into the kitchen through a swinging door with spring-loaded hinges. The door went "wump wump" closing behind him. We heard yelling from the kitchen as we continued to pore over the painting.

Behind us, we heard the kitchen door's "wump wump" again, and a moment later, there was an "Excuse me!" as the wife barged between us, her bulk forcefully shoving us aside. She had a bottle of Windex in one hand and a wad of paper towels in the other, and before we could stop her, she was spraying the painting and scrubbing it in a circular motion. In a few moments, the painting was completely ruined, the surface covered in swirls of looping scratches and smeared paint. It was a total loss. She turned and barged back into the kitchen, the door making those wump wump sounds behind her. More heated yelling emanated from the kitchen.

I wrote "painting damaged beyond repair by owner" on our bill of lading and had the old man sign it before taking the work down from the wall. It was heartbreaking to witness that beautiful painting destroyed.

The next morning, I called Irving in New York, and with much trepidation, I explained what had happened. He refused to believe me. "Nonsense! It can't be that bad. Send it to me," he insisted. A week later, an angry Irving Blum called from New York, his voice louder and more booming than I had ever heard it. "What the hell did you do to my painting! Jeeeeeeeeezus! It's a total loss! Unbeleeeeeeeeeeeeeevable!"

Weinberg

Daniel Weinberg could be a difficult man. There were rumors he started in the rag trade manufacturing clothes and parlayed that into becoming an art dealer. I don't know that it's true, but it made sense to me. The garment trade was brutal, with low margins and high overhead. To survive, an entrepreneur had to be tough, ruthless, and tight-fisted—the same attributes Weinberg used to ensure success in the art world.

He started a gallery in San Francisco and later moved to Los Angeles, leaving his art in storage with Atthowe in Oakland. Once he re-opened in LA, he began hiring me to install exhibitions and deliver art to clients. I got my first look at the way he did business when he asked me to send a truck to Oakland to pick up his art from Atthowe and put it into our storage warehouse in Los Angeles. He assured me he had made the arrangements with Atthowe, so I took him at his word—and our truck returned to Los Angeles empty. It turned out that Atthowe had not been paid for several years of storage and refused to release the shipment when my truck arrived. Scott Atthowe called me to discuss the problem, letting me know he would only release Weinberg's inventory when he received payment. He also warned me about extending credit to Weinberg, saying he was often slow to pay for services.

Weinberg was also unpredictable, with contradictory attitudes toward the artists he exhibited and the artworks he displayed. When he hosted the first Jeff Koons exhibition on the West Coast, he was very demanding. The show was composed of canister-style shop vacuum cleaners encased in large, thick-walled acrylic boxes, and Weinberg wanted the art and boxes to be pristine. We spent hours polishing surfaces, using Plexiglas non-static cleaning paste and soft cloths. We rubbed until our arms ached to remove every speck of lint or dust, first on the inside of the Lucite boxes before inserting the vacuum cleaner with hose attached and accessories, and then the outside. Inevitably, though, once we'd put the vacuum in the box and closed it, we'd see a pesky hair, fiber, or speck of lint had come with it, and Weinberg would insist we start over. This was extreme Finish Fetishism, and I wasn't sure if it came from the artist or Weinberg's desire to ensure the objects would be presented perfectly to collectors.

On the other hand, he could be surprisingly unconcerned about certain works of art. When we received a shipment of Julian Schnabel plate paintings from New York, I opened the crates and discovered each of the paintings had shed chunks of porcelain cups and plates during their cross-country ride, and loose shards littered the floors of the crates. I immediately called Weinberg to inform him of what I thought was a disaster, but to my surprise, he told me to mend the pieces myself. Incredulous, I asked if he was serious. "Just glue the goddamn things back on the paintings. It's no big deal, just take care of it," he said and hung up.

I leaned the first painting against a wall in our warehouse and organized loose fragments of plates, teacups, and other porcelain parts on a table. It was impossible to be precise. There had been several paintings in each crate, and who knew which shards went to which paintings? And what about the pieces that had shattered into multiple shards when they hit the crate floors? It looked like those decisions would be up to me.

Schnabel had stuck the ceramic pieces to his canvases with Bondo, a thick, putty-like substance that auto body repair shops use to fill dents. It appeared that Schnabel's process was to paint the canvas using acrylic or oil paints, add fragments of porcelain with Bondo, and then apply additional layers of paint, often across the surfaces of the attached ceramics. The trick to reattaching the loose fragments was to look for the outline in the Bondo that matched the outline of the fragment. But the paintings were large, often measuring six or seven feet in each direction, and their surfaces were covered in a complicated matrix of thick paint, colors, Bondo, and lots of still-attached pottery fragments. Finding the original attachment locations was a puzzle, especially now that some fragments were in smaller pieces.

Weinberg said he had no photos for reference, so I did my best to eyeball the pieces back into their original positions and Bondo them in place. However, adding Bondo also changed the original artwork, and guessing the positions of fragments further deviated from the painting's original state. If I couldn't find where a hunk of plate or cup had been attached, I made my own aesthetic choice about the optimal visual location.

I admit that working on these paintings probably raised lots of ethical questions. But maybe Schnabel didn't care any more than his dealer did. Either way, I "restored" a dozen Schnabel paintings in this manner, and to this day, no one has ever noticed, so did it even matter? And is that a commentary on the relevance of the artwork? I wondered if what I'd done was any different than an artist's assistant painting on his canvases. Many of the Old Master artists had assistants adding landscapes and backgrounds to their paintings to expedite the completion of commissions. Was I doing any more for the Schnabels than I had done for Richard Diebenkorn when I worked as his assistant, stretching and priming his *Ocean Park* canvases and mixing his paints? My efforts were sometimes visible under the paint he added to the surface, but that didn't make them my creations—and that is my philosophy about the Schnabel's.

I got on fine with Dan Weinberg until we had a falling out over a painting by Robert Mangold, one of the pioneers of minimalist art. My employees delivered the wrapped and cardboard slip-cased Mangold to the Weinberg gallery, and several weeks later, I received an angry phone call from Weinberg telling me the painting was damaged—possibly beyond repair. What was I going to do about it, he demanded? He said I had better place a claim with my insurance carrier as soon as possible, adding that the value was $100,000.

I listened, and without agreeing to accept the claim, I said I would look into it. I was relieved to find that our copy of the delivery receipt indicated the painting had been accepted "in good condition" at the time of delivery with no damage or other exceptions listed. Liz, Dan's girlfriend and gallery assistant, had signed for it. But when

I reported this to him and said I didn't believe an insurance claim was warranted, he began cursing and slammed down the receiver.

The next morning, I went to his gallery and asked the receptionist if I could examine the painting. It was sitting on a shelf in a backroom storage area, and I could see a three-inch-long gouge down the center that had penetrated the paint layers and exposed the underlying canvas. The canvas wasn't ripped, but the fabric weave was frayed and spread open from what appeared to have been an impact. It looked like the corner of a crate, or the frame of another painting might have fallen against it. Only a painting conservator of great skill would be able to restore the surface—if it could be done at all on a minimalist canvas like this. Mangold's simple monotone colors would easily show repairs.

While I was mulling over what could have happened, Liz walked in. She and I had an uncomfortable history. A few months before she began working for Weinberg, she applied to work for me, but I had not hired her. Our interactions involving gallery affairs remained business-like when she went to work at Weinberg's gallery, but I always had an uneasy feeling she could be carrying a grudge. I wasn't sure if it was because I rejected her for the job or if she'd had romantic ideas, which would magnify the bad feelings, but there was something unresolved between us.

I asked her why she signed our bill of lading if we had delivered a damaged painting, and she said no one had seen the gouge until the painting was unwrapped. Figuring Weinberg had called me as soon as the damage was noticed—which was only yesterday—I was certain they would still have the wrapping materials, and I asked to see them. She replied they had been thrown away. None of this rang true to me, and I left, letting the issue sit.

Weinberg began calling periodically over the following weeks. He would start by speaking in a civil, business-like manner, but when I politely denied his claim, he would veer into shouting and cursing.

Finally, I ran out of patience and asked my insurance agent, Tom, to meet me at the gallery to view the painting and possibly get our insurers, Lloyds of London, involved. Lloyds would be unlikely to pay the claim because Weinberg had not declared a value or purchased our insurance. But involving my insurers would stop Weinberg from harassing me, at least for a while.

When I told Weinberg I was bringing an insurance representative to view the painting, he seemed pleased. "It's about time you did something," he said. But when Tom and I walked into the gallery several days later, I immediately noticed that Weinberg wasn't happy to see Tom and became uncharacteristically closed-mouthed, with a wary look in his eyes. He took us back to look over the damaged painting, and after a few minutes, Tom began reminding him of some previous claims, implying there had been problems with them. Weinberg's face turned red, and abruptly, he left the room.

Several weeks later, at an opening reception of another gallery, I bumped into the young woman I recognized as the Weinberg gallery's receptionist and learned she had recently quit. When I mentioned I'd met her during my visit to view the damaged Mangold, she said, "Oh! Liz damaged that painting while she was putting it in the storeroom after your company delivered it." The revelation added another unwelcome layer to the Mangold insurance claim. True, it explained what happened and exonerated my company. But if I told Weinberg his girlfriend damaged the painting and was covering it up, I knew he would refuse to believe me and would likely go totally nuts.

Weinberg's calls finally tapered off, and after several months with no word, I thought he might have given up. One day, however, he called to invite me to lunch. I was wary, but his voice sounded cordial, and I deluded myself into thinking that perhaps his girlfriend had confessed and the invitation was a way of making peace. I doubted Weinberg had ever apologized for anything, or that buying lunch was his way of apologizing—but the stress of dealing with the situation was warping my judgment, and I agreed to go.

I met him for lunch at an airy restaurant on the corner of La Cienega and Melrose boulevards. He was pleasant enough while a waiter took our orders, but there was a glint behind his eyes. My apprehension about the meeting had killed my appetite, and I knew I'd just pick at my salad.

He was still on his good behavior when the food arrived, and I was just beginning to relax when suddenly, without any warning, he slammed his fist on the table, causing a portion of my salad to jump from my plate onto the white tablecloth. His face contorted in rage, and he began yelling at the top of his voice, jabbing a finger at me: "I've had enough of your fucking lame excuses! I don't want to hear any more bullshit about why you won't take any fucking responsibility for the damage you caused! You're going to pay me for that painting! Don't think you will get away with it!" He continued ranting, and in my peripheral vision, I could see everyone in the restaurant staring at us.

The maître d' rushed over with a look of alarm. "Is everything all right, sir? Can I be of help? Could you please keep your voices down? You're disturbing your fellow patrons."

In response, Weinberg hunched over his plate, eyes cast down, and sullenly began shoveling food into his mouth. I ignored the salad scattered on the tablecloth and nibbled on the remnants of my plate, wondering what was going to happen next. My sphincter muscles were numb from anxiety. Should I bolt for the door? Would he physically assault me? If he did, could I handle him? He would likely come after me if I told him his wife had damaged the painting, but at least that wasn't going to happen. I was too afraid to say a word.

Several long minutes crept by in awkward silence while he sat red-faced and fuming. Abruptly, he leapt out of his chair, knocking our tablecloth askew and spilling his water and silverware on the floor. "Fuck it! Fuck it! Fuck it!" he screamed. "I'm sick and tired of talking to you. You are going to damn well pay me for that painting!"

The maître d' rushed over again with a frightened look on his face. "Sir, I am going to ask you to leave immediately!" he said. "We cannot tolerate bad language disturbing the peace and quiet of our patrons." He escorted us out the door while the entire restaurant watched in wide-eyed silence. Even the kitchen staff had come out to see what the commotion was about.

When we reached the sidewalk, I began walking away, but Weinberg whirled and blocked my progress. We were on the street corner in front of the restaurant's open patio doors as he continued yelling and cursing, a rant that went on for several minutes, and the entire restaurant could hear him. There wasn't anything management could do about the disruption now that we were on city property, but they might still call the police. I started to worry about the possibility of getting arrested for disturbing the peace when Weinberg abruptly stopped yelling. He turned his back on me and walked away with a stiff-legged gait. It was the last I ever heard from him. Venting finished, he didn't call me again.

Kienholz

Even the most ordinary day of art handling can put you in danger of getting maimed or killed by falling objects—or being arrested or sued for unforeseen and entirely innocent actions. And all of those risks are heightened when dealing with artists like Ed Kienholz, whose works and temperament both tended to be larger than life, with a volatile edge that could appear without warning. During the summer of 1986, Kienholz called and asked me to pick up eight concrete TV sculptures. He had used the wooden cabinets of large, old

1960s floor model televisions as molds, poured concrete inside, and then removed the wood, leaving cured concrete shapes with TV screens and control knobs embedded. These were heavy objects weighing up to 300 pounds, and Ed said they were being stored in a room above a single-car garage behind his hillside house. The access was along a dirt road, he said, and we'd need an all-terrain forklift to get them down to ground level.

I rented one and had it delivered to the site a few days later. It was an enormous machine with balding front tires that were over four feet high, so I decided I should be the one to drive it. With two of my employees directing, I entered the narrow lane that went downhill to the garage, and immediately noticed there wasn't much gravel left on the track to give me traction. A second problem was that the lane wasn't level in front of the garage. After years of erosion, it had a pronounced downhill tilt sloping away from the garage, and there were no guardrails between the edge of the lane and a very steep drop-off that angled downhill. Any false move would result in calamity, sending the forklift tumbling down three hundred feet toward the swimming pools and roofs of the houses that lined the street below. As if to underline what that could mean, the sounds of laughing children playing in their backyards drifted uphill in the wind as I sat surveying the site, trying to figure out how to position the machine so I wouldn't risk killing them.

Kienholz's two-floor garage, which dated back to the 1920s, stuck out of the steep hillside above the track. It was constructed from concrete marked with the outlines of the boards used to cast it. Both levels had old, wooden double doors painted in fading green and locked with hasps and padlocks. Because the stairs to the upper level were rotted away, we had to use the ladder that leaned against the outside to reach the upper doors. When we opened them, sunlight poured inside, and the tops of the televisions came into view. No thief was going to steal those sculptures.

I put the forklift into low gear and turned it toward the garage so the fork blades could begin retrieving the TVs. But each time I drove within a few feet of the garage, the tires lost traction on the slope, and the forklift skidded back toward the cliff. I tried to gain the extra distance by revving the engine, but the tires simply spun in the loose sand. Suddenly, an angry, red-faced Kienholz jumped up beside me and tried to push me out of the seat. He was yelling and swearing: "Goddamn fucking piece of crap! I'm going to shove this piece of shit over the cliff! Get out of the seat so I can send this pile of junk to hell!"

Kienholz was heavier than I was, and I struggled to stay in the seat while clutching the steering wheel as tightly as I could and keeping my foot shoved on the brake. As he thrust a sweaty shoulder against me, he tried to jam the gear shift lever into reverse. In the art moving business, the customer is always right—unless the customer is attempting to unleash mayhem on the homes and innocent children below. Ed managed to dislodge me from the seat so I was cantilevered halfway off the forklift, but I desperately gripped the steering wheel and managed to keep my right foot on the brake.

Suddenly, he jumped down, ran up the lane, and disappeared, leaving me shaking and gasping for breath. I turned the forklift off and put away the keys. Once I regained my composure, we lowered the TVs by hand, using ropes.

Kienholz and I had another powder-keg meeting in 1993 after I received a phone call from Peter Goulds, owner of LA Louver Gallery and Kienholz's dealer. Goulds was British, and in his proper English accent, said, "Bryan! Please send a couple of your men and a truck to meet Ed in an hour. He is in LA from Hope, Idaho, and needs you to pick up a sculpture. You may send your invoice to my attention." Peter gave me the address and hung up. I knew who he meant when he said "Ed," and little warning bells began ringing in the back of my head. I decided to accompany two of my art handlers . . . just in case.

We arrived in the parking lot of a four-story brick loft building in the Toy District of downtown Los Angles and waited. Twenty minutes later, Kienholz pulled in driving a black Crown Victoria sedan, a "Crown Vic" in police parlance. Cops loved their powerful Crown Vics, and Kienholz, too, loved a big car—so much so that when he died, he was buried sitting in the driver's seat of his restored '40s Packard, a collector's car.

He unwound from behind the steering wheel, stepped out, and looked us over. "Good morning, boys!" he called. He walked to the back of the car and opened the trunk, pulling out a sledgehammer. The hair on the back of my head started prickling. Before I had time to ask what was going on, he barked, "Follow me, boys!" and entered the building, trotting up flights of stairs with us close behind. He led us to a corridor on the top floor that was lined with locked doors and stopped in front of one of them.

"Stand out of the way!" he yelled.

I barely got clear before he began pounding the door with the sledge. He swung it sideways like a lumberjack using an ax to fell a tree, and on the fourth blow, the door flew inside with a crash, leaving bent screws protruding from the hinges. We appeared to be involved in a breaking and entering felony. I looked up and down the hallway to see if anyone would come out to investigate the noise. How much time did we have before the police arrived and we ended up in jail? Kienholz shouldered the sledge, stepped on the fallen door, and walked into the room, which was full of art. I suddenly realized that this was the storage inventory of the Nicholas Wilder Gallery. I recognized it because it had been in my warehouse until Nick removed it several years earlier, after closing his Los Angeles gallery and relocating to New York City to start a second career as a rare book dealer.

Kienholz paused to look around, and spotting a sculpture with several paintings leaning against it, said, "Grab that one." He began moving paintings and crates until he found another sculpture: "Here's another one I want you to take." In all, we lugged four human-sized sculptures made of stone and glass downstairs and loaded them into our truck. These were not Kienholz pieces, and I asked him who the artist was, so I could accurately fill out my bill of lading inventory. He explained that the pieces belonged to one of his neighbors in Hope, Idaho—a young artist who had complained to Kienholz that Wilder refused to return his unsold work or pay for sold pieces. Ed promised to retrieve the sculptures the next time he went to Los Angeles, and today was the day. Hearing this made me feel better about our burglary, and I watched as he climbed into the Crown Vic and roared out of the parking lot.

An hour later, I was back working at my desk, and my drivers were unloading the sculptures into our warehouse when my phone rang. It was Peter Goulds, and he sounded worried. "Bryan! I had nothing to do with any of this! I never called you and will deny having done so. I do not know anything. You are strictly on your own, Bryan, and please do not implicate me in any way."

I envisioned Kienholz returning to the gallery and gleefully describing how he broke down the door and grabbed the sculptures, scaring the hell out of Peter, who probably thought he'd wind up in jail for being an accessory to a burglary.

After my drivers finished unloading the sculptures, I sent them back with a sheet of plywood and screw guns to close up Wilder's storage space. It was too late to call him in New York, so I waited until the next morning to tell him what we'd done. Nick didn't seem the least bid perturbed and actually laughed in amusement. "Typical Kienholz!" he said, adding that he would send someone to repair the door. Several weeks later, I went back to check on the repairs, and seeing that our plywood still covered the opening, I sent a couple of my craters to reinstall the door. They called back to tell me they were standing inside the room—and the roof was missing. Thinking this was preposterous, I drove over, and sure enough, the room was open to the sky. Only the overhead support girders remained above all the paintings, sculptures, and flat files full of drawings and prints. A couple of pigeons sat on a girder, watching us. The entire art inventory was covered in dirt and debris, and poop from the pigeons. There didn't seem to be any roofers working, so I decided to send a crew and trucks to evacuate the art, clean it up, and place it in our warehouse.

Wilder never paid money for any of these services and did not seem very concerned about the welfare of his collection. But shortly before he died, he did give me a couple of works of art as payment.

Billy Al

Like Ed Kienholz, Billy Al Bengston was one of the original Ferus Gallery artists. Billy's best works were the elegant *Dentos* series, glossy automotive paint on thin, metal panels that were bent and distorted. Billy's studio was on the second floor of a former Elks meeting hall in Venice, California. It seemed that anyone who wanted to be considered an important LA artist during the '60s and '70s had to have a Venice studio. The influential LA gallerist, Riko Mizuno, once refused to visit an artist's studio because it wasn't in Venice, saying he "couldn't possibly be a very good artist if his studio isn't located there." And you could easily make a case that it was true, as the greatest California artists—Richard Diebenkorn, Sam Francis, Larry Bell, Robert Irwin, and Ed Ruscha—all worked in the neighborhood.

A long, wide wooden staircase led from the front entrance of the old Elks building to the second floor where Billy had his studio and residence. There was also a metal fire escape at the back of the building. I was familiar with both. I once delivered a *Dentos* from a museum to Billy—wrapped in glassine and not much bigger than a piece of writing paper, it weighed less than an ounce or two. As I carried it up the front stairs, I could hear Billy and his girlfriend Penny shouting at each other in a heated argument. This wasn't surprising because they often fought like cats and dogs, but it made me tense because it meant Billy would be in a lousy mood and unpredictable. I rang the doorbell and waited. The yelling continued without a pause, so I rang it again. After a few moments, Billy appeared, looking at me with an angry face, and shouted, "Servants' entrance is around the back." His painting was so diminutive he easily could have taken it, but instead, he slammed the door in my face as I heard locks being set while he resumed yelling at Penny. I felt humiliated but turned and trudged back down the stairs, around the building into the back alley, and up the fire escape.

The back door didn't have a doorbell, and although I knocked loudly, the argument drowned me out. I stood on the landing for ten minutes, pounding on the door to get attention. Finally, the door was yanked open, and a red-faced Billy Al shouted, "What the hell do you want!" I held up his painting, and he snatched it out of my hands, once again slamming the door in my face.

Several months later, I returned to his studio to pick up a painting on canvas. This time, I dutifully walked up the back stairs and banged loudly on his door. He opened it and looked coolly at me: "You don't need to kick the crap out of my door to get my attention. I can hear it if you knock civilly." He ushered me inside and pointed at the painting. It stood nearly six feet tall and almost as wide. I began to worry about how I would get it safely down the stairs and over to my truck, which was parked more than a block away.

"Excuse me, Billy," I said. "I wasn't expecting your painting to be so large. Could you help me carry it to the truck, please?"

He looked at me disdainfully. "Don't be a wimp. It doesn't weigh anything. You can handle it by yourself." He turned toward the entrance, his body language indicating it was time for me to get going.

I looked behind the painting and saw there was a crossbar in the middle so I could get my hands around without my knuckles pushing against the back of the canvas. Billy always bought prefabricated stretcher bars from art stores, probably Aaron Brothers, and they keyed together with mortise and tenon fittings—no screws, nails, or glue. The crossbars also keyed into slots in the center points of the stretcher sides. When the canvas was stretched over the bars, all the parts were held together by tension. The design worked well, but the materials were flimsy.

Billy was standing impatiently with one hand on a hip and the other holding the back door open, so I grabbed the painting and carried it onto the landing. As soon as I was outside, he closed the door, leaving me on my own. I carefully descended the stairs, trying to keep my balance while holding the painting high enough to keep it from hitting the treads.

I reached the sidewalk, thinking the worst was over, but as I was walking toward the truck, a strong gust of wind hit my back, turning the painting into a sail and pulling it forward along the sidewalk with me in tow. Struggling to hold on, I tried to turn the painting parallel to the wind to relieve the pressure, but it began yo-yo-ing back and forth, much like a kite on a short string does in a strong wind. Suddenly I heard the crack of wood splintering, and I found myself holding just the cross brace as the rest of the painting flew fifty feet down the sidewalk. Its corner touched the ground causing it to cartwheel, and it kept going until it hit the mirror of a parked car and came to rest. I ran to retrieve it, still holding the cross brace in one hand, likely making me look like a crazed Christian pilgrim. The painting was unscathed, though, and that was a true miracle.

Chris Burden

Occasionally, we got the chance to help Chris Burden with shipping. I say occasionally because many of his pieces were conceptual, and there was little or nothing to ship. He was a genius at constructing an indelible experience from minimal materials, something I learned when I went to see a piece he set up inside an empty warehouse in an Irvine industrial park. It consisted of a seventy-two by thirty-inch-wide platform suspended from the ceiling by chains attached to each corner. The platform hung eighteen feet off the floor and twenty-four inches under the ceiling. To reach it, you had to climb a sixteen-foot stepladder, grab one of the chains and hoist yourself up onto the swinging surface—while remaining face down. This was a cloud-viewing perch, and to see the sky, you had to carefully roll over to face the ceiling without losing balance while the platform swayed. It would be easy to knock over the ladder in this process, which could have left you stranded for hours until someone came to set up the ladder and rescue you. Amplifying the danger, there was no safety net or padding on the floor far below, and when I went, there was no one staffing the exhibit either. I was the only visitor, taking my chances alone.

The clearance between the ceiling and the body of the platform was only eighteen inches, and the platform was covered in slippery, white Formica, making it even riskier to climb onto. Burden had cut an aperture in the roof and attached a conical-shaped eyepiece, similar to ones you might look into as you cranked an old-fashioned carnival peep show. Looking through the eyepiece at clouds drifting by while lying on the gently swinging platform induced dizziness and vertigo, probably by design.

Once you'd had enough, climbing off the platform required hanging over the side eighteen feet in the air while desperately trying to find the steps of a wobbly ladder without knocking it over. Once you committed to dangling off the edge, there was no turning back, and if you misjudged the ladder, you could fall and be hurt or killed. It was absolutely terrifying.

But if you survived it all, you'd never forget that platform, ladder, and vertiginous sky.

Conceptual artists like Burden are rare, which is fortunate for art handlers who need physical objects to justify our occupation. We felt lucky when Burden ventured brilliantly into the world of things, and he called on us to assist. In 1990, he was working on a large sculpture titled *Medusa's Head* for an exhibition at White Cube Gallery in London when he asked me to come to his Topanga studio compound to take a look and give him an estimate for crates. When I arrived, he was applying rough cement to masses of chicken wire that he planned to use as armatures to support four wedge-shaped segments as they were being fitted together to become a large ball. The ball was intended to hang from a ceiling to represent an asteroid covered with railroad tracks and other industrial age symbols, signifying Earth's destruction from pollution and industrial development. I liked the concept, but I could see right away that his armatures were going to be too flimsy. Each rested on three thin legs he made from the same square tubing used in cheap office chairs. Manufacturers liked it because it was easy to bend—which is exactly why he shouldn't have used it.

I bluntly told him he was making a mistake and should beef up the legs before he made the segments heavier by adding more cement. A month later, we delivered the crates to begin packing, and my heart sank when I saw the same skinny little legs sticking out the bottoms of the beefed-up masses of concrete, which weighed hundreds of pounds. The concrete was now colored a dull black and brown to mimic an asteroid seared from entering the Earth's atmosphere.

We crated the segments, doing our best to add blocking under the bottoms to support their weights and keep stress off the legs.

I called both the White Cube registrar and the art handling company receiving the crates in London, asking them not to uncrate or even touch the sculptures until Burden was present. Unfortunately, he decided to hang out in France on vacation before going to London, and White Cube, worried about getting the sculpture installed on time, couldn't wait. They pulled out the pieces, and the legs on one of the segments buckled, collapsing under its weight. When Burden saw it, he thought it had been damaged in transit and blamed me.

I did wind up working with him again, though. In 2012, Suzan Şengöz, a registrar from the Los Angeles County Museum of Art, asked me to meet her at his studio in the hills above Topanga Canyon to work out how to safely deliver segments of a piece called *Metropolis* II to LACMA. Its multiple parts were carefully engineered to fit together to form a room-sized model of a cityscape—with buildings, freeways, and rail and trolley tracks. Burden had assembled a team of model builders, overseen by a project manager, to construct his metropolis, and when fully operational, the mesmerizing sculpture was a kinetic masterpiece. Dozens of matchbook cars frenetically raced around a convoluted system of freeways and highways as miniature trains, and trolley cars traversed levels of tracks.

The piece had been built in sections for transport and to fit through doorways, and all the components had built-in leveling so they could be perfectly aligned. This was crucial because the tiny, gravity-fueled cars could only work properly if their freeway courses lined up. An escalator system raised the cars to the top, and from there, they rocketed downhill and around a maze of roadways through the miniature city at a pace that mirrored our crowded city and automobile culture. For LACMA, we'd be moving not only the complex terrain of *Metropolis II* but also the cars, including thousands of extras Burden had purchased to replace the ones that wore out after hundreds of hours of racing around the tracks. He kept each new car in its original cardboard box.

When it came time to load and deliver the whole works to
LACMA, I determined we needed to use twenty-four-foot flatbed
trucks. Anything larger couldn't negotiate the narrow, winding roads
out of Burden's rural mountain studio. There was one steep, hairpin
S-turn, in particular, that was so precipitous a loaded truck wouldn't
have enough power to back up if it made a mistake negotiating the
curve. There was no room for error—a driver who chose the wrong
path could go over the edge. Somehow, it felt like that Burden per-
formance piece all over again, but this time with other people's lives
at stake. When we got to the treacherous spot, I stayed in front of
each truck, walking backward and using hand signals to tell my drivers when to turn.

We set up a crane in Burden's yard to load the segments, and with
great tension and trepidation, we got them safely to LACMA. That
brought Burden back as a customer, and I worked for him several
more times before he passed away in 2015, not from accident or gun-
shot, as his history might've suggested, but from melanoma. It was
all too soon for the brilliant creative genius.

Spafford

I thought it was a hoax when the caller identified himself as Ken
Eikenberry, the attorney general of Washington state. Why would he
be phoning me? I had a flash of paranoia and was trying to remember
if I had violated any laws there when he explained he was looking for
a company with the expertise to remove several murals from the
state capital building. Would I be interested in taking on the project? There was some controversy over the removal, he added, but
it would be easier to explain in person if I was willing to schedule a
site visit. As the state would provide an air ticket, a rental car, and

a hotel in Olympia, I accepted, thinking it would be an interesting and fun excursion. I have in-laws in Seattle whom I enjoy visiting, and I like salmon fishing in the Pacific Northwest, so I'd been in the region often but had never stopped in Olympia.

It turned out to be a charming town with a long history of lumbering and fishing. The state capital building is an impressive, stately edifice—its interior walls covered in white and grey polished stone and floors in intricate designs. Louis Comfort Tiffany designed and manufactured the ornate bronze light fixtures and balcony railings and the massive central atrium chandelier. The building's stone came from various European quarries, once used as ballast for sailing ships, until it was unloaded from the vessels to be replaced by lumber destined for Italy and other European countries.

As with most state capitals, the House occupied one wing, and the Senate occupied the other. Eikenberry first took me into the House chamber and pointed to two murals on upper balconies, behind the spectators' seating. Set in arched alcoves, one on each side of the chamber, they both looked down on the legislators' desks. They were black-and-white abstracts, comprised of geometric stick figures that represented stories from mythology. My immediate thought was how jarring, and out of place, they seemed in contrast with the sedate and stately building and antique wooden furniture. They were excellent paintings—and exhibited in a gallery or a modern building—they would've been a handsome addition. However, in this staid setting, it seemed as if the artist was imposing his artistic will without regard to the surroundings.

Eikenberry explained that the murals, titled *Twelve Labors of Hercules*, were by local artist Michael Spafford. They had been hidden behind drapery for several years because the legislators not only disliked them but also thought some portions were pornographic. One female legislator was particularly aghast at a section apparently depicting a rape. The matter was currently being litigated in court, where the artist and local arts groups contended that the murals could not be removed without irreversibly damaging them. We walked upstairs to the balcony, and a close look showed that the first mural was painted on ten sheets of 3/4 inch plywood attached with panel adhesive to the ten-foot-long wall. For some reason, the artist had cut out the shapes matching the figures and interlocked them like a jigsaw puzzle. But those seams were invisible from the floor below, so Spafford could have saved the trouble by simply painting on full panels. It was also apparent that all the panels were initially painted white, and the stick figures, outlined in masking tape, were applied on top in black, using paint rollers.

Eikenberry asked if the murals could be taken down intact. I suggested that the state find out by attaching a test panel to the wall with the same adhesive the artist had used, waiting for it to cure, and then trying to remove it using wedges and pry bars. If it worked, it would demonstrate to the court that the removal would be safe and allay the concerns about damage. I also recommended bringing in a Santa Barbara-based conservator named Scott Haskins, who had extensive experience with mural restorations from working in Italy. Having such a proven expert overseeing the removal, if it were approved, would ensure that we wouldn't damage the murals and would tamp down any concern about professional handling. I told him it was likely Haskins would apply a protective facing of tissue and varnish to protect the panels for storage, and that we could provide crates and packing materials and house the murals in sections.

The AG asked me to send a quote, and six months later, the state sent me a contract.

Within a week, I began receiving angry, threatening phone calls from Seattle activists and art professionals. Word of the contract had reached the press, stirring a hornet's nest, and I faced a difficult decision. While I sympathized with those fighting to keep the murals in place, I didn't feel too badly about removing them because the state had paid for and owned them and could do what it wanted. More importantly, state officials were taking prudent measures by spending funds to protect them, rather than destroying or painting over them. My motive for agreeing to the project wasn't entirely profit-driven. I also liked the challenge. Plus, I had made a commitment, and I wanted to see it through. Still, I gave myself a week to carefully think it over before moving forward or quitting. What finally decided it for me was that the piece was clearly out of place in the historic building and making a lot of people unhappy. I had no problem saying yes.

Before we could get back to Olympia, the project was delayed for months by some unexpected legislative maneuvering. But finally, I arrived at the capital with two of my employees and our expert Scott Haskins. We were just beginning preparations to remove the panels when the artist, Michael Spafford, arrived with a TV reporter and camera crew from a Seattle television station. He positioned himself in front of his mural, looking sad and dejected while being photographed and interviewed. The episode had a feel of theater to it. Finally, though, we were able to complete the removals, carefully packing all the panels into ten crates, which we delivered to an unoccupied government office building at the Renton Municipal Airport, near Seattle. Workmen inside an empty cafeteria were busily constructing a false wall three feet in front of an existing wall. Before they completed it, we placed all our crates inside, then stood by watching as the workers sealed the opening with drywall and painted it over. When they finished, there was no evidence the *Twelve Labors of Hercules* was entombed inside.

Nearly a decade later, I received a call from the president of Centralia College near Olympia asking about the artwork. He explained that the state had given the mural to the college, and they had spent a large amount of money designing and building special walls for mounting them inside a new auditorium. The president was worried because no one remembered where the murals were. They had carefully searched the vast capital basements where they were supposedly being held, but had, of course, come up empty-handed. He sounded relieved and excited when I told him they were at the Renton airport and gave him the address, describing the false wall and the crew and equipment he would need to dig out the crates. I also told him he would need to hire a conservator to remove the panels' protective facings.

The college unearthed the paintings, and the murals now have a better-suited home in a beautifully designed modern building where people can enjoy them. They look spectacular inside the auditorium, mounted on pedestal-like walls that thrust forward from each side above the audience. The college loves having them and pointing out their controversial history to visitors. But artists can be contrarians at odds with their collectors, and I read an interview where Spafford said he wasn't pleased, because he had painted his murals specifically for the capital building, and they wouldn't work in another location. Sometimes, though, it wouldn't hurt an artist to admit that the client might actually be right.

Dentist

In the art moving business, you run into all sorts of quirky and eccentric characters. The art world just seems to attract them, whether they've found their way to the center of it or are orbiting the periphery in a place like Fresno, home of one of the more memorable eccentrics I've encountered. Fresno, a city of half a million in California's Central Valley, is surrounded by vineyards, orchards, and farmlands but is not a particularly fertile place for art. It has several small museums and not much of an art scene. For decades, though, my company has made deliveries and pickups for Fresno's slice of the art world—the Fresno Art Museum, along with a few private collectors and a couple of corporate collections. In all that time, I think I've only picked up from one artist—a dentist with the unfortunate name of Dr. Hertz.

I was sent to Dr. Hertz's home when I was a driver for Cart & Crate, which ran a shuttle truck up to the Bay Area every two weeks. Hertz wanted us to pick up a dozen paintings, and though I arrived in the evening after dark, it was still hot outside when I rang his doorbell. He took me to a painting studio converted from a bedroom and pointed out the twelve twenty-four-inch-square canvases leaning against the walls, side by side. I took in the details: the stretcher bars were well made, and the canvases were evenly stretched without distortions or wrinkles. It appeared he had used acrylic paint taken directly from jars and thickly applied it using spatulas and pallet knives. And he'd only used primary yellow, blue, and red—no hues or mixed colors. The work could possibly look good on the waiting room walls of a dental office, but with its jarring color scheme it would have been disturbing to someone undergoing a root canal.

Hertz asked me the question I always dread: "How do you like my paintings?" As I paused to formulate a diplomatic reply, he saved me by jumping in with his own appraisal. "Aren't they beautiful?" he enthused. "I am such a genius, another Van Gogh! I called your boss and told her I wanted to store my paintings in your warehouse right next to Nick Wilder's storage area, and she agreed. Nick has a great reputation for finding new talent, and when he sees my paintings, he'll definitely want to represent me in his gallery."

I was stunned by the wackiness of this idea. For one thing, Nick Wilder never came to Cart & Crate to look at his art, and even if he did, he would dismiss this decorative schlock outright. I looked more closely at Dr. Hertz, who sounded a little delusional, to see if he really was nuts. But I decided he just had an outsized ego. That was confirmed when I told him I needed to go out to my truck for plastic and tape to wrap the paintings, and he stopped me, saying, "Oh no. If you wrap them, Nick can't see the subtly of my technique. No, they must not be wrapped or obscured."

So, I loaded the paintings and drove back to LA. In the morning, I reported to my boss that Dr. Hertz said she had agreed to give him space in the storage rack next to Nick Wilder's.

"He's dreaming," she replied. "Put his paintings on top of the racks where there's some space under the roof."

I protested that if we put the paintings on top, no one would see them, and the doctor wanted them to be visible.

She gave me a hard look. "Just do as I say."

A year later, Dr. Hertz asked us to return his paintings, and when I arrived at his home, he greeted me sadly. "I don't understand it," he said. "Why didn't Nick contact me? He had to have seen my paintings when he visited his storage." He looked sharply at me. "You didn't wrap them, did you?"

I couldn't bring myself to tell him the paintings had been stored well away from Wilder's and out of sight.

I went outside to my truck, carried the first two paintings into the house, and tried separating them as Dr. Hertz stood watching. I couldn't get them apart. I began to sweat from anxiety and to gain a little time to figure out what was wrong, I moved them over to his work table.

The paintings had been placed in storage racks face-to-face and back-to-back on a shelf, proper technique, but we had left them unwrapped at his request and stored them only twelve inches from the ceiling. The roof wasn't insulated, and a year of heat had cooked the paint and bonded the canvases together. What was Dr. Hertz going to do when he realized his precious work had been ruined?

I got a reprieve when a phone rang in another part of the house and the doctor left to answer it. Grabbing the two canvases, I pulled with all my strength, and the paintings separated with a ripping sound, patches of paint pulling off one canvas and remaining stuck to the other. Each canvas was left with areas of missing paint—white gesso showing in the cavities and chunks of paint imprinted with the pattern of the companion canvas's weave.

When Dr. Hertz returned, he looked intently at both paintings, one hand under his chin while the second held his elbow. I waited for an explosion, but he didn't say a word as he walked around, viewing them with a bewildered look on his face.

"My God!" he said finally. "These paintings are pure genius! I haven't seen them in a year and had almost forgotten that I invented this unique technique. Aren't they amazing?"

I went back outside and began struggling to separate all the canvases inside the truck. Every painting suffered losses and paint transfers, and after I carried the remaining separated canvases into the house, he thanked me for "safely returning his masterpieces."

I had to agree that the "new technique" had been an improvement.

Deutsch

Back in Los Angeles, I encountered another eccentric artist—a prolific painter named Boris Deutsch, though he was already dead when my path crossed his. A sleazy attorney had somehow taken control of the art from Deutsch's estate and called me for a meeting to provide an estimate for moving and storing the collection. Deutsch had a rising reputation in the 1920s and '30s and even received a commission from the Works Progress Administration to paint eleven murals at the Terminal Annex Building, a post office near Union Station in Los Angeles. His work is in the collections of the Smithsonian and the Los Angeles County Museum of Art, among other major venues. But according to the attorney, Deutsch had fallen out of favor following a beef with the art critic for the *Herald Examiner* newspaper. The resulting bad reviews, the lawyer said, had been poison for his career.

Walking into Deutsch's home was one of the saddest experiences I have ever had. The house, on a residential street in the Mid-Wilshire area near Vermont Avenue, was built in the early 1900s, with a front porch and bedrooms on the second floor. Its clapboard siding was badly in need of paint, and the interior and its occupant had apparently been deteriorating for years. Right inside the front door was a couch covered with old blankets and a pillow in a dirty, greasy pillowcase. Within reach on the left side was a stool with an electric hot plate and a saucepan of congealed pork and beans sitting on the cold burner. Just to the right was a painting easel holding an unfinished canvas, and next to that, a small table with a well-used, old-fashioned artist's pallet, thickly caked with layers of dried paint, and an open paintbox piled with desiccated and twisted paint tubes. A handful of brushes sat in a coffee can still partially filled with turpentine, indicating the artist had died not very long ago.

Leaning against the walls and furniture were hundreds and hundreds of small paintings, Deutsch's artwork, which was stuffed into every square inch of every room in the house. A narrow pathway led through this forest of paintings to the kitchen refrigerator, then to a sink full of dirty dishes, and on to a bathroom. Other than that, there was no space left to walk in any other part of the house.

As we began to peel back the years of art accumulation, it became evident that Deutsch had lost his way. The early canvases were somewhat good, realistic figurative depictions—some possibly studies for murals or much larger paintings. But later, his style and subject matter began to go off the rails, and the quality declined while he seemingly searched for a new direction. Looking at those paintings, I could almost read his mind as he became increasingly desperate to return to relevancy. He painted in a cubist style, mimicking

Braque and Picasso. He experimented with Abstract Expressionism on small canvases, not seeming to understand the gestural concepts and large scale these paintings needed. He attempted hard-edge paintings without realizing the edges had to be sharp and crisp and not painterly—and he dove into pop art without a clue about what it really meant. Being an artist must have consumed his entire being, and for years he kept doggedly painting, in the process literally painting himself into a corner, where he finally died alone on his couch, still working on yet another canvas.

For me, it was enormously sad to think about the man and how many other artists there are in the world who die in similar desperate obscurity. But as we sorted through the detritus of a man's life's work and dreams, all the attorney cared about was how much the art was worth and how much money he'd make selling it. I decided I didn't want any part of the attorney's schemes. He might've helped Deutsch if he'd come along earlier, but at this point, the only beneficiary was his own greed. I told the lawyer I wasn't interested in storing the art, paid my respects to Boris Deutsch, and silently wished him some peace.

Gothic

A loan officer from the Bank of New York asked me to meet him at the residence of Brett-Livingstone Strong, an Australian artist who specialized in portraits of celebrities. The bank wanted me to store Strong's entire inventory of paintings, sculptures, and copious amounts of prints. The paintings—twelve of them, all forty inches by fifty inches—were hanging in Strong's mansion inside a guard-gated enclave near Mulholland Drive. (Several years later, Arnold Schwarzenegger and Maria Shriver moved nearby and became Strong's neighbors.) The loan officer explained that the collection was collateral for a $10 million loan the bank was giving Strong for a construction project in downtown Los Angeles.

The first thing I noticed when Strong showed us into the living room were several framed photos of the artist standing alongside Michael Jackson, both dressed identically in band leaders' uniforms with epaulets and brass buttons. The loan officer was impressed. Strong claimed to be good friends with MJ and showed us two of his paintings, which he said were the only portraits Jackson had ever commissioned of himself. One was a somewhat murky painting of Jackson called *The Book*, and the second showed a romantic Jackson and Lisa Marie Presley standing belly-button deep in a pool of water at sunset while being attended to by three or four naked nymphs. The remaining paintings were more mundane, hackneyed subjects like whales. The loan officer, who I gathered had not participated in the bank's loan negotiations, asked Strong a question about his project. Strong invited us into his studio, unfurling a roll of drawings and laying them on a white Formica drafting table. The drawings showed dark, brooding Gothic building façades for a downtown Los Angeles commercial complex that reminded me of Batman's Gotham City. With a flourish, Brett pulled out a drawing illustrating a sword-wielding angel standing atop a 700-foot spire. More than twice the height of the Statue of Liberty, it was the signature piece of the project, and it would become Lady Liberty's West Coast rival, he said. He explained that the other drawings showed designs for the complex's hotels, a theater, entertainment, and shopping centers. I looked more closely at Strong. There are dreamers and there are scam artists, and it is often difficult to tell them apart. Was he sincere? Or was it a clever way to monetize his unsold inventory of artwork? Either way, I thought the project, called Angel City, was absurd and unlikely ever to get built. But that wasn't for me to say.

We removed and individually crated the paintings. From another storage location, we picked up eight or ten stone sculptures, several of them large, and a dozen crates containing stacks of prints that appeared to be photo reproductions of the paintings. I didn't hear anything further about Strong's project until several years later, when the *Los Angeles Times* architecture critic, Nicolai Ouroussoff, wrote a piece that completely eviscerated the grandiose plan.

"If Angel City is built, it will do more than damage Los Angeles' long-standing efforts to transform downtown into a credible cultural hub," Ouroussoff declared. "It will become a permanent blot on the city's civic and cultural identity. There is no shortage of irony here. Strong began his career carving tombstones in Australia, and the design for Angel City has a surprisingly morbid look for an entertainment complex geared toward family fun. The skeletal steel frames of a dozen pseudo-Gothic buttresses creep up the City of Angels monument's base on all sides. At its top, the monument's cylindrical form evokes a blend of rock 'n' roll erotica and funereal kitsch. Picture a giant tombstone for the city."

That frank assessment may have killed the project. Soon after, City National Bank withdrew its portion of promised financing, and Strong declared bankruptcy. The Bank of New York began the process of liquidating Strong's art, but after months of trying, it was unable to find any buyers. The bank finally transferred the inventory to General Motors Assurance Corporation for an undisclosed sum. But GMAC couldn't sell the art either, even after we transferred the twelve crated paintings to the Beverly Hills Gallery, where Strong thought the celebrity content might appeal to the clientele. When the gallery returned the paintings unsold after a year, GMAC held a public auction for all the art. The winning bidder was Matt Patisso, owner of a

New York real estate investment company called "Liquid Brick" that dealt, among other things, in distressed properties. The following day Patisso came to our offices with Strong to see his acquisition. Almost immediately after Patisso took possession of the work, our storage fees stopped being paid, and as the months passed, the balance owed ballooned. In response to our requests for payment, Patisso began making veiled references about missing paintings, saying he recently saw one of them hanging at Strong's house. I told him we hadn't released any of the art, but I wondered about that Beverly Hills gallery.

Then one day, Patisso called, saying he had sold the Jackson/Presley painting and asked me to do a condition report. I unpacked it and examined it with a magnifying glass. Oil paint brushstrokes were present, but something seemed wrong. Then, I saw pixelizations and realized someone had substituted one of the prints for the original painting and attempted to disguise it by adding paint to the surface. Patisso settled his account in 2004 and had everything picked up. In October 2019, what was supposedly the original Jackson/Presley painting was sold by Julien's Auctions for $4,480.

A few years ago, *The Book* resurfaced, its owner claiming it had been purchased in 1990 by a Japanese businessman named Hiromichi Saeki for $2.1 million and transferred to them in 1992 as payment for a debt and put in storage. Oddly, we were storing what was ostensibly the same painting at the same time for Bank of New York. The current owner says he has offers to buy the painting, which he believes is worth $5 million.

I recently got a call from a gentleman who said he wanted to store a valuable collection related to Michael Jackson, worth millions. I asked him if the artist was Brett-Livingstone Strong and heard the uncertainty in his voice as he asked. "How did you know?"

I didn't go into the story. I simply said I wasn't interested and hung up.

Fragile

Art made of glass, while beautiful, is the bane of every art handler. That no doubt has been the case ever since the Egyptians and Romans began crafting designs from the seductive material, whose fragility becomes part of its value. Damaged glass is nearly impossible to repair and almost always a total loss—so as delicate work survives through time, its vulnerability and brushes with destruction become part of its mystique.

Take Marcel Duchamp's *Great Glass: The Bride Stripped Bare by Her Bachelors, 1915 – 1923*, now on permanent display at the Philadelphia Museum of Art. Considered one of the most important Dada masterpieces, it stands nine feet tall with two evenly size panes of glass in a single frame, stacked one above the other. Duchamp used thin wire to draw outlines on the clear surface. He used colored varnish to glue the wire—along with other objects he found—to the glass, mimicking the leading that holds glass panes in stained glass windows. He even incorporated areas of the dust that had settled on the surface as it lay on a shelf during the periods he stopped working on it.

The piece, eight years in the making, was damaged while being shipped to a collector—likely the crate had been dropped or fallen over. But Duchamp was supposedly happy when he saw the spiderweb cracks radiating from the sides of his glass panels and decided to embrace the cracked glass as part of his work. He was interested in notions of chance in art, and chance had just asserted itself. His laissez-faire attitude was a rarity, though, and today the fear of lawsuits and insurance claims keeps art handlers in fear of fragile works. That doesn't mean we veer away from them. Mostly, we learn to apply layers of caution and packing materials to buffer the pieces from damage and then steel—and insure—ourselves against the inevitable.

One of my clients, DeWain Valentine, seems irresistibly drawn to fragile media. He specializes in cast resin wedges and concave circles done in transparent colors—pieces ranging from a few feet in diameter to eight feet or larger. Resin may be a plastic, but it damages as easily as glass, and from the time a piece is cast, preventing cracks is a constant challenge. The first threat comes from the massive amounts of heat that can build up inside the mold as the resin cures—a by-product of a chemical reaction between the liquid resin mixed with a catalyst that makes the plastic harden. DeWain dealt with that by working with Hastings Plastics in Santa Monica and a large chemical company that manufactured resins, who helped develop resin varieties with extended curing times and cooler temperatures.

There were other pitfalls as well. If the resin and catalyst are not blended thoroughly, the resin won't harden evenly. And if the materials aren't blended fast enough, the resin will start to harden as it's being mixed. So, before he could fabricate the enormous pieces he became known for, DeWain had to invent a mixing apparatus that would let him quickly and completely blend large volumes of catalyzed resin. Once he had done that, he was able to cast more massive sculptures, including a translucent black wedge measuring twelve feet long by forty-two inches wide on its bottom and standing seven feet high. The sculpture, a commission for the corporate headquarters of a Chicago bank, weighed nearly two tons, and I saw it days before it was to be installed.

Fresh from its mold and an arduous and time-consuming finishing process that involved sanding and polishing every surface, it gleamed. But getting it to that point had put DeWain behind schedule, and now he needed me to crate it at his studio and have it rush shipped to Chicago. I checked with several airfreight companies, who told me it was too large to ship that way and wouldn't arrive in time. I got the same answer from the trucking companies. I called DeWain to let him know. But when we arrived at his studio to do the crating, he announced he had found an airfreight forwarder who guaranteed delivery before the opening.

I was skeptical and warned him that he should be careful, but he went with the company anyway. The crate arrived several days too late—with two forklift puncture holes in its side. Unfortunately, this wasn't just a nick. The holes went all the way through the crate, and the sculpture inside was shattered, a total loss.

I had more encounters with DeWain's large wedges over the years. His art dealer and girlfriend, "Melinda," loaned one to the curator Katherine Plake for her inaugural show at the Palm Springs Museum. We crated and delivered it, and before the exhibition ended, Melinda left DeWain and moved to New York to marry a wealthy real-estate developer and art collector. Later, DeWain moved to Hawaii and married a woman named Kiana. When he returned to Los Angeles many years later, he called to ask if I knew the whereabouts of the Palm Springs sculpture, saying he had lost track of it. From then on, whenever I went to his studio, he and Kiana would pester me about where the wedge was. I began to realize that DeWain was convinced I had it stashed in my art storage warehouse—as though I'd want an extra two-ton sculpture in my space, albeit a beautiful one. Assumptions like that inevitably cause rumors and suspicions, which can adversely affect reputation and customer trust, both of which are paramount in the art services business. So finally, after years of politely fending off their queries, I got fed up and called the Palm Springs Museum to find out if they had any records of where the sculpture had gone. They did. It seemed Melinda had instructed the museum to return DeWain's crated piece to a Bekins Van and Storage company in North Hollywood.

I googled the company and learned it had gone out of business many years earlier. DeWain didn't get his piece back, but after I gave him the information, he stopped insisting that I was holding onto his sculpture.

We moved another large wedge from DeWain's studio in Torrance to the J. Paul Getty Museum in 2011 for the first *Pacific*

Standard Time exhibition, a massive project tracing the birth of the Los Angeles art scene after World War II. DeWain's sculpture had to be pulled out of a sea container he was using for storage behind his studio. It was in a crate that was too rickety for safe transport, so we constructed a new one and worked out the logistics for the moving and repacking with the Getty's art handlers, led by Kevin Marshall and the museum's excellent conservation staff. Our plan was to use a crane to lift the sculpture out of the container, re-crate it, and then truck it to the Getty.

When we got there with our crane, however, we found that DeWain had tried to get a head start moving the crate with his own forklift, which was now stuck in the mud, blocking our way. We extracted it, and then the crate, only to discover it had been nailed shut, which meant we'd have to use pry bars—very carefully—to get it open, as the Getty staff watched nervously.

Once the sculpture was exposed and the Getty conservators inspected it for condition issues, we lifted and packed it into our crate for a flatbed truck delivery to Jack Brogan's workshop for polishing. Jack's expertise was in nontraditional and industrial materials. And he was a genius at assisting artists with technical solutions—from new fabrications to fixing damaged McCracken planks to repairing artwork made of resin.

The Getty had three conservation staff members watching us work and a camera crew recording our every move, so it was a nerve-racking project. Just when I thought we were finished and was beginning to relax, DeWain told the Getty folks he had another large, crated piece he wanted them to look at, saying he thought it was even better than the one we just finished packing. The Getty agreed, so we craned it out of its sea container and used our gantry to lay it flat on a large polishing table inside DeWain's studio. When we opened the crate, though, it was obvious that a corner of the sculpture was damaged and missing a chunk several inches across.

DeWain immediately said he wanted to make an insurance claim and pulled a prepared claim form out of his pocket, asking me to sign it. But the missing chunk of resin wasn't anywhere to be found—it was obviously a preexisting damage issue. The Getty talked him out of the claim, though it was a reminder of how you have to be wary in the art moving business and always watch your back.

In the late 1980s, DeWain moved from working strictly with plastics that had the surface polish and translucence of glass and began working with the thing itself, building sculptures from 1-inch-wide strips that he'd cut from sheets of 1/4 inch thick, single-strength glass. He joined these strips to create three-dimensional lattice shapes similar to bridge trusses, using silicone as an adhesive. Glass is actually flexible up to a certain stress level before it breaks, but it was often compromised by the many silicone glued joints in DeWain's structures. Silicone is rubbery and has an elastic "memory." When distorted, it wants to return to its original position, so as we moved a sculpture, and the silicone joints moved, the attached glass would try to flex as well. Multiply any displacement or distortion across the many joints of the structure, and it was inevitable that one or two glass segments would eventually break—no matter how carefully the sculpture was handled. We constantly worried about not just damaging the pieces but about getting cut.

At first, DeWain repaired the sculptures himself—a relatively easy task accomplished by cutting away the silicone and inserting a new strip of glass. But then, he began charging for the repairs, and soon he wanted to declare a sculpture with any breakage a total loss and collect the full value on an insurance claim. At that juncture, I refused to continue handling those pieces—but not before delivering and installing one last eight-foot-long sculpture for a couple living in Sherman Oaks.

To hang a Valentine construction, we'd attach multiple "L" hooks to a wall, generally spacing them sixteen inches apart to keep the glass from sagging, and carefully lower the sculpture onto those. The ½ inch raised throat of the hook was sufficient to keep the sculpture from falling off in an earthquake.

But when we arrived at the Sherman Oaks house, the husband had other ideas. He wanted DeWain's sculpture hung on an uneven flagstone-faced fireplace with a stone hearth bench extending across the bottom. As he showed us the spot, he handed me a package of flat-head screws saying, "Use these. I don't want to see those ugly hooks you've got there."

I protested that the heads of his screws were too shallow, and using them placed the sculpture at greater risk of falling off, but he was adamant. "I'm paying you," he said imperiously, "so do what you're told."

I wrote on our delivery paperwork that we were using his hardware against our advice and had him sign it. I also had him initial the "no insurance" box, and we hung the piece as he asked.

Several weeks later, his wife called to say the sculpture had fallen and was damaged—and, what was I going to do about it? I said I would call back. I knew the sculpture wouldn't fall on its own because we had solidly inserted the screws into the fireplace, so I decided to go look at it and called to make an appointment. The couple's teenage daughter answered, and when I introduced myself, she sounded upset, stifling sobs.

"Oh, please, please can't you do something?" she pleaded. "My dad is so pissed off at me, but it wasn't my fault! The sleeve of my cashmere sweater caught on the corner when I walked past, and the sculpture just fell off!"

I said I would get back to her and waited until the next day before calling again. This time I got the wife. I told her I was on my way. Her reception was frosty and self-righteous. The sculpture had fallen because of my ineptitude, she said, I would have to compensate them for the loss. She led me to their living room, where a pile of shattered DeWain Valentine glass littered the hearth. But the screws where it had hung were still intact. Viewing the mess, I decided it would get their daughter into even more trouble if I revealed what she had told me. So, I simply told the wife the damage wasn't our responsibility and left.

Several weeks later, I received a summons to appear at small claims court at the downtown Los Angeles courthouse. The couple was suing me. When I arrived for the trial, they were with their son and a very nervous-looking daughter, who didn't make eye contact. They asked the judge to award them financial damages, claiming I had incorrectly and negligently installed the sculpture. When the judge looked at me for a response, I walked over, and without saying a word, I showed him my bill of lading, pointing to the signatures and the note about the hooks. He immediately ruled in my favor. The whole family, including the daughter, was at the bench arguing with him as I walked out of the courtroom.

Having felt the visceral anxiety that glassworks can produce, I appreciated the way Guy Dill, another Los Angeles sculptor, exploited it in a series of long thin sculptures he made by clamping one or two-inch-wide strips of glass on one end of eight-foot-long stainless steel. Once he mounted the steel-glass sandwich vertically or horizontally on a wall, he'd insert a metal wedge on the open end between the steel strip and glass and push it inward until the glass bowed under pressure into a parabolic shape. By trial and error, Guy worked out the exact degree the wedge could be forced before the glass would snap. The viewer could see the stress being exerted on the glass and feel how close the glass had come to breaking. It was a brilliant conceit. And one I'd just as soon enjoy from afar.

Dogs

EVERY DELIVERY MAN, postal worker, and service person visiting a home is at risk of a dog attack, and all of us have dog stories to tell. Dogs are naturally territorial, with instincts honed to protect their masters and their homes from intruders—even invited ones—making them yet another common hazard of the art handling business.

Mostly, they're a nuisance nipping at our heels and getting underfoot, but I have had several experiences that put me at risk of serious injury, even death. Worst, perhaps, was one in which an art collector allowed her dog to target me.

I went to install several paintings at the woman's home, which sat uphill seventy-five feet away from the street, with a paved walkway curving through immaculate green grass to the entrance. When I rang her bell, my client, in her 50s with a helmet of salon-styled black hair, met me and looked me over disdainfully. She smirked as she let me in, and as soon as she closed the front door behind us, I was confronted by a large, white standard poodle—the ends of its legs and tail groomed into poodle pom-poms. It jammed its long, pointed nose into my crotch, pushing hard, and bared its teeth in a low, guttural growl. I felt its hot wet breath as my client stood by without a word. She glanced down and smiled sadistically, obviously enjoying my discomfort.

Dog trainers teach a way to prevent dogs from jumping against the stomach or chest is to raise a knee to fend the animal off. But carrying a heavy, metal toolbox, I was off-balance, jammed against the door, and boxed in by my client, who made no effort to grab the dog or move out of my way. The woman waited a few long moments, glancing again at my crotch before demurely asking: "Is my little Pierre making you uncomfortable? I could lock him up if you would like."

After she led the dog away, I worked for an hour installing her paintings, pissed off by what felt like a deliberate attempt to humiliate me, and I struggled to tamp down my anger. When I completed the installation, the client signed the paperwork and apologized for her dog, but her tone felt perfunctory, less an apology than a way to remind me she had the upper hand. She closed the door behind me, and I walked toward my truck. Then I heard the door closing again, and turning my head, I saw Pierre charging down the hill toward me. Behind him, I could see my client peering from between her window drapes with a grin on her face.

Standard poodles were originally bred for retrieving game during hunts, and Pierre thought I was his target. He was closing in, and there was no way to outrun him because my truck was too far away. The only option I saw to save myself from serious injury was to stand and fight. Pierre was snarling as he launched himself at my throat. I waited until he was in the air and swung the toolbox into his path. His nose connected squarely against it with a loud crunch. He rolled backward, blood splattering on the walk, and yelping in pain, took off running back to the house. His owner opened the door to let him in and began angrily screaming, accusing me of attacking her dog, though she was the one who set him loose. She was threatening to call the police as I drove away.

Retriever

A client in Beverly Hills scheduled us to uncrate a large painting and re-stretch it. The painting, like many too large to fit through doorways or be shipped by airfreight, was folded in two halves for easier handling. Making a painting "foldable" involves cutting its stretcher bars in the center and reattaching them using mending plates. Then, whenever the painting requires folding, the mending plates on the back can be unscrewed, and the staples pulled for several feet on either side of the center to loosen the canvas so it can be curved around a Sonotube. The larger the tube diameter, the farther the canvas should be loosened in each direction from the center to prevent tearing the painting. Once the canvas has been loosened, we insert the Sonotube underneath the painting's center and lift it straight up, causing the canvas to arch over the tube snuggly and evenly. We position the two stretcher bars parallel to each other, and the bars become legs. Then, we add wooden braces to hold the Sonotube firmly against the painting and still more braces to keep the "legs" evenly spaced. Paintings prepared in this manner can stand upright and be safely transported or crated and shipped.

We were hired to unpack and re-stretch the painting to its full width and install it. That involved folding it face-up on the floor and lifting off the Sonotube. Then, we would carefully turn the painting over, reattach the mending plates, and stretch and staple the loose canvas flaps. To do all that, we'd need a large, undisturbed space.

My four-man crew arrived at the residence and found the homeowner hosting lunch for a group of friends, all of them sitting on high stools around the kitchen's center island. The house was "open concept," so the kitchen and dining area were essentially part of the living room, where the crew would be working. That meant they'd be within feet of the guests. As the homeowner and friends carried on a lively conversation, fueled in part by several bottles of wine, the crew moved couches, coffee tables, and chairs to open up enough floor space to work.

They opened the crate in the garage, and as they brought the folded painting into the living room, they passed a large golden retriever sprawled on the kitchen floor next to the client's feet. When my crew suggested it would be prudent to lock the dog up while they worked, he acted irritated about having his party interrupted. But he got up and shut the dog outside in the backyard.

My crew spent several minutes carefully unfolding the painting face-up and was ready to flip it over for re-stretching when suddenly the dog burst back into the room. Excited at rejoining the crowd, he bounded toward the party, running straight across the face of the painting and tearing around the guests while the owner yelled for him to stop and tried to grab his collar. The dog scampered back across the painting, around the room, and trampled the painting for a third time while my employees and the guests all lunged as he passed, trying to stop him. The dog, who thought this was a fun game, made yet another pass across the painting before he stopped to sit down in the center, just out of everyone's reach.

After he was finally locked up, the client and my crew assessed the extensive damage to the painting. The dog's claws had carved crescent-shaped gouges on the surface, penetrating the varnish and the underlying paint. Many of the deeper gouges caused indentations in the canvas, some of which went all the way through. There were dozens of these divots across the entire canvas. The painting was a mess.

The next morning the homeowner called me to ask who my insurance carrier was so he could file a claim. This was another one of those instances where the client is always right, unless he's being totally unreasonable. I pointed out the obvious—that *we* hadn't damaged his painting. He countered that we never should have had the painting lying face-up on the floor. I explained that it was part of the process and is safe but not dog-proof. I held myself back from saying none of this would've happened if he hadn't been looped at lunch. He hung up after angrily threatening to get his attorney involved, and I never heard from him again.

Rottweiler

Sonny and Cher's Holmby Hills mansion was decorated by Ron Wilson, a noted interior designer in the 1970s. Wilson charged $100,000 per room for his services, plus the cost of furniture and accessories, which he bought cheap and presented to clients with substantial markups. He also ordered and purchased freshly made "antique" furniture from Mike Hamilton, who operated out of a carpentry shop on La Peer Drive in West Hollywood. Unctuous odors of lacquers and acetone permeated the street from their shop, which was directly across the street from Cart & Crate, where I was working at the time.

Hamilton built his pieces from wood salvaged from barns and old houses to enhance the antique feel of the made-to-order furniture they specialized in, adding "wormholes" with electric drills and attacking the wood with chains to give it an even more worn appearance. This was called "distressing the furniture" to age it. Mike and his employees were often high and loopy from spray painting finishes and breathing the fumes, and I frequently heard them squealing and singing as they gleefully whipped an armoire or breakfront.

Buying "rapidly aged" furniture kept Wilson's ultimate decorating promise—that his busy clients would receive rooms and homes that felt completely out of the box, requiring minimal participation from them. Weeks before decorating a home, he would hire Cart & Crate to accumulate all the furniture and accessories—books, lamps, ashtrays—needed to fill the house. Some of these items were recycled from previous decorating jobs, then updated or redone. His first step was always to completely strip the client's house so he could decorate from the floors up. Some of the furniture was sent to be reupholstered and used again, while the rest we'd haul to Goodwill, where we also went regularly to purchase books for Ron. Any title would do as long as it had an embossed cover or un-torn slipcover and "looked important." He or one of his assistants would sift through the boxes we brought back, pulling out volumes good enough to put on clients' bookshelves to give an impression they were well-read and sophisticated. It always amazed me that someone would want to live in a house with hardly a single personal object. Why not live in a hotel?

Wilson was phobic about having clients around while he worked and would demand they go far away on a weeklong vacation until he was done. His goal was to complete a house in five days or less, which was a tall order for mansions in Bel Air. He would schedule floor refinishers, painters, and wallpaper and drapery installers with military precision, hovering over the craftspeople to ensure they completed work promptly and with perfection. We followed on their heels with truckloads of furniture and accessories. Often the floor finishes were not completely cured by the time we arrived, and we had to wear socks inside as we delivered furniture, sliding on the slippery floors and struggling to carry a heavy armoire or large overstuffed couch without falling. Dropping a piece of furniture or sliding it over a floor was never an option. If a floor or wall finish were ever scratched, Ron would have had a meltdown.

Wilson expected us to finish delivering and placing all the fur-niture and accessory items in one eight-hour day—no matter how large a home was. To save time, we studied his decorating methods to learn his tastes, and soon we were able to install rooms while he was elsewhere in the house. He would rush into a room intending to tell us where things should go, only to see everything already in place. Looking perplexed and confused, he would turn on his heels and run off to another part of a house, leaving us to get on to the next space.

When a project was nearing completion, I would intentionally install an object out of place as a test to see if anyone would notice. In Sonny and Cher's house, I turned a silver-framed photograph of their child upside down on the grand piano in the living room. On return trips to the mansion over the next few years, I noticed the photograph was never righted.

A few months after completing our work at Sonny and Cher's, Ron Wilson sent me back to install some small paintings and mirrors. I drove my Chevy van up the long driveway, through the ornate wrought-iron gate, and into a large motor court outside the front door. The parking area, about sixty by eighty feet, was unpaved and covered with a deep layer of pea gravel.

I parked the van on the far side of the drive, grabbed my tools and, with feet crunching on gravel, walked across the courtyard to ring the front doorbell. A diminutive Mexican maid answered. She was skinny, likely weighing less than ninety pounds, and wasn't even five feet tall. I thought she might be from Oaxaca, whose people often have small frames.

She showed me into a round entry hall with a polished marble floor. A hallway on the left led to the kitchen, and another on the right led to the living room. She told me to wait and disappeared in the direction of the kitchen.

After a minute or so, I began hearing scraping and clicking sounds. The sounds grew louder, and suddenly an enormous Rottweiler emerged from the right hallway, looking straight forward with dead eyes. His black and tan snout bobbed up and down as he loped across the floor toward the kitchen, fur rippling over heavy muscles. A wide, black leather collar with metal studs adorned his neck.

I froze and held my breath, praying he wouldn't notice me. He was about to enter the left hallway when he suddenly sensed my presence and scrambled to turn toward me, emitting a rumbling growl. His paws slipped on the floor, causing him to fall several times, which frustrated and enraged him even more as he straightened out and began picking up speed. I backed against the wall waiting for the impact, and he was almost on top of me when the little maid rushed in from the kitchen, screaming curses in Spanish. She dove like a football tackle onto the dog's back, grabbed his collar with both hands, and hung on with all her might. I backpedaled around the curved wall trying to reach safety as the dog gave chase, dragging the maid who was desperately clinging on his back and flopping up and down like a rag doll. The little maid screamed louder, and with one free hand, she repeatedly whacked the dog on his right ear until he yelped, subdued, and began to obey her.

Still holding his collar in a tight grip, she led him out the front door to a dog run at the edge of the car park on the right side of the house. The run, enclosed by an eight-foot-high chain-link fence, had a concrete floor, and I watched her lock the dog inside with a padlock. He stared at me through the mesh with hatred as she returned to the house, sweating and breathing hard. "That dog is trained to kill! You are very lucky!" she said.

She led me into the living room, and I finally started hanging paintings. The dog incident unnerved me, but I remembered to check the piano for the upside-down photograph, and the humor of seeing it there, just as I'd left it, calmed and cheered me. After installing art for thirty minutes, I needed a tool from the van and walked outside, leaving the front door ajar to avoid being locked out. Halfway across the parking court, feet crunching on the gravel, I glanced over to the dog run. It was empty. The gate was still locked, but the dog was nowhere in sight. He somehow managed to jump over an eight-foot fence, his enormous mass defying gravity. Just the thought of it worried me. I quickly looked around and, seeing nothing, I cautiously got down on my hands and knees to look under the van. The Rottweiler's ass stuck out from behind the driver's side front tire. He was hiding there, stalking me, waiting to ambush me when I returned to my truck.

His butt and short tail tensed as he realized he'd been discovered, and I desperately ran for the front door, hearing his paws on the gravel and his deep-throated growl as he closed in behind. I rushed inside and slammed the door in his face. The heavy wood vibrated and shook as he repeatedly launched against it, growling and snarling, claws scraping. The fearless maid went outside and led him back to the run, cuffing his ears and yelling Spanish curses as she went. This time she attached a chain to his collar and secured him to the fence before locking him inside the run. Sonny and Cher's front door was a beautiful antique, an original Spanish Colonial constructed with heavy lumber and hand-forged iron fittings. It was pristine when I arrived, but now it was scarred with deep claw marks that started seven feet high, extending down to the bottom. The Rottweiler was still locked up when I left, glaring malevolently at me and growling.

Movie Stars, Moguls, and Hollywood Types

Queens

THE ART AND MOVIE WORLDS overlap in LA, and over the years, I have provided services to dozens of movie stars, entertainers, and Hollywood heavyweights ranging from Elizabeth Taylor to David Bowie. I never know if I'll get a brush with glamor or lose a few illusions.

Raquel Welch once asked me to ship a neon cross dating from the 1930s that she found in a small tabernacle church, from Taos, New Mexico, to Los Angeles. I delivered and installed it in her home, plugging it into a wall socket before leaving. She called several months later to tell me it had "burned out and severely damaged the electrical circuitry." I didn't see how this could've resulted from a mistake made with the installation, because all I did was plug it in. But, in good faith, I went to her Trousdale Estates home to take a look and discuss repairs, expecting I might be asked to pay for an expensive electrician to rewire her home. As it turned out, though, the damaged "circuitry" was in her boyfriend's boom box. To settle the matter, I bought him a new one.

There wasn't a hint of drama when I went to Elizabeth Taylor's home to determine the logistics for installing a sculpture in her garden. I assumed I wouldn't see her at all, but just as I was preparing to leave, her houseman came outside and said she wanted to meet me. Could I wait? I basked under the glow of a warm sun in the beautiful surroundings for forty minutes, and at last, Elizabeth came walking down the path and greeted me. I was stunned because although she was seventy years old, she still looked beautiful and young. Her famous violet eyes were hypnotic, and staring into them, I had a strong feeling she was flirting with me. I instantly understood how easily the world's greatest actress could evoke any emotion and had wrapped so many leading men around her little finger. I can hardly remember what she said, but just being in her presence was one hell of a thrill—and the only tip I needed.

Andy Williams

In autumn, swirling hot winds routinely arrive in Southern California, often bringing havoc. For much of the year, prevailing winds and breezes come from the west, sweeping across the Pacific and carrying cooling air across beaches and inland. In winter, those winds bring rainstorms. But when ridges of high pressure build aloft in the fall, the winds shift, sweeping in a dry heat from the desert regions to the east as they funnel through mountain passes on their way to the coast. These are the legendary Santa Anas, which can reach hurricane-force winds and lower relative humidity to nearly zero—with the air so dry your eyes water, and skin itches. Under these conditions, it only takes a downed power line or some nut with a Bic lighter to start a catastrophic brush fire. Often these fires originate twenty or thirty miles inland, in the valleys on the eastern side of our coastal mountains. They rapidly grow in strength, fueled by dry chaparral, growing up to twenty feet high, densely covering the ranges extending from Oxnard to the north, along the coast to Santa Monica in the south. Within a few hours, flames can crest the slopes and sweep south toward Malibu, reducing houses to ruins along the way. When these conditions build, we are often called by desperate collectors to rescue art collections from private homes. In one dire event, our trucks were summoned to stand by in case the Getty Museum's collections needed to be carried to safety.

On my way into work one morning, I heard a radio announcement that a brush fire jumped the 101 Freeway near Thousand Oaks and was burning up the mountain slopes, heading in the direction of Malibu along the coast. I knew it was going to be a busy day.

Just minutes after I sat down at my desk, Andy Williams called, sounding worried and scared. "The fire is coming in my direction, and it's looking bad," he said. "I'm watching on TV, and there are houses already burning in the hills above Malibu. How soon can you get out here and rescue my paintings?"

I said we would leave immediately and get there as quickly as we could.

Williams, a singer with a silky voice and a lot of gold records, had a home on a Malibu beach, and owned several important contemporary paintings, including a beautiful Morris Louis that he treasured. Louis painted on raw, unprimed canvas using Magna color, a fast-drying acrylic resin paint. His painting technique involved pouring colored bands of thinned paint on an inclined, stretched canvas, steering the direction of each band by tilting the canvas as the paint traversed the pristine surface. Because Magna dries so fast, Louis could apply multiple veils of paint without waiting days for it to dry. Over time, he learned to thin the paint with turpentine to give it the transparency he wanted without bleeding into the canvas along the edges, resulting in a blurred, fuzzy appearance. His work was glowing and vivid. The only problem was that Magna, and the solvents he used, were toxic, and breathing in the fumes eventually killed him.

From an art handling standpoint, Morris Louis paintings are challenging. The raw canvas shows every speck of dust, scuff, and fingerprint and must be handled with the utmost caution. They are also virtually impossible to clean, especially after the raw canvas naturally ages and oxidizes, developing a mellow golden hue. Using a cleaning solution might remove an offending fingerprint, but the remedy would also brighten the canvas where it had been applied and draw attention to itself.

The Morris Louis was one of William's favorite paintings. I moved and installed artworks often enough for Andy to learn he didn't collect on the advice of an art consultant or interior decorator—he collected pieces he loved. And now he was panicked about the possibility of losing one. It took over an hour of driving through smoky air and flakes of falling ash before we made it to his door and knocked. Andy was white-faced, trembling, and nearly in tears as he led us to his living room. The Morris Louis leaned awkwardly against a couch, its canvas partially hanging off the stretcher-bar. A thirty-six-inch tear extended from the top center edge into the center, cutting through two of the painted bands and into a section of raw canvas, leaving torn threads dangling. We stood side by side, sadly looking down at it, and seeing how distraught he felt, I was tempted to put an arm around his shoulders to comfort him, but I kept my professional distance.

"I thought you weren't coming, and my only option was to remove the painting from its stretcher bars and roll it so it would fit into my car," he mournfully explained. "I was trying to pull out the staples when it ripped."

I knew the painting was ruined but decided not to say anything that could make him feel even worse. All of us evacuated, and I took the torn canvas with me.

Several weeks later, Andy called and asked me to ship the painting to Goldreyer in New York City. Goldreyer was a painting conservator with a reputation as a miracle worker for damaged contemporary paintings. No one knew how he could take a virtual mess and return it several months later as a flawless painting showing no signs of repairs. He kept his methods so private that whenever I went to his studio to deliver and pick up paintings, he never once allowed me inside. Even if the painting was large and needed two art handlers, he would take it from us at the door and disappear, carrying it inside.

He kept Andy's painting for a year before shipping it to me so I could return it to Malibu. When we opened the crate and unwrapped the painting, I was stunned. The canvas was perfectly intact without any sign of repairs, even in unpainted portions of the raw canvas. I looked closely at where the torn area had been, front and back, and I couldn't see a blemish in the woven threads. How was this possible? How could torn and frayed fibers be repaired without showing any evidence? I knew better than to ask.

Joan Rivers

I met Joan Rivers after her personal assistant called to say the comedian was selling her house and might need my services for her art collection. We made a date for a consultation and the P.A., a young woman, answered the door when I arrived at Rivers' home. She told me to wait in the entry foyer while she went to tell her boss I arrived, and since there wasn't any seating, I wandered a bit, sticking my head through a side door into what appeared to be a living room. Two small, white corgi dogs were sleeping blissfully on a large white couch, one with pink ribbons above its ears and the other with blue—it was hard to believe they were descendants of wolves. Rivers' husband Edgar stood in the center of the room, staring straight ahead. He didn't move or notice my presence.

I quickly returned to the foyer, and a moment later, the P.A. came back to usher me into an office. Joan Rivers was seated behind an ornate Louis the 16th table, and instead of a welcome, she gave me a cool stare, sizing me up with her eyes. "An offer has been made on our house, so it looks like it is sold. I want you to give me an estimate for moving and storing my art collection. I hear you have a good reputation. Is that really true?" She stared at me with a look of skepticism. "How do I know I can trust you to take care of my art? What makes you any better than some Tom, Dick, and Shmeezle I could hire off of a street corner?"

I said nothing, deciding not to take the bait.

"All right," she said. "Mary will take you around the house and show you my collection." With a flick of her wrist, she dismissed me and turned her attention to paperwork on the desk.

Mary led me through the house, which was full of French antiques. I counted nearly sixty paintings and drawings and several additional sculptures. When we finished, I asked her if there was an inventory listing the art we could use to identify and label it for storage. I stressed the importance of having this list to account for the items and control our storage inventory. She said she would ask. I figured the packing and loading would take four men two days to complete and sent Mary an estimate.

Several months passed before she called again. "Miss Rivers wants to keep her art until the very last day," she said. "Escrow closes next Friday, and she wants you to move her on Thursday." I reminded Mary about needing the inventory, and she told me she was taking care of it.

On moving day, I showed up at the house with six art handlers and three trucks for the rush job and asked Mary for the inventory.

"Oh," she said. "There isn't an inventory, but I will be with your guys to identify each painting."

But Mary was no expert, and an hour passed with virtually no progress as she fumbled through a pile of purchase receipts attempting to identify paintings one at a time. She disappeared briefly and then came looking for me with a worried expression. "Miss Rivers wants to talk with you."

I went to the office, and Rivers gave me an angry look, both hands thrust forward, palms down on her desktop. "This is outrageous! Your men are standing around doing nothing. Why am I paying you if you are incapable of doing the work?"

Remembering that escrow was closing and the house had to be vacated by the end of the next day, I knew I was holding an ace card, so I replied contritely, "I am terribly sorry for the inconvenience. I was hoping there would be an inventory we could use to properly identify your paintings for storage. The lack of an inventory has greatly slowed us while we wait for Mary to identify the art. I deeply apologize. We'll leave now and return when she has had time to prepare the list, and we won't charge you for our time today."

I left her office and told my employees to round up their tools so we could go. But as I was walking across her expansive lawn toward my car, I heard her shrill, hysterical voice yelling behind me. "Here, Cook! Cook! Cook! Here, Cook! Cook! Cook! Cook!"

My first thought was that Rivers was calling one of her dogs. Was one of the corgis named "Cook?" Then, as the yelling continued, I realized she was calling *me*. I was incredulous. Mary rushed out of the front door and ran toward me, wide-eyed and breathless. "Miss Rivers wants you to come back. Please come back."

I walked toward the house as the strange call continued and once again stood in front of the ornate desk. Rivers was looking up at me with a wild look in her eyes, and though I was standing just three feet away, she continued yelling at the top of her voice: "Here, Cook! Cook! Cook! Here, Cook! Cook! Cook!"

This went on for almost a minute while I calmly stood, meeting her gaze. Abruptly she stopped. "What do we need to get my art moved out?" she asked.

I had won but was very careful to maintain a neutral expression. I explained there was not enough time to inventory her art, and we would need to store it by piece counts. She agreed, but I knew, like all powerful, important people, she did not like losing to an underdog, and I would need to be cautious if there were any future dealings.

Ray Stark

One of the most impressive private collections of modern sculpture I worked with in California belonged to Ray Stark, a film producer with a long line of successful hit movies including *Lolita*, *West Side Story*, *Funny Girl*, and *Annie*. Ray and his wife Fran—the sister of actress and comedian Fanny Brice—lived in the house that once belonged to Humphrey Bogart and Lauren Bacall. Looking at period publicity photographs of the stars sitting in the living room or outside in the garden, I could see the Starks hadn't changed the place much—except for the artworks they placed around the rolling Holmby Hills grounds. Ray Stark was great to work for, always fair, and easy to talk to. And his good eye for art led him to buy pieces by Maillol, Noguchi, Barbara Hepworth, George Rickey, and other important artists, including several large Henry Moore bronzes. He kept one of the Moores on the side of the front entrance motor court, seated on a plinth made of railroad ties and surrounded by a bed of Ivy, and once, he asked me to move it. I hired a crane with a couple of riggers for the job—big, tough, construction-work-er types. It was an unexceptional, no-drama job, but I remember it because as the workers were holding onto the sculpture to guide it and the crane began lifting, a dozen rats scurried out from underneath, squeaking and scattering in all directions. I laughed to see the macho guys dancing around and shrieking in a panic.

Ray kept some of his collection at a ranch in Los Olivos, a beautiful little town about an hour north of Santa Barbara, where he raised thoroughbred horses. His ranch sat on the upper half of a hill. The lower half—plus the valley floor and a vineyard—belonged to Douglas Cramer, a television producer, and fellow art collector. Their ranch entry gates were side by side, and my visits over the years took me through both of them. Ray's ranch had original buildings, including a leaky clapboard house and barns, but his mark on the landscape was hard to miss. A fourteen-foot-tall Henry Moore bronze with a shiny gold patina stood in the middle of a horse corral near the ranch house, and whenever I stopped at the ranch, there would be one or two horses leaning against the Moore or scratching their backs against it.

Ray bought a Fernand Léger sculpture for the ranch from another of my clients, Gene Klein, owner of the San Diego Chargers football team, who lived in Rancho Santa Fe, a community of large estates near San Diego. Klein and Stark had a common interest in raising thoroughbred horses and collecting art, and they handed me more of a challenge than I'd bargained for when Ray asked me to move the Léger up to Los Olivos. Before sending me to fetch it, Ray mentioned the sculpture's footing was concealed under dirt, so I took a pick and shovel when I drove down to figure out how to move it.

The large, whimsical figure titled *Walking Flower*, was made of brightly colored ceramic elements fixed together with grout. It stood more than nine feet tall, not counting the buried base, and I was concerned if we attempted to lay the sculpture horizontally, we would damage it. So I decided to measure the entire height, base to tip, to ensure we could safely transport it standing upright. It took a couple of hours of hard digging to reach the bottom, and when I did, I discovered that the Léger was affixed to heavy timbers that would be risky to remove. They'd have to come too—and the total height could pose problems. To prevent unpleasant surprises, I drove the route we'd be taking to Los Olivos, stopping to measure the clearances under any overhanging branches. The small ranch roads near Klein's place merged into a larger two-lane road leading out of the area and connected to the main highway. One major obstacle along the way was a low overhead bridge, and I carefully measured the clearance from the road crown to the underside of the bridge girders. Back in my LA office, I called a trucking company with a double-drop frame, lowboy trailer that would hold the sculpture closer to the road to improve its chances of fitting under the bridge. But when I measured its height, I realized with the sculpture loaded, we would be ten inches too high. Fortuitously, the Léger was topped with a ten-inch, pyramid-shaped ceramic piece, and I received permission from the Léger Foundation in Paris to temporarily remove it by cutting at the grout line.

We loaded the Léger with a crane and slowly drove several miles to the bridge, only to discover we were still one inch too high. We let air out of the trailer's tires and squeezed underneath by a heart-stopping, paper-thin margin. The rest of the trip was routine, and after delivering and installing the Léger, all that was left to do was grout the top piece back on and send photos to the Léger Foundation for their okay. As expected, they approved.

When Ray died, he left his art collection to LACMA, and my penultimate job for him was to pack up the pieces at his house and the ranch, then remove all the sculptures and place them in our warehouse. LACMA intended to install them in a memorial garden in honor of Stark, but nothing went as planned. Eli Broad was funding the construction of Broad Contemporary Art Museum, BCAM, his gallery pavilion at the museum, and I heard he might have objected to having Ray's sculptures near his project. Later I heard that construction delays on the LACMA campus meant the museum couldn't meet a stipulated deadline to install Ray's sculptures. Whatever was true, LACMA ultimately didn't get the bequest, and instead, in 2005, we made one last trip for Ray, delivering all the pieces to the J. Paul Getty Center, where they are installed in courtyards and gardens. The Léger is there, but one of my favorites, placed on the museum's grand plaza steps, is *Air*, by Aristide Maillol. The piece depicts a horizontal nude woman resting on her hip yet seeming suspended or caught in the motion of falling. The huge figure weighs 1,500 pounds, but cast from lead, which has a soft visual warmth, it feels impossibly light.

Squirrel

Ray wasn't the only local Maillol fan and collector. One of the artist's *Air* sculptures is in the gardens of the Norton Simon Museum, and we once crated and shipped it to Paris for restoration and installed it upon its return.

Another Maillol lead cast sculpture, of a standing, life-size female nude, was owned by Norton Simon's ex-wife, Lucille Ellis Simon, a LACMA Trustee who had her own excellent art collection installed at her home in Los Angeles. The house, located at the Wilshire Country Club with a beautiful view of the golf course, had a back lawn that blended into the fairway's grass without any fencing, giving the impression that her property extended for acres. The Maillol stood near the fairway's edge, where for years, it miraculously escaped getting dimpled by errant golf balls.

One morning Lucille walked out to her patio to enjoy her coffee in the warm sunshine and noticed the Maillol figure was missing its left big toe. She called the police to report that the piece had been vandalized and hired security guards to protect her sculpture collection at night. She also had us epoxy all the outdoor sculptures onto their concrete plinths as security against theft.

LACMA's conservation department replaced the missing toe with a matching lead prosthesis, but a few weeks later, that too disappeared, and the surgery had to be repeated. Lucille assumed the security guard had been sleeping and fired him. She then installed an ugly chain-link fence across the back of the lawn for protection, along with security cameras around the property.

The cameras solved the mystery: the security footage showed a squirrel gnawing on the injured toe. Whether this was a mineral supplement or a tooth sharpening exercise was unknown. But guards and fences were not going to keep squirrels away from the property, so we moved the sculpture to our storage warehouse. When Lucille died, LACMA asked me to remove the other outdoor sculptures. We had secured them so well it took me an entire day to chisel them loose.

Douglas Cramer

Douglas Cramer, developer and producer of *The Love Boat* and *Fantasy Island*—low-brow television hits that made him wealthy—spent a good deal of his money on leading-edge contemporary art. He particularly liked Ellsworth Kelly and owned several large, pristine paintings, as well as a 1,200-pound steel sculpture we bolted to his living room wall after wrestling it into his house. Cramer kept much of his collection at his ranch and vineyard, which sat below Ray Stark's place in Los Olivos. His large hacienda was on the side of a hill, sixty feet above a narrow valley floor, with views of his vine-yard and the golden, oak-covered hills on the other side. The house was basically two stories, although several floors were split-level. Water cascaded from a small pool on the lower level into a larger pool at the bottom, which was surrounded by an expansive patio, a bathhouse, chaise lounges, umbrellas, and cabañas. The setting was sophisticated and superb.

We had been making regular trips to the ranch for several years to deliver and install art when Cramer decided to build a gallery to display more of his growing collection. He chose a site against the hill on the far side of the vineyard and asked me to meet his architect there to discuss designs for a loading dock, workroom, and storage space. He flew me out of Van Nuys Airport on his private jet—which would've been a great perk except for the winter storm that turned the trip into a white-knuckle flight.

Cramer was especially proud of a portrait Julian Schnabel had done of him, a piece in which his likeness was actually discernable on the crusty Bondo-broken ceramics surface. The painting mea-sured thirty-six by thirty-six inches, and with its stretcher bars and raised surface, it jutted out eight inches but sat inside a twelve-inch-wide maple frame, angled on each side to touch the wall. We hung it in the house's round central, a hub from which hallways, doors, and stairs led to different parts of the house. I couldn't help but notice in the center of the atrium's Mexican tiled floor, someone had in-stalled a steel David Shapiro sculpture shaped like a house that was about the size of a shoebox and very heavy. Its low profile in such a high-traffic area looked like a trip hazard to me, but no one was asking for my opinion, and there it remained.

Several years after I installed the Schnabel, Cramer's secretary called and, in a matter-of-fact voice, told me the piece had fallen off the wall and was seriously damaged. Cramer wanted me to go to the ranch the following morning to meet with his insurance agent and attorney. I drove up from Los Angeles and walked into the house to see the Schnabel lying cockeyed, face-down on the floor, with chunks of paint and Bondo scattered about. A woman and three men, all in business attire, stood across the room, talking quietly.

Seeing that they were occupied, I looked closely at the painting. It had been hung on two half-inch-diameter steel lag bolts that were screwed into lead shields embedded in the masonry wall. The two lag bolts together could have suspended a refrigerator, and there was no way the painting would have fallen on its own. One of the bolts was still embedded in the wall but bent at an angle. The other was attached to the painting, with the lead shield and a fist-sized chunk of masonry attached to it. There were also scrape marks on the curved wall indicating that the painting had moved sideways as it fell, defying the laws of gravity. Next, I looked closely at the Shapiro sculpture and noticed by the accumulated floor wax around it that the sculpture had moved out of position by 3/4 inch. A staircase came down behind the Shapiro. From those clues, I deduced that someone had run down the stairs, rushing to another area of the house. They'd likely tripped over the Shapiro and fallen forward into the beveled Schnabel frame. That would've caused the painting to lurch sideways on the curved wall, bending one lag bolt and yanking the other out of the wall before the painting fell to the floor.

How might the accident have happened? My guess was that it probably involved Cramer's boyfriend, Craig. Craig seemed nice enough, but unlike Cramer, he seemed totally disinterested in the art around him. On our many visits to the ranch, I often noticed him hanging out near the pool with three or four boisterous young men wearing tight Speedos, and I could imagine them chasing each other down the stairs when one of them tripped over the Shapiro and fell headlong into the Schnabel.

The insurance adjuster was representing Chubb, which was also my insurer. When she asked how my insurance company was going to handle the damage, I explained my conclusions about the likely cause. I saw the realization growing in her eyes, but in the end, the solution was that Chubb paid Cramer's claim and charged me my deductible of $10,000. I kept working for Cramer, though, and a few years later, when he sold the ranch and moved to New York, we shipped his collection there, including the fallen Schnabel, which a conservator had restored.

I stopped by the ranch several years ago and saw the airy, modern cube that was once Cramer's gallery was now a winery, with fermenting vats, aging barrels, and a tasting room occupying the space. The only connection to the past was a framed poster announcing a MOMA exhibition. It was still on the restroom wall, where I had hung it thirty years earlier.

Brad Pitt

Brad Pitt asked me for advice on moving a large, carved stone tub into his bathroom. It weighed over 2,000 pounds, and no one could figure out how to get it up to his hilltop home. His contractors were stumped, and a crane company couldn't set up close enough to lift the weight. His house was in the Hollywood Hills at the end of a narrow, dead-end street, with a street-level garage. A steep flight of stairs next to the garage climbed fifty feet, ending at the left side of the single-story house, which ran across the crest of the hill. When I met the contractor on site, Brad and his girlfriend at the time, Jennifer Aniston, were home and looking very happy with each other.

It took me a few minutes, but I saw a solution to the tub problem—we'd convert the stairs to a ramp and use chain hoists to pull it up. I asked Pitt's general contractor to build a heavy-capacity plywood cover for the stairs. Meanwhile, we'd start constructing a hoist system by standing railroad ties on end and sinking them into four-foot-deep holes at the top of the incline, one on either side of the stairs. We wrapped rigging straps around the ties and attached a chain hoist to each. Then we ran a chain from the top of the ramp all the way to the bottom and attached that to a dolly we'd built—a heavy one with six wheels and enough capacity to carry the one-ton tub safely. Its ride to the top began as we used one of the chain hoists to winch it up the ramp. When one chain hoist was fully reeled in, we extended the other one, hooked it to the chain, and unhooked the first hoist. The relay system worked perfectly. Brad and Jennifer got their bathtub, and I got the astonished respect of the contractors who saw the kind of problem-solving we art handers regularly do on the fly.

Jimmy Stewart

Our client, Planet Hollywood, ran a chain of restaurants decorated with film props and memorabilia. Planet Hollywood was a joint venture by Sylvester Stallone, Bruce Willis, Demi Moore, and Arnold Schwarzenegger. The group employed a curator to find and purchase props from movies, which we would deliver and install at the various restaurants. When they bought a desk from the 1939 Jimmy Stewart movie *Mr. Smith Goes to Washington,* the curator asked us to deliver the desk to Stewart's Beverly Hills home so the actor could autograph it and be photographed as he did.

We drove the desk to his place, and after unloading it, rang the doorbell, which was answered by a very bald Jimmy Stewart. Seeing the photographer, he said, "Wait here while I get my hairpiece," and ran back into the house. He returned a minute later carrying a wig, which he casually put on in front of us as if it were a hat. As he did so, the real Jimmy Stewart magically appeared. The curator showed him the desk and handed Jimmy a felt-tip marker. Stewart stared incredulously at the desk. "I don't remember this. Is it really from the movie?" he mused. "Well . . . I suppose it has been a long time. . . ." He shrugged his shoulders and "authenticated" it with his signature.

Anthony Quinn

Some actors in real life are just like their movie personas, and if you're lucky, you'll meet the likable version of the characters they play. Luck is unpredictable, though. When I delivered a small, framed Monet painting to Anthony Quinn, I halfway expected the exuberant Zorba of *Zorba the Greek*, but instead, I got someone more like the volatile warrior he played in *Lawrence of Arabia*.

Quinn's mansion was in Bel Air, guarded by an ornate gate framed with decorative pillars. Through it, I could see a cobblestone driveway that curved uphill to a motor court at the top. The sides of the driveway were planted with dense ivy, and the sprinklers were on to keep it green. I rang an intercom next to the gate and heard Quinn's voice answer. He sounded angry.

"What do you want!" he snapped.

I explained I was here to deliver his painting.

"Don't bring a truck up here. Walk it up the driveway!" he ordered, abruptly hanging up.

I unloaded the painting from my truck as the driveway gate swung open and began dutifully trudging up the long drive, careful to stay in the center to avoid any spray from the sprinklers. The cobblestones were wet, and I walked cautiously so I wouldn't slip and fall. I heard a car door slam up ahead and the throaty roar of an engine starting. An Alfa Romeo convertible sports car with the top down suddenly appeared, bearing down at me as the driver shifted gears, picking up speed. Quinn was behind the wheel, eyes looking directly at me, and I realized he wasn't going to stop. I ran for my life, feet slipping on the cobbles, and jumped into the ivy holding the painting high over my head to protect it from the sprinklers. The knee-high plants soaked my shoes and pants, but I kept the painting dry. Bedraggled, I reached the front door and waited a long time until an unfriendly housekeeper opened it. She looked disapprovingly at my dripping shoes and told me to wait outside.

Five minutes later, she returned with an armful of towels, laying them on the floor to make a path to an opposite wall. She told me to stay on the towels and lean the painting against the wall. I did as she requested, and as I turned to go, I asked if she would make certain the gate remained open until I could get out. She seemed to agree, but when I reached the bottom, the gate was shut, so I trudged all the way back up the hill, rang the front doorbell, and stood there the requisite five minutes until she reappeared. She scowled, giving me a dirty look, and said she would wait until I got to the bottom before opening the gate. She apparently took me for a slow walker. It was fifteen more minutes until the gate opened, and I could finally leave.

Dinah Shore

My orders from LACMA were to pick up a painting from the singer Dinah Shore. She was adamant, they said, that I arrive at 10 a.m. on the dot. But when I got to her home, exactly at 10, a butler dressed in a tuxedo and tails ushered me into the entry hall and told me Miss Shore was still asleep, so I'd need to return later. He looked perturbed as I relayed my instructions and insisted on carrying them out, and he left through a doorway, returning with two maids and a cook. The maids wore black dresses with white lace aprons, and the cook was in white with a white apron and a chef's hat. It looked as if they'd just stepped out of one of those Depression-era movies where wealthy people's servants always wore such uniforms. They argued in French, their hand gestures indicating that none of them was willing to wake up their boss, and finally, the butler went back to the kitchen and returned with a box of wooden matches. He pulled out four matchsticks and broke a piece from one, then turned his back and arranged them in his hand, so the short one didn't show. The group took turns choosing a match, and one of the maids turned pale and looked like she was about to faint when she pulled the short stick. The other three, visibly relieved and still speaking in French, pointed down the hallway.

The unlucky maid stood frozen for a few long moments but finally, head bowed, she walked in that direction as if to face a firing squad. She disappeared, but I heard her knocking on a door and saying, "Excuse me, Miss Shore, the man is here to pick up the painting."

All hell broke loose as the very familiar voice of Dinah Shore began yelling about being woken up and spouted a long string of curse words that would have embarrassed any longshoreman. The little maid came running back toward us, sobbing uncontrollably, and disappeared into the kitchen. It was brutal, but I left with the painting.

Max Palevsky

Max Palevsky, the tech mogul, venture capitalist, and movie producer, owned half a dozen Calder mobiles and several large outdoor Calder sculptures. When I worked for Cart & Crate in the 1970s, he asked for a crew of six art handlers to move a medium-size Calder stabile at his Palm Springs home. The job would require bathing suits, he said. When we arrived, we saw that the sculpture was standing on a small island in the middle of his swimming pool, hence the need for swimwear. Palevsky liked beautiful women, who always seemed to like wealthy men like him, and he was lying on a chaise lounge next to the pool surrounded by six gorgeous women in skimpy bikinis. His butler, dressed in a white jacket and black slacks, was mixing drinks at an outdoor bar while keeping an eye on the food that was cooking nearby on a built-in barbeque grill.

We put on our bathing trunks, and a couple of us swam to the island to figure out how we were going to get the sculpture out of the pool. It was six feet high and too heavy to hold while swimming, so we decided to wrap it in layers of truck pads and let it drop to the bottom of the pool, reasoning that the pads would cushion it when it landed and also act as a water "sail" slowing the descent. After wrapping it securely, we tied a rope to the middle, and while a couple of guys pulled from the side of the pool, we carefully guided it off the island into the water, where it sank to the bottom. Four of us swam down, grabbing hold to get our feet planted on the bottom, and by bending knees and lifting in unison, we were able to shift it a foot at a time toward the shallow end. Eventually, all six of us lifted the Calder, none the worse for wear, out of the pool at the shallow end—to the cheers and applause of Max and his girlfriends.

When Max died in 2010, he bequeathed each of his grandchildren a mobile. Unfortunately, one grandchild was disappointed when the Calder Foundation declared his as a fake, rendering it worthless. The foundation has absolute authority over restorations and authenticating Calder's sculptures, which are relatively easy to fake. I wondered if Max knew it was a copy or what he would have done upon learning a dealer had sold him a worthless piece.

The estate's executors asked us to send two of Max's large Calder stabiles to Christie's, New York, to be auctioned—one from Palm Springs and the other from Malibu. I had installed the Malibu piece, titled *Red Curlicue*, years before in the gardens of Max's elegant Spanish hacienda-style house, which was beautifully situated on several acres on a bluff overlooking the Pacific. Johnny Carson was a neighbor a few properties over. Max had married twice, and after his divorce, he purchased the neighboring property for his ex, so they were next-door neighbors. The trees along the edges of the properties had grown too high for us to use a crane to move *Red Curlicue*, so the only way to remove it was to take it out in sections. Calder used old-fashioned square-head bolts to fasten sections together and often stamped them with the letter "C" to show they were original and authentic. Each of the sculpture's sections was attached by ten or more bolts, and as we dismantled the piece, we were careful to preserve them and their nuts.

When we arrived, I was surprised to find the sculpture painted yellow and asked the house manager why *Red Curlicue* was now *Yellow Curlicue*. She said that Palevsky received permission from Calder to change the color, but I was skeptical. I had never encountered a single instance where an artist was willing to change a finished artwork to satisfy the whims of a collector. While my crew was busy taking the Calder apart, I walked to my car, passing an open garage door, where I noticed gallon cans of enamel house paint sitting on a shelf. The cans had drips and splashes of the same yellow as the Calder. Evidently, Max had grown bored with the red and took it upon himself to repaint the Calder in a color he liked. We crated and shipped *Yellow Curlicue* to Lippincott in Connecticut, where it was stripped and repainted to restore its original color before it was sold at auction. To avoid paying sales taxes, the new owners sent it to Montana, where it spent a year and a day on the grounds of a university and was clearly subjected to some harsh weather conditions. When it was returned to us to install at the home of Terry Semel, the former Warner Bros. CEO who was now running Yahoo, we found rust, fading paint, and scratches. Many of the original "C" stamped bolts were missing as well.

The other Calder was at Palevsky's second Palm Springs home, which he bought in the 1980s after selling the place with the sculpture in the pool. We were the ones who had installed the piece we were now taking away, and back then, I had used a large crane to lift it over the house and onto the swimming pool deck, which perched at the edge of a steep overlook with sweeping views across the Coachella Valley. But Palevsky later added guest quarters and a larger garage, as well as a tennis court in front of the original house. Now, there was no place left to set up a crane to get it out. The stabile, made of thick-gauge steel, was heavy, and it had a multi-colored paint scheme, with paint covering the bolts holding the sections together. It would be impossible to remove those bolts without damaging the paint, so we would need to lift the whole sculpture over the seven-foot glass barrier that surrounded the pool deck.

Given all the other obstacles, we decided our best plan would be to clear a path several hundred feet long through the desert around the side of the house and use it to drive up a small Japanese crane. With shovels and pry bars, we began digging out and moving cacti, small trees, and boulders until we cleared a path wide enough for the crane. The crane precariously set up its outriggers between the pool glass and the very edge of the precipice, but it couldn't get close enough to completely lift the weight of the sculpture. However, it was able to tilt it enough that we could insert dollies under two of the Calder's legs. Then the crane tiled it in the other direction, and we got a dolly under the third leg. That done, we could roll the sculpture across the patio and place it close enough to the fence for the crane to lift it over onto our temporary road. The crane would retract its outriggers, move forward, set up again, lift the Calder, swing it around, set it down, and move again. We repeated this "crab walk" multiple times until we got past the house and could load it onto a truck for delivery to New York. Calder might've enjoyed the sight of his stabile temporarily gaining the freedom, if not the grace, of his mobiles.

Cowboys

WHEN I WAS EIGHT YEARS OLD, cowboys and Indians were a big thing with all the kids, our version of superheroes. We would endlessly play at being gunslingers, shooting at each other and imposing our own rough justice. On one occasion, I made a noose from a piece of clothesline and told a younger kid we were going to hang him. He thought we were serious and ran home crying to his mother, who called my dad—who thought it was hilarious. Those were the days when cowboy movies were regular features in the movie theaters, and radio programs broadcast the Lone Ranger, Roy Rogers, Hopalong Cassidy, and Marshall Matt Dillon of *Gunsmoke*.

Gunsmoke was the only western where the bad guys got shot and often didn't get up. Marshall Dillon was tough as nails and a dead shot, while the good guys in other radio westerns, cowboys like Roy Rogers, always shot the guns out of the bad guys' hands, which made for more wholesome entertainment. My mother said *Gunsmoke* was too violent for a young boy, so I built a crystal radio that had a headphone, and by carefully adjusting a wire across the crystal, I could pick up the program and listen in my room.

Eventually, westerns fell out of fashion, and their stars began fading from memory. In their retirement, Roy Rogers and his wife Dale Evans opened a museum in Victorville, on the high desert outside of

LA. The museum, its façade resembling a western fort, was visible from the freeway, and a giant, rearing palomino on a pedestal stood sentinel in front. The palomino was an oversized fiberglass replica of Roy's horse Trigger, which he rode in his movies and television series.

As years passed, fewer and fewer people remembered Rogers, and attendance at the museum dropped. Roy and Dale's son Dusty, who inherited the museum after they died, decided the best way to keep it going was to move it to Branson, Missouri. Branson had fashioned itself as a country music entertainment center, with theaters featuring live music, a large amusement park, and other honky-tonk ventures. Dusty hired a van and storage company to move the museum's collections, and their people asked me to bid on handling all the packing because they were uncomfortable taking on that kind of specialized work. Whenever I hear that, I know there is often a hidden agenda: to pick my brain for information so they can do the job themselves. But, remembering my childhood love of westerns, I decided it would be fun to spend an afternoon at the museum and drove out there.

The museum displays were dated and poorly lit, with lots of fading photographs and books, along with costumes and some weapons. There was one large, glass showcase, however, that held something that made the trip worthwhile: a taxidermy stuffed palomino. It was Trigger himself, rearing up on his hind legs and wearing Roy's saddle. I climbed inside the case and measured him for a crate, surprised to find myself standing next to the very horse I had seen Roy Rogers ride so many times. Watching TV back then, I had no inkling that fifty years later, I would be looking into Trigger's glass eyes. That would be our only meeting, though. As I predicted, the van line agents ended up doing the packing and moving themselves. The museum in Branson lasted until 2009, and its collection dispersed the following year. Trigger found his way to Fort Worth, where he's now at home at the Cowboy Channel.

Autry

The megastar of cowboy cinema from the 1930s and '40s was Gene Autry, whose career eclipsed nearly all the others. Not only did Gene act in ninety-three feature films, but he had a wonderful singing voice and enjoyed a long string of recording successes. A businessman with broad media interests, he became the owner of the Anaheim Angels baseball team and later opened what is now the Autry Museum of the American West in Griffith Park, across from the Los Angeles Zoo. With the aim of creating an institution with the collections and scholarship to be taken seriously in the museum world, he hired an excellent staff to oversee the Autry's design, development, and construction—creating first-class exhibition spaces, storage areas, and conservation labs, along with a significant roster of exhibitions.

In 1990, the Autry Museum contracted me to collect stagecoaches for a show called *Stagecoach! The Romantic Western Vehicle*. I traveled around Southern California with a truck and crew, picking up stagecoaches from ranches and the homes of private collectors, even taking one from inside Santa Barbara's city hall. Years earlier, a construction project walled-off city hall's original large entrance, so we had to dismantle the coach in the lobby to get it out of the building.

Our last stop on the stagecoach roundup was the ranch of a man named Ed, one of Autry's close and longtime friends. During the Great Depression, when Autry came to Hollywood from the Oklahoma Dust Bowl, he brought Ed along, setting him up in the prop business to provide gear for western movies. Ed did well during the days of westerns, renting buckboards, saddles, and stagecoaches. He used the money to buy the large ranch in Brawley, California, where we met him, now in his 90s and taciturn as hell. When western movies dried up, Ed moved many of the props, including the coach we wanted, to his ranch, storing them in a big barn next to his house.

When I called him to schedule an appointment, he said he didn't like going out in the summer heat anymore and told us to come after sundown.

It was pitch black when we arrived, the only light in the area coming from the windows of his house. I could dimly make out crops growing on the thousands of acres Ed farmed, but I couldn't tell what they were. And it was still scorching, at least 100 degrees. Ed opened his front door and gave us a stern looking-over before walking to the side of the house and flipping a switch, lighting a long driveway that led to a big barn. He walked us down and opened a heavy door that slid on rollers. The barn was filled with western equipment, a virtual museum in its own right, and the stagecoach we needed was behind several buckboards and buggies, which we rolled outside to make room. We strained to move the coach outside and pushed it up the gravel driveway to the street, where our truck was parked.

As we were positioning the coach to roll it backwards up a ramp into the truck, Ed drove up in his white Cadillac and shone his headlights at the rear of our truck to illuminate our work area. The big, white Caddy had fins, six-shooter door handles, and a set of Texas longhorns as a hood ornament. I wondered if Ed was tongue-in-cheek about these cowboy ornaments or was serious about his decorations. I decided it would be unwise to ask.

The car sat idling with its windows up so Ed could stay cool in his air conditioning, and because the windows were darkly tinted, we couldn't see him. We began rolling the coach up the ramp by grabbing the wheel spokes and using them to lever the wheels. This was hard, slow work, and we were almost at the top when suddenly the wheel I was holding fell off in my arms, and the wheel nut bounced off my shoe and clattered into the street. I shouldered the wheel back onto the axle and held it there to keep the coach from falling over, but we were stuck on the ramp, uncertain what to do.

The Cadillac slid into gear and very slowly pulled up next to the ramp. I heard the whirring of the electric window being lowered and the sound of Gene Autry's voice crooning a western ballad emanating from inside. "Boys!" Ed said in his twangy Oklahoma drawl, "When you roll a stagecoach backward, the wheels will fall off. They stay on real tight when a coach is moving forward." With that, the window whirred shut, Gene's voice fading away as the Cadillac slowly backed down the street to its original spot. We rolled the coach back down the ramp while I shouldered the wheel to keep it on the hub until we could replace the nut. And then we turned it around and, without incident, rolled it back up.

Hoolihan

The Autry Museum was well established when it took over the ailing Southwest Museum of the American Indian—a once luminous institution that had occupied a striking Mission Revival building since 1914. The building sat on a hilltop overlooking the Arroyo Seco, the historic canyon the Pasadena Freeway follows from Los Angeles to Pasadena. Founded by journalist and Native American rights activist Charles Lummis, the Southwest Museum had a stunning collection of more than 200,000 Native American artifacts, primarily from the Western United States. But it suffered decades of neglect, and by the 1980s, the facilities were rundown and badly outdated. Large portions of the collections, including fragile, priceless baskets, had been carelessly stored in a tower that stood above the main museum buildings, with objects stacked on top of each other and shoved into corners. Because the tower lacked climate control or air conditioning, the artifacts had been subjected to the vagaries of temperature and weather, as well as plenty of insects and vermin. The

Southwest's merger with the Autry in 2003 wasn't without controversy, but it was a lifeline for the museum.

The Southwest had struggled for decades to correct itself. In 1981, it hired a new director, Patrick Houlihan, who began improving the buildings, renovating galleries and installing climate control in some, and updating the lighting and exhibit cases. Houlihan was a respected scholar of Southwestern Indian cultures and the author of several books. I met him when he began using my company to assist at the museum by delivering artifacts to conservators and shipping them to entities back east. We conferred on several occasions to discuss the best way to handle certain fragile pieces, and I found him likable and friendly.

He called one day to ask me to help him with a painting he had just discovered in the tower. We climbed the creaky stairs, and he pointed to the back of a shelf, where I could see the end of the rolled, dust-covered painting poking out from behind stacks of haphazardly stacked pots and baskets. To get to it, we carefully removed several of the fragile objects, laying them on the floor as there was no room on the shelves. The rolled canvas was thirty-six inches long, and I cautiously lifted it off the shelf, looking to see if there were any black widow spiders or roaches lurking. We carried it downstairs and laid it on a work table, carefully unfurling the roll to reveal a Thomas Moran oil painting. It was a stunning find but also a mystery. Why would someone remove a painting by such an important artist from its stretcher bars and roll it without protective interleafing materials? Why hide it on a shelf? Judging from the accumulated dust, it had been there for decades. Perhaps someone intended to steal it and later lost their nerve or left the museum before they had the opportunity. Houlihan had me deliver it to a painting conservator to be re-stretched, cleaned, and repaired, and I later crated and shipped it to New York City.

He called me again after the 1987 Whittier Narrows earthquake struck Los Angeles. The tower suffered extensive damage, a major blow to the museum, which could not afford the elaborate repairs it now needed. Then one day, he was gone. I found out he had moved to Taos, New Mexico, to take a position at the Millicent Rogers Museum, which also specializes in art and culture of the American Southwest. In 1992, I was stunned to read he had been indicted for selling pieces from the Southwest Museum's collections—using the money to purchase a ranch in Arizona. I called the Millicent Rogers and asked to speak to him, but he had resigned a few days earlier, and I just missed him.

Houlihan was convicted and ended up going to prison. Still, I had difficulty believing he stole from the Southwest Museum for personal gain after devoting so much energy and hard work to turn it into a modern institution. My guess is he may have improperly de-accessioned objects to raise funds to make those improvements. He admitted at his trial that he *had* taken items from the collection but said he used them in legitimate transactions to acquire important pieces. Whatever his intent, he made me an unwitting accomplice by hiring me to ship and deliver many of the pilfered artifacts. The temptations are many in this realm, and I've always been sad to see otherwise good people succumb.

Earthquakes and Petty Tyrants

Lear

THE GREAT NORTHRIDGE EARTHQUAKE of 1994 rumbled through the Los Angeles basin, causing tragic loss of life and substantial damage everywhere. My wife and I live in Santa Monica and were awakened at 4:30 a.m. to a deafening roar as our house violently rocked up and down. The furniture in our bedroom was upended, and drawers shot out of dressers. The television set crashed to the floor, paintings flew off their hooks, and the clamor drowned out my voice as I yelled at my wife to get under a door jamb for safety. The quake's final jolt lifted our house at such a severe angle that I thought it was collapsing on top of us. A sculpture that had been leaning against a wall soared across the room but, by a miracle, landed flat on the carpet in the midst of overturned furniture and debris without hitting anything and was undamaged.

The neighborhood's power was out, and with a flashlight, we found our way downstairs, where the doors stood open with their locksets torn out. The entire house was a shamble. The kitchen floor was covered in ten inches of broken cups and plates, along with the

entire contents of the refrigerator, freezer, and virtually every cabinet. In the living room, most of the furniture, including the couch,
was toppled over. There was a strong smell of natural gas outside,
and we learned that a gas pipeline running under the street two
blocks away ruptured. It howled like a jet engine being revved for
takeoff, and we worried that it would blow up or start a massive fire.

When daylight arrived, we went outside to see how our neighbors
fared. Across the street, a beautiful Greene and Greene craftsman
house from the early 1900s—which had been lovingly restored by its
owners—was turned ninety degrees on its foundation, its corners
overhanging in a star pattern. I helped my neighbor go inside and
salvage all the period fixtures before his house, like two others on
our block, was red-tagged by the city and later demolished.

My collection of Native American pottery, purchased from the
artist Tony Berlant, was broken. A rare bottle of vintage Bordeaux
wine, a gift from the actor Tony Curtis, lay smashed. In the after-
math of the terrible event, there were many things to be bummed
about, but the thought of how I would never taste that wine was
somehow extra disheartening. I noticed the bottle's neck was sitting upright amid the smashed glass littering the floor and still held
an ounce of wine, so I waded through the debris and found paper
towels, along with the solitary wine glass that remained intact in a
cabinet. I used the paper towel to filter out glass shards as I poured
the wine into my glass, and I got to taste the wine. It was sublime
and lifted my spirits.

The telephones began working again, and at 7:30 a.m., Norman
Lear called. He sounded desperate, saying his house had been destroyed. He wanted me to send art handlers with trucks to rescue
his art collection. Lear's newly constructed house was located on a
ridgeline above Mandeville Canyon, and when he moved in—only a
few months earlier—we had delivered and installed his art collection. I left my wife to deal with the chaos at our house and called

several of my employees, asking them to bring a truck and meet me at Lear's as quickly as possible. Mandeville Canyon runs north of Sunset Boulevard near Santa Monica, and despite the blinking streetlights and emergency vehicles on the roads, it only took twenty minutes for me to arrive.

A long hallway led from Lear's front door to the house's interior, and five alcoves in the walls along each side displayed ten large, magnificent pre-Columbian terracotta figures. Those now lay in shattered heaps on the tiled floor. Fortunately, the shards were large, and the artifacts could be restored, so I went looking for containers to pack them in. When I couldn't find anything in the house, I returned to the hallway to stand guard and protect the pieces until my employees could get there.

A few minutes later, though, the Suits began to arrive—Lear's camp followers, accountants, attorneys, agents, and producers, all in suits and ties. They entered through the front door in pairs, looking around in disbelief and agreeing with each other in hushed tones how terrible it was that poor Norman's house lay in ruins. I attempted to stop them, but they brushed past as if I were invisible. The first one through the door simply held out his arm and wordlessly pushed me aside. None of them looked at me or even seemed to notice I existed. They didn't notice the broken pottery either. They simply walked down the hallway, oblivious to the way their shoes were crunching on top of the shards. I yelled for them to stop, but they crunched on, and in less than twenty minutes, the shards had been pulverized into sand. It was heartbreaking.

Once my employees arrived, we walked through the house, assessing the damage to the rest of the art collection. Lear owned a large, important Robert Rauschenberg painting, *Rodeo Palace (Spread) 1975*, which we had installed in his living room on the wall directly behind the long, L-shaped sectional couch that wrapped around a four-by eight-foot glass coffee table. The couch and its side extension, both upholstered with soft, gray leather, were large enough to easily seat ten people. Two easy chairs covered with the same leather sat opposite the coffee table, and with the couch formed a long "U" shape around the table, which was bare except for a tall, ceramic "Conehead" peanut jar sitting in the center. It was modeled after the space aliens John Belushi and Dan Ackroyd played on *Saturday Night Live* and shaped like an artillery shell.

The Rauschenberg was a heavy painting, as it was stretched over plywood and included wooden doors. We had lag bolted it into the wall studs for extra security because it would be so close to people sitting on the couch. But the force of the earthquake tore the studs out of the wall, and the painting, still attached to fragmented drywall and two-by-four studs, was lying face down across the tops of the couches and chairs. At first glance, I thought the painting had landed safely, cushioned by the soft upholstery. Then I saw the point of the peanut jar poking out through the back. Luckily the Conehead had missed hitting the doors, including a screen door, that were part of the painting, as those would have been difficult to repair. We packed all the art pieces, including the damaged Rauschenberg, and stored them for eighteen months while the house underwent extensive repairs. During that time, Robert Rauschenberg visited our warehouse at Lear's request and, after examining the damage, asked me for glue, brushes, paper, and other supplies. He proceeded to spend a day repairing the painting.

Nearly two years later, Norman Lear's young personal assistant called and asked me to deliver and install his entire art collection at the house the following week. He was pushy and self-important, something I've often noticed with personal assistants, who channel the importance of their celebrity employers to give themselves the power to boss others around.

The afternoon before we were scheduled to deliver the art, I stopped by the house to assess the conditions there. Driving up the street, I saw dozens of work trucks parked for hundreds of feet on both sides. When I walked in, the house was buzzing with feverishly working painters, plumbers, door installers, electricians, and other tradespeople. I located the general contractor's onsite supervisor, who looked harried and stressed, and asked when the work would be done. Not for another week, he replied. Hearing this, I called Norman's assistant and strongly suggested we hold off on delivering the art to minimize the chances of it being exposed to damage or theft by workmen in the chaotic environment.

"Nonsense!" he said. "Do what I tell you to do. I told you to deliver and install Norman's art tomorrow, and I expect you to obey my instructions."

So, we followed his instructions, arriving the next day to hang the paintings, even though we had to work our way around and between the workmen who seemed to be everywhere. We were careful to have the personal assistant check our inventory and sign off that he had received all of the artwork, but the next morning, he called to tell me two paintings were missing. "What are you going to do about it?" he demanded. I replied that we had delivered every single work, and he had verified and signed for everything.

"Not true!" he argued. "I didn't agree to receive those missing pieces. Norman is holding you responsible."

Signed paperwork or not, Lear may have thought we really had lost his paintings. We didn't work for him again for another twenty years.

Ovitz

The same afternoon we evacuated the art from Norman Lear's residence, Michael Ovitz, the Hollywood mega-agent, called asking for immediate help at his house. We handled or stored all of his extensive art collections and couldn't refuse to help, although we were all tired and dealing with the damage at our own homes. I only had four hours of sleep, and nothing to eat, so I was running on fumes, but I went with my crew over to Ovitz's. We had installed all the art in the place, and our work was sound because it was all still intact, and nothing had fallen or was in danger. But likely thinking he dodged a bullet and might not come out of the next quake quite so well, Ovitz was intensely focused on taking down his entire collection. We went to work wrapping and removing dozens of paintings, and after hours of labor, we reached the end at 2 a.m. All that remained was a large, aluminum Frank Stella—a three-dimensional assemblage painting that hung in the dining room. I was numb with hunger and exhaustion and looking forward to going home when Ovitz asked me if I thought the Stella could remain hanging safely. We had installed it several years earlier, and for several long moments, my mind went blank, and I couldn't remember how it was attached to the wall.

Ovitz took my hesitation as a fatal shortcoming, and his reaction showed he no longer trusted me. From that point on, he hired installers from the J. Paul Getty Museum for his mount-making and technical installations. There was irony in this because the Getty routinely hired my employees, so he was using people who received much of their training and experience working for me.

In the early 2000s, he called and asked for a personal favor. He wanted me to pack up the art and antique collection of one of the partners at his agency, Creative Artists Associates. It was an emergency, he said. The partner's house sat on a Pacific Palisades bluff overlooking the Pacific, and the bluff was crumbling fast. Several neighboring properties had already collapsed and sat in heaps of rubble several hundred feet below. The partner's house was in danger of being condemned because it might do the same. When I arrived with trucks and a packing crew, the house seemed normal, except for a small crack in the foundation below the front door. It took more than a week to pack and remove the hundreds of antiques, paintings, and other artifacts inside. When I stopped by on the final day to check on my crew, I was shocked to see the house had already slid nearly five feet down the hill, and my packers were using an eight-foot stepladder to climb up and down from the street to the front door. Inside, the floors were twisting and tilting, and there were constant groaning and creaking sounds emanating from the floor and walls. I admired the courage and tenacity that let my employees stay on the job without complaining, but the situation was so clearly dangerous by then that I ordered everyone to grab their tools and evacuate immediately. There were still some collection pieces inside, and I told the partner we would remain to pack them if he would bring them out to us. I wasn't surprised when he refused. The next morning the house abruptly collapsed and slid in a pile of splintered rubble to the bottom of the hill.

After Ovitz received our invoice, he called to complain about how high it was. I don't think he ever understood how much danger he put us in or how much we had done to rescue his associate's art.

Guillotine

Two months after the Northridge quake, I received a call from a couple living in a West Hollywood condominium, who asked if I would come and look at a painting hanging unevenly on their wall. The company that had originally installed it wouldn't come back to work on it, they told me, and they hoped I could help. I wondered if they had stiffed the original company, but I agreed to meet them the next day.

They took me into their bedroom, where a large painting—about seven-feet-by-seven-feet and encased in a heavy Plexiglas frame—

was hung over the head of the bed. They didn't have a headboard, and the painting, which was directly above their pillows, was tilted, with one side drooping several inches lower than the other.

I walked next to the bed to look at it from the side but couldn't get close enough to see what was causing the problem. I asked if I could stand on the bed to lift the corner of the painting and examine the picture hangers. With their assent, I took off my shoes and climbed up, pulling the pillows away so I could stand directly under the painting. I reached up and barely touched it when suddenly it fell, almost guillotining my toes. Luckily, my reflexes were quick enough to let me grab ahold and keep it from trampolining off the bed and being damaged.

The painting was installed using two "bulldog" hooks, the kind that are attached by nails hammered into the drywall at a downward angle until the back of the hook is flush against the wall. The nail angle acts to counter the downward pull exerted by a painting's weight. But during the earthquake, which lasted forty-five seconds, the bouncing and swinging of the painting caused the nails to seesaw up and down, cutting through the drywall until the hooks were dangling. My slight touch was all it took for the nails to fall out of the wall and drop the painting. This couple had been sleeping for weeks underneath a booby trap, which at any moment could have killed or maimed them, and I had literally saved their lives. But instead of thanking me, they immediately focused on who was going to pay for reinstalling the painting. I had caused it to fall when I touched it, they said, and therefore it was my responsibility to re-hang it at my expense. I was stunned by their chutzpah. Never mind that I had come to look at the painting without charging or that I had risked my toes and pulled them out of harm's way. All they could think about was the money. When I told them I needed help to install it and would charge for the service, they ordered me to leave immediately. Let no good deed go unpunished.

Matches

Many elements can make a work of art dangerous—the materials used, the way it's installed, the thoughtless preferences of its keepers. All of those came into play when a young woman working for Ace Gallery phoned and asked me to pick up a life-size sculpture of a horse's head by artist David Mach. I was to deliver the sculpture to a high-rise building in Westwood and install it in the residence of the gallery's client, who wanted to live with it before deciding whether to buy it.

At the time, Ace Gallery was on the second floor of the historic art deco Desmond's Building on Wilshire Boulevard, several blocks east of LACMA and the adjacent tar pits. It was a tricky location to service. Reaching the gallery required climbing up a narrow flight of stairs or stepping into an ancient elevator piloted by an elderly man who had spent most of his life working inside it. The elevator lacked modern controls, so the door had to be closed by hand, and a second folding gate pulled across it. The operator turned a wheel until the elevator slowly moved up or down. The tiny cab could only hold a couple of people or very small art. Larger works had to be carried up or down the fire escape at the rear of the building. The fire escape's metal steps could be slippery, especially in wet weather, and the stairs were especially dangerous to navigate with a heavy or unwieldy painting or sculpture.

A curt young woman with blond hair met me at the Ace reception area and led me to one of the galleries. She pointed at the sculpture hanging on the wall, which I was surprised to see had been made by gluing together hundreds of matchsticks. The sculpture was of a horse's head in the style of the Hellenistic Elgin Marbles, and it was quite beautiful. The matchheads faced out, giving it a pixilated appearance, making it a sort of a pointillist sculpture. But these weren't safety matches. They were the old-fashioned wooden kind, which meant that one miscue, or a simple scrape or nick, could light the entire head on fire. Carrying it would be like carrying a live bomb. I carefully lifted the head off its hook, noting that the hanging hardware was too small to adequately hold its size and weight, and carried the piece toward the front entrance.

"Not that way!" the woman ordered, "The service entrance is over there." She pointed toward the fire escape and walked away, leaving me struggling to open the door. Because of its automatic closer, it resisted my efforts as I strained to push it open while holding the sculpture away from the doorjambs. To free my hand and turn the doorknob, I had to lift my knee underneath to help support the weight, which left me balancing on one leg. Finally, I managed to open the door and hop outside, and as soon as I did, the door slammed shut and locked, leaving me standing on a metal balcony. I needed both hands to carry the sculpture, so I couldn't hold onto the railing, and I descended cautiously, one stair at a time.

A few days after I installed the head in Westwood, the young woman called again, saying the sale hadn't gone through, and ordered me to return it to the gallery. This time I took the elevator and held the sculpture while the operator shrank against the wall, keeping as much distance from the matches as he could, his eyes never leaving them. The bossy blond woman, who was sitting behind the reception desk, didn't greet me. I could tell by her expression she wasn't happy to see I had used the forbidden route.

"Take it to the gallery and hang it back on the same hook," she ordered.

I carried the head into the gallery and carefully laid it on the floor. Testing the hook, I discovered it had begun to pull out of the wall. The nail was loose, making the installation very unsafe. Worse, it was only a five-pound picture hanger, and the head weighed at least twenty pounds. I headed down to my truck to get a larger hook, but as I walked past the reception desk, the woman stood up and said, "Where do you think you are going?" She wasn't satisfied when I told her. "Why can't you understand simple instructions?" she said. "What did I tell you to do? Go back and hang it on the same hook."

I tried to explain that the hook was precarious and would only take a few minutes to replace. "Do as I say," Her voice was rising, "I am not going to tell you again. Do it now!"

So, I went back to the gallery and hung the head on the wiggly hook while she followed and stood, hands-on-hips, glaring at me. I wrote on my bill of lading, "Signer refuses to allow replacing of the hook. Existing hook is unstable and dangerous." She signed without bothering to read it. It was a Friday.

On Tuesday, the gallery opened at 10 a.m., and at 10:15, I got a call from the blond. "The head fell off the wall and my boss, Douglas Chrismas, is holding you entirely responsible for the damage," she raged. I bit my tongue and said I was on my way over to look at it.

When I walked into the gallery, the head was gone. In its place was a scorched patch on the floor with a pile of twisted, charcoaled matchsticks littering the center. The bottom of the wall was also scorched, and the picture hanger, with the nail still attached, had fallen to the base of the wall. The blond looked deflated and avoided eye contact. But at least Ace Gallery hadn't burned down that time.

Nails

The art moving business comes with free season tickets to the theater of the absurd. It's filled with episodes like the angry phone call I got from the preparator of a New York gallery for whom we'd crated and shipped a valuable painting. The young man was so upset he was practically apoplectic. "I am so pissed off I can hardly breathe!" he fumed. "So absolutely pissed off. It's outrageous! How could you pack a painting like this? It's the worst crating job I have ever seen. You shouldn't be allowed to stay in business. You are morons! Total, idiot morons!"

I was taken aback by his vitriol and confused by what he was saying but fought the urge to go Irish on him and decided to be polite. "I'm sorry to hear you have encountered difficulties," I said. "Could you explain to me what the problem is with our packing, please?"

"It's nailed shut," he sobbed. "Why would you nail the crate shut? And it even has glue! I had to use a hammer and a crowbar to get the crate open, and the crowbar punched a hole in the painting! You people are totally responsible, and you need to notify your insurance company!"

This confused me. Why would one of my craters glue and nail a crate shut? I asked him where the crate was now.

"It's here on the floor right in front of me," he said.

I told him to turn the crate over and heard his receding footsteps, a grunt of exertion, the clunk of a crate on the floor, and footsteps returning to the phone.

"Okay, I turned it over, now what?" he said.

"What do you see?" I asked.

There was a long pause, and suddenly he screamed: "Screws! Oh my God screws! Never mind!"

Calder

Alexander Calder's mobiles are among the most beautiful sculptures ever created. Hanging from ceilings on thin wires, his pieces seem to float effortlessly in perfect balance, gracefully moving in the slightest breeze, their components dancing in harmony. He liberated sculpture by freeing it from gravity. Calder created these masterpieces by painstakingly balancing the varying weights of his metal cutout shapes and the lengths of rods connecting them. He married the rods using hooks and loops so they could freely pivot and would bend the thin steel rods to have them ride correctly. His process involved trial and error to find perfect balance points and rod lengths. Even the paint he used to coat the steel components could affect balance and had to be compensated for.

When handling or installing a Calder mobile, it is important to never disrupt its synergy. Accidentally bending the rods disrupts their action and could ruin the sculpture. It may not be obvious damage as scratching or chipping paint, but it is damage nonetheless, and once a metal piece has been distorted, it is very difficult to re-bend a wire or rod back into its original shape.

My client "Betty" seemed oblivious to this precise and careful balancing act when she scheduled me to install a Calder mobile. She and her husband owned a talent agency and lived in a Beverly Hills home with a large and important art collection. In the 1970s, many Los Angeles art collectors were the wives of rich and powerful men who seemed drawn to collecting as a means of enhancing their social currency and perhaps even finding meaning as they grew older. The wife could boast to her friends about what they paid for the art and which prominent gallery they purchased it from, and if the purchase was made in New York or London or Paris, all the better. The big auction houses, Sotheby's and Christie's, had great difficulty keeping showrooms in Los Angeles because many clients preferred the prestige of going to New York to bid in the art auctions there.

An art handler had to consider all the social dynamics whenever a newly purchased work of art arrived and needed installing. It was imperative to remember how significant this event was for the wife, who likely spent weeks anticipating the shipment's arrival from New York or Europe. Installation day was her opportunity to oversee the work involved and take credit for its success with her friends when they came to admire the important addition to the collection. Quite often, a party was arranged, with guests invited to view the new acquisition and witness the collector's wealth and connoisseurship. If the shipment arrived late, we were usually put under pressure to unpack and install it before the party began. This happens so regularly there is a saying in the art handling world: "More art gets damaged because of a party than any other way." When it comes to art, haste can definitely make waste—and parties are whirlwinds of haste.

I arrived at the house on the Beverly Hills flats with a ladder and tools and rang the doorbell. I could hear muffled chimes coming from inside. The door opened, and Betty greeted me curtly—an indication she felt it was never a good idea to get too friendly with the help who needed to know their place. The front door opened to a large atrium, and on one side, a wide staircase curved to the second floor.

Betty instructed me to unpack a shipping crate sitting by the wall and install the Calder above the stairwell. She left while I opened the crate and laid out the components. There were two ways to install the mobile. I could fully assemble it, then lift it as one piece and hang it. Or I could hang the central armature and attach the remaining arms. Because I didn't have any help that day, I decided on the latter method, which would make it easier to control the akimbo arms. I had brought a spool of thin aircraft cable and the ferrules I'd need to attach it from an eye in the ceiling. Aircraft cable, which has high tensile strength, is a stainless, flexible cable used to connect pilot controls to a small airplane's elevators and rudder. It is carefully tested to ensure it conforms to the stated tensile-strength specifications and comes in different diameters to carry different amounts of weight. Unlike copper wire or braided picture-hanging wire, it cannot be twisted around itself to form loops or attachments to the eyes on the backs of paintings. Rather, I'd use the ferrules to create loops. They're soft metal tubes with two parallel shafts. I'd thread my aircraft cable through one shaft and insert the free end in the second shaft to make a loop. I'd then use a pair of special pliers to crimp the ferrule, squeezing it tightly shut and making the loop permanent. I had purchased the perfect cable for the job and was certain Betty would be pleased. It was so thin that it wouldn't visually stand out and detract from the appearance of the mobile, but it was rated to hold one hundred pounds, beyond adequate for the Calder, which weighed less than fifteen.

When Betty returned, I opened my toolkit and removed the spool of aircraft cable to show her. "Oh no! No!" she exclaimed. "That will never do! I don't want to see anything hanging my beautiful Calder." She picked up her purse and pulled out a roll of clear monofilament. "The man at the fish store said I should use this. It's clear, and we won't see it." This was absurd. Even a clear "fish line" would still be visible. She thought she brilliantly figured out how to install a work of art worth several hundred thousand dollars by going to a fishing tackle shop to ask for an "invisible line." And a clerk who didn't know anything about art, except possibly reproduction prints of LeRoy Neiman paintings, was happy to make a sale. I'm sure he didn't know or care about the consequences of his advice. My heart sank as I realized I was stuck in a losing position. Betty had already made up her mind. If I tried to talk her out of it, she would interpret my actions as questioning her judgment and get upset. But if I hung the Calder on her "fish line," it would eventually fall, and I would get the blame. It could hang for months before the monofilament inevitably failed. And how often would I wake up in the middle of the night wondering when the phone was going to ring? I didn't even want to think about how the mobile could be damaged.

I examined the fishing line. It was clear nylon, and according to the label, it was eight-pound test, totally inadequate for the mobile's weight. Worse, fishing monofilament is designed to be elastic so it will stretch to absorb the shock of a fighting fish. The fishing pole also flexes, and the combination enables a skilled angler to play a fish weighing much more than the line's rating. But fishing line is not intended for static, dead loading, where the weight keeps the line continually under tension. The line will continue to stretch over time until it breaks. It will also degrade from exposure to UV. It was completely unsuitable for the job.

When I attempted to explain this to Betty, she became defensive and angry. "Why are you arguing with me? I'm paying you to follow my instructions. Just do what you are told." Famous—and ridiculously common—last words. I tried one more time to tactfully reason with her, but it only made her angrier, so I climbed up my ladder while she stood below, lips angrily pursed, hands-on-hips, and watched me. When I completed the installation, we stood back looking up at the mobile, admiring it while its arms gently rotated past each other in a rhythmic pirouette. It was a beautiful piece. Her hands returned to her hips as she turned and said: "I told you! Didn't I tell you my fish line would look . . ." At that moment, the line snapped, and the Calder plummeted straight down, bouncing off a step with the loud clanging of metal hitting metal and rolling end over end down the remaining stairs. As it moved, it looked like a discombobulated slinky toy. In an instant, even before it reached the bottom, Betty turned on me: "Didn't I tell you not to use the fish line? Why did you use it when you knew it was wrong? Didn't you listen to me? If my Calder is damaged, you are going to be 100 percent responsible!" She turned and stomped out of the room.

I was stunned by her sheer audacity. I was also amazed how quickly she thought to deflect blame from her own mistake, which showed what a hard-ass she was. Most collectors would have been down on their hands and knees in tears, inspecting the sculpture for potential damage. Not Betty.

With trepidation, I walked over to inspect the Calder. By some miracle, it was undamaged, probably because it had fallen on carpeted stairs, and I re-hung it using my aircraft cable. Betty didn't return to the room and instead sent her housekeeper to sign the paperwork and show me out the door. That was the last time I worked for Betty. Seeing me again would be a reminder of her mistake. Better to punish me for my impudence at being right.

Graham

In the early '80s, the sculptor Robert Graham was awarded a hefty commission to create a sculpture for the United Nations Plaza. It would be built from four hollow, bronze drums, each measuring forty inches diameter by sixty inches long and covered with figures of nude women and other symbols. Stacked on top of each other, the drums would be a modern-day Trajan's Column.

Bronze is the preferred metal alloy for many sculptors because it is easy to cast and takes on lustrous patina finishes. It is also weatherproof and long-lasting, and many bronze figures and artifacts go back centuries. I still think about the magnificent bronze horses overlooking San Marcos in Venice, Italy, which may date to Hellenistic Greece. The sculptures have since been moved into a museum and replaced with replicas, but in 1974, while they were still in situ, I climbed over a railing and onto their balcony to pat their butts and run my hands over their flanks. The artist had likely run his hands over them many times while creating them until satisfied with the contours and subtleties, and to touch them was to have the same experience. One of the privileges of being an art mover is getting to develop a tactile sense of an artist's genius, and I was always happy to have a chance to work with an artist like Graham, whose work we moved, installed—and touched—over many years.

We picked up the finished drums from Graham's Venice studio and had them packed in crates for a next-day airfreight shipment to New York. Graham's studio assistant, his cousin, called to say he was stopping by my shop to inspect our packing. He arrived just as we were closing for the day, carrying two large and heavy metal toolboxes he wanted us to include with the shipment. When I told him we would need to stay late to crate them and would charge overtime rates because the flight was leaving in the morning, he demanded we open the crates and proceeded to place his toolboxes inside two of the round drums.

This wasn't a good idea, I cautioned, because while bronze is sturdy, it's also soft and can easily be bent. But the cousin insisted, and he waited while we sealed the crates. The inevitable happened. A week later, Graham's office manager called to say he was extremely upset because the drums had arrived distorted and no longer fit together. She also said Graham would no longer be using our services and would send an invoice to repair the columns.

People tend to think about art being threatened by the ravages of war and nature, but it's human nature that so often does it in—the need to rush, the insistence on being right at all costs, and the everlasting desire to pinch a penny, save a dime.

Rain

When Herb Moskowitz, the chief registrar of the Metropolitan Museum of Art, asked me to return a small painting to a lender in Westwood, near UCLA, I immediately arranged a delivery date. But I later called to reschedule when I saw heavy rain in the forecast. This seemed reasonable and prudent, and I was surprised by the collector's strong response: "Certainly not! I do not want my painting to stay away a minute longer. Young man, I demand you return it promptly at 10 a.m. on the day we agreed to." I attempted to explain the obvious risks of transporting a painting in a rainstorm, but she took this as a challenge to her authority: "If you don't deliver my painting when I want it, I will complain to the Met!"

Indeed, it was pouring on the morning of the delivery, and fearing that it would be unsafe for both me and the painting to go out in the storm, I called again. The collector was unmoved. She furiously demanded I deliver her painting at once and accused me again of challenging her authority. So, I wrapped the painting in several layers of plastic and taped them shut. I drove the painting—a small, ornately framed Cezanne painting—to Westwood in our van. The rain was cascading in sheets, and the street was a flowing river when I arrived in front of her stately, single-story home. To make the delivery, I'd have to carry the package up a long cement walkway from the curb to her front door. Her front lawn was recently replanted, and the saturating rain had turned it into gumbo soup. Half an inch of ochre-colored mud and manure slurry flowed over the walkway, and ungerminated grass seeds floated in the muck while the heavy raindrops splashed several inches into the air. I sat inside the van, looking out at the scene. The painting was secure against the rain, but I wondered how wet my feet would get. Would my shoes be ruined? I had a rain jacket with a hood, but the intensity of rain guaranteed my pants would be soaked. It was tempting to turn back and cancel the delivery, but I knew the woman's reaction would be severe, and so I stepped outside, grabbed the painting, and gamely splashed through the slop to ring the doorbell. The door was opened by a middle-aged woman who stood in a living room carpeted wall to wall with a white Berber carpet, a very expensive one. I started to hand the painting over, but when she didn't respond, I realized she expected me to unwrap and re-hang it. She stood looking past me at my footprints on the muddy walkway, then down to my mud-covered shoes, and finally at the dripping wet plastic covering the painting.

"What were you thinking?" she roared. "Why would you deliver my precious painting in weather like this? You're responsible if the painting is damaged. Take it away immediately and deliver it when the weather is good!" She slammed the door in my face, and I slogged her valuable artwork back into the rain.

Martha

One of my longstanding clients was Walter Annenberg, the wealthy publisher, art collector, and philanthropist. Walter was a multi-billionaire in the 1980s when few in the world had amassed that kind of wealth—all the more impressive as a billion dollars in 1980 is worth over three times as much today. The Annenbergs hailed from Philadelphia and had strong ties with the Philadelphia Museum of Art, which coveted their stunning collection of Impressionist paintings, multiple Van Goghs, Monets, Cézannes, Renoirs, Picassos, and other influential works. The Metropolitan Museum also hoped—and lobbied—for a bequest.

In the late 1970s, the Annenbergs built an art-filled compound they called Sunny Lands on 600 acres along the edge of Rancho Mirage. Their home sat on top of an old sand dune with views over the Coachella Valley and nearby mountains and was surrounded by a private nine-hole golf course. The entrance to the property was through a manned gate strategically placed at the end of a long driveway, and guards with direct connections to federal government sources to check the IDs and criminal records of any visitors. A stone wall and electronic sensors sealed the perimeter, and security personnel riding in golf carts patrolled the grounds. The high levels of security and privacy, along with the beautiful golf course, made Sunny Lands an ideal destination for world leaders and VIPs—the

Nixons were friends, and other guests included Ronald and Nancy Reagan and Queen Elizabeth and Prince Charles.

The Annenbergs wintered in Rancho Mirage, returning to Philadelphia in early May to escape the desert heat. Before they came for their desert stay each fall, they would hire my company to take down and dust paintings as well as the sculptures. Their fifty-five-piece art collection remained in Sunny Lands year-round, and when paintings were loaned for exhibitions, we handled the shipping. Occasionally we rearranged art in the house or installed a recent purchase. And sometimes, if the Annenbergs were hosting an important visitor, we would install one or two of the Van Gogh paintings or other masterpieces in the guest bedrooms.

On one occasion, Herb Moskowitz of the Met contacted me to crate and transport the two Monet paintings going on loan to the Met—pond scenes from Monet's Giverny studio gardens, where he had also painted his famous *Lily Ponds*. The Met was a stickler for tradition, and the precious paintings would have to be packed using brown paper and a shredded wood called excelsior. This was a protocol that dated back to the 1930s, even though most museums were quickly turning to foam padding and plastic wrapping. The Met also wanted its crates lined with asphalt paper as a moisture barrier. It was a paper impregnated with petroleum, the same material used for paving roads and roofs, and was primarily used in construction as an underlayer for roof shingles and as a waterproof barrier under wood or stucco siding. It smelled like roofing tar and let off considerable gases, filling a sealed crate with fumes. It definitely was not archival material and had the potential to cause long-term damage to certain works of art. It pained me to use it with these works.

The Met also specified using it to bolster and pad paintings and sculptures inside crates. To make bolsters, we would have to roll the asphalt paper into long tubes and stuff them with excelsior, the way you'd roll tobacco to make a cigarette. Excelsior was awful to work with too. It was scrap wood that had been shredded into straw- or hay-like strands and compressed into large, heavy bales held together with baling wire. We'd have to cut the wires and pull slabs of excelsior off the bale, then tear apart the slabs to loosen and expand the material. It was a dusty, sneeze-inducing, eye-watering mess. The Met's rules called for us to lay stuffed tubes inside the crate and place a painting wrapped in brown paper—another Met-required material—on top, facing up. We'd then fold the tube over the frame to contain the painting and attach the crate lid. The last part of the Met's laborious process was to bolt the crate shut. We'd have to rout notches into the lip of an open crate every sixteen inches or so around the perimeter and attach threaded plates, then attach matching plates to the crate's lid. We'd insert 3/8-inch bolts through the plates to fasten the lid.

We were making the crates and preparing the tubes for packing at Sunny Lands when I ran out of bolts. These had to be made of high-quality steel to endure the torque strain applied by a wrench, so I generally chose American-made brands—but the clerks at the hardware store told me the bolts I liked had been breaking and advised me to purchase some made in Korea. The store was sold out of them, though, and so was every other hardware store in a fifty-mile radius.

I was stuck using the American bolts, and when we drove the crates down to Sunny Lands to meet Herb, I was apprehensive. We wrapped the two Monets, carried them outside to the patio where the crates were being staged, and packed them into the "cigarette" lined crates. Mr. and Mrs. Annenberg walked out and stood watching, something they'd never done before. I had many previous interactions with them, which usually involved changing the placement of art around the house, but they always left once the actual installation work began. I inserted the first bolt and was carefully tightening it when it snapped. The second one worked all right, but the third and fourth broke. At this point, my frustration and tension boiled up, and I blurted, "These darn American-made bolts!" Out of the corner of my eye, I saw Mr. Annenberg stiffen, and Herb, fast on his feet, said, "You mean those Korean-made bolts?"

"Oh yes! Sorry," I replied. "The only bolts we could find were these Korean ones, which are definitely not up to American quality." Mr. Annenberg smiled and nodded his head in agreement, and he and Mrs. Annenberg walked back into the house.

My company handled the Annenberg's entire collection in 2002 when it went on tour to the Philadelphia Museum of Art, the Met, and LACMA—the three top contenders to receive the works when the Annenbergs died. At the Annenberg's request, the Philadelphia Museum contracted with me for the packing and crating, as well as a climate-controlled trailer delivery to LAX. I was also asked to set up airfreight to Philadelphia and arrange an armed security escort. The museum sent a young assistant registrar, Martha, to oversee the project and condition report all the art over a two-week period. She called me the second day with measurements for each crate so we could build and deliver them on the following Monday and begin packing them for a Friday delivery to LAX for an overnight flight to Philadelphia. I set my craters to work and hired three off-duty Los Angeles police officers with two private cars to provide escort in front and back of the semi-trailer, plus one additional officer to ride in the tractor with the driver. I also booked pallet positions with American Airlines to ensure the shipment wouldn't get bumped.

My art handlers delivered the crates on Monday and began packing them. Late Thursday afternoon, Martha called in a panic to let me know she overlooked a painting and a sculpture, and could I please help her by getting those crates made and delivered on time? My craters worked late into the evening, and I drove the two crates out to Sunny Lands the next morning. When I arrived, I asked my crew where Martha was, and they pointed toward the swimming pool, where a skinny, blond woman in a bathing suit was lying in the sun. My guys said she spent most of her time out there while they were inside packing the crates.

We completed the packing and loading of the trailer around sunset with adequate time to get to American's airfreight before its cutoff. My security cops arrived right on time, and I began to relax as I gave them and the trailer driver instructions. But suddenly, a blood-curdling scream came from the other side of the truck. It was followed by more screams in rapid succession, and I thought Martha had been severely injured, perhaps getting her foot caught in the lift-gate. I ran around the truck and found her standing there. She stared at me with an unhinged look in her eyes, and although I was only three feet away, she continued screaming at the top of her lungs. I waited for her to calm down and found out she was upset because she would be riding to the airport with one of the security officers and didn't like the size of his car. She demanded a larger one, preferably a limousine, and said she wasn't moving until I got it for her.

I went into the house to ask the Annenbergs' house manager if there was any place in the valley where I could rent a large car or book a limousine. The manager said she wasn't surprised by the outburst because Martha spent most of her time on the project lounging around the pool while the Annenberg staff waited on her. The manager had worked for years with the Annenbergs, and I knew from the aggravated tone of her voice that she would probably give them an earful about Martha. She began calling car rental places and limousine services in Palm Springs, but it was Friday evening, and nothing was open. I went back outside and pleaded with Martha to either go with one of the officers or ride in the truck, which had large seats and plenty of room. She stubbornly refused, standing with her arms folded and giving me hostile looks.

We were running out of time, and if we didn't leave promptly, a billion dollars' worth of masterpiece-quality art would be stranded for three days until we could put it on a Monday evening flight. So, I let Martha know we were going—with or without her—and told the driver and security guards to head out. One of the cops opened his passenger door, and after giving me a withering look, the petulant junior registrar climbed in, and the shipment left for a safe flight to Philadelphia. A year later, Annenberg announced he was bequeathing his collection to the Metropolitan Museum. The Met sent Herb Moskowitz, their erudite, highly professional head of collections, to oversee and assist when we packed the two Monet Lilly Pond paintings, and I watched the way he had charmed the Annenbergs. They were fastidious about protocol and highly protective of their beloved collection. I'm sure they were less than impressed when the Philadelphia Museum not only put a junior staffer in charge of their entire collection but chose one who placed their precious art at risk.

My guess is Martha's behavior helped steer the bequest of those treasures. There may have been other factors in play, but I'm willing to bet she shifted the balance toward the Met while she focused on her tan and limousine.

Clocks

In the art moving business, we routinely work with clients around the world and must understand the customs and sensibilities of many different cultures to avoid inadvertently offending someone. I learned much about doing business with the Japanese from my client Kaz, who oversaw art shipping transactions for the Los Angeles branch of an enormous shipping conglomerate headquartered in Tokyo. I recognized his accented voice on the phone one afternoon when he greeted me as "Mr. Bryan" and asked me to meet him the next day at their offices near the Los Angeles Airport. "Please be here at 8 a.m.," he said. "Very, very, important, Mr. Bryan!" He hung up without further explanation.

In business dealings with the Japanese, I found it was often necessary to read between the lines. Americans are used to being straightforward and blunt, whereas Asian cultures are often more oblique and less direct as a matter of politeness. My dealings with Kaz came during the 1980s when Japan was riding high in the world with a strong economy and lots of money to spend. Politeness was always mandatory on both sides, but I noticed subtle shows of superiority over the Americans had also become the norm. Japan suffered many years of humiliation and poverty after World War II, but it had risen from ashes and rebuilt and now had a vibrant economy. There was a strong sense of resurgent nationalistic pride, particularly in having surpassed the United States in many ways.

Traffic was terrible as I drove to LAX the next morning, and I tried to tamp down my anxiety level because it was almost eight when I finally got off the freeway near the company. After my long, slow drive, I desperately needed to consider food and bathroom options. If I drove around looking for a gas station, it could make me late. I wondered if Kaz would consider it an affront if I asked to use the company's toilets before our meeting started. And if I were late, would it be considered even more ill-mannered to cause a further delay by using the urinal? By luck, I saw a McDonald's and pulled into the parking lot. Using their restroom solved one problem, but it was three minutes to eight, and I didn't have time to pick up an egg McMuffin to solve the other. At Kaz's, I parked in the lot where a sign said "Visitors Only" and walked quickly toward the office entrance. A gray passenger van was parked at the curb in front, and standing next to it were five middle-aged Japanese men dressed in suits. I was wearing slacks and a shirt and began to worry I was underdressed. As I walked past the men, I heard a voice call out my name. "Mr. Bryan, please come with us." Kaz walked toward me and gestured to the sliding door on the side of the van. "Please be seated."

He looked me in the eye, but the other four looked past me, and I waited, showing good manners by letting them climb inside first, while also ensuring that I could sit next to the sliding side door. Being close to an exit door is smart when flying in a plane or sitting in a theater, and especially when being driven by someone unknown.

As the men climbed into the van, they took off their suit coats and neatly folded them across their laps, doing this in such close sequence that their actions appeared to have been choreographed.

The van left the parking lot with Kaz driving, and the men began talking to each other in rapid-fire Japanese, laughing at some humorous point. We entered the 405 freeway heading south, and after a few miles, all five men pulled packs of cigarettes from pockets. There was a show of politely insisting the others accept one of theirs, and once each had a cigarette, they took turns lighting their neighbors'. All talk ceased as they took deep pulls and exhaled against the ceiling. It was cool outside, so the van windows were closed, and soon the interior was enveloped in a blue haze. It occurred to me that if I could see their exhaled smoke, I was also seeing their breath. How many germs would be in that breath? Did cigarette smoke kill germs? What were the odds that at least one of the five men had an infectious malady of some kind? My sinuses were becoming congested, and my eyes began watering.

My mother had smoked when I was a kid living back east. During winter, with the car windows rolled up, the heater on, and snow blowing outside, her second-hand smoke was unbearable. Inevitably I would become carsick, green, and miserable. I didn't like this situation much better. At least I had taken that pee, or I would have been in real trouble.

Our two-and-a-half-hour drive took us to San Diego, where we left the freeway and entered a hilly residential area. Kaz parked the van near a corner, and we piled out onto the sidewalk. I had spent the trip tamping down queasiness and was ecstatic to breathe fresh air again.

Forty narrow, concrete stairs led from the street corner to a modest, two-story house on the hill above us. The five men began climbing up in single file, with me in the rear, and the first one up rang the doorbell. We waited for several minutes and rang again. After several more minutes passed, I became impatient and squeezed past the men to reach the door, where I pounded my fist hard. That got results. Moments later, a balding man in his 60s yanked the door open. He was wearing a sleeveless T-shirt and hadn't shaved in several days. Though my sinuses were still congested from the ride, I caught a whiff of sweat and booze. He briefly glanced at me and then focused on the Japanese contingent on the stairs. A cunning, avaricious grin spread across his face, and he stood aside: "Welcome! You all come on in!"

With no room to step aside, I walked into the living room ahead of my Japanese clients, and as soon as I entered, I realized why no one had heard the doorbell. The walls, fireplace mantle, end tables, and bookshelves were all covered by clocks. Grandfather clocks stood everywhere. The wall next to the stairs going up to the second floor had more clocks. There were at least 200 of them, and the tick-tock racket was nearly unbearable. For occasional moments there was an odd effect when all the ticking sounds seemed to sync in harmony before descending back into cacophony. Anyone living in this noisy environment had to be either insane or drinking heavily to keep their sanity.

The owner took an open spot on one side of the living room next to a grandfather clock, while the five Japanese men clumped together on the opposite side, arms folded and hands shoved under their armpits. This was likely intended to avoid having to shake hands with the owner, whose hygiene appeared questionable. I was in the middle.

Kaz came over and, in a low voice, instructed me to tell the owner that the management team was honored to visit his home. I delivered this message, and I returned to Kaz, who told me to offer $7,500 for all of the clocks. I then realized I would be doing the negotiating while the Japanese watched and listened to the owner's replies. I had seen this tactic before, where counterparts in the negotiations would have to carefully explain their position to the interpreter, who in turn would repeat it in Japanese. The Japanese men understood English, but this tactic would give them time to formulate a response. It would also keep the clock owner off balance because he was being forced to negotiate through an intermediary.

I walked over to the owner, and when I told him the $7,500 figure, he gestured emphatically around the room with a sweep of his arm: "Bullshit!" he fumed. "That's only pennies on the dollar. These damn clocks are worth a hell of a lot more than a measly $7,500!"

I went to the other side of the room to consult with Kaz, who in turn began speaking with the others. This took five minutes, after which I was sent back with a "very generous" $10,000 offer.

Each time an offer was rejected, my Japanese clients took longer to discuss it. And you didn't have to speak the language to understand what was going on. They "argued," and one would hold out, scowling and making it clear he wasn't going to spend another dime of their company's money. The others would appear to plead with him, gesturing toward the clocks and speaking in urgent Japanese. I figured this was an intentional delaying tactic to wear the owner down. There weren't enough chairs, and the room was crowded, so none of us were sitting, and as the negotiations progressed, the owner was beginning to look tired. Maybe he needed a beer? On the other side, I wondered how badly nicotine cravings were affecting the Japanese men. Who was going to give in first?

As I presented the fifth offer, all the clocks interrupted, announcing the noon hour. Cuckoo clocks, Big Ben bongs, chimes, and more rang out in a deafening racket. This cacophony may have marked a planned event because suddenly, a door at the top of the stairs flew open with a crash, and a heavy-set woman dressed in a pink bathrobe, worn slippers, and a plastic shower cap appeared in the opening and looked down at us. She had a cigarette sticking out the corner of her lips and was carrying a Colt .45 automatic pistol in her right hand. She stood at the head of the stairs and began waving the pistol in the air while screaming at the top of her lungs: "Japs! Dirty Japs! Stinking dirty Japs! I'll kill you, you Goddamn fucking Japs! Get out of my house! Get your fucking yellow Jap asses out of my house! I'll kill all of you Jap bastards!"

Startled by this onslaught, the Japanese men stood staring up at the specter, momentarily immobilized and wide-eyed, before bolting toward the front entrance door. They collided with each other in their haste to leave—good manners vanished. The scene was so ludicrous, I stayed behind to see what would happen next. I wasn't a "dirty Jap" so she wouldn't shoot me, would she?

The owner started yelling at the woman. "Go back to your room now! Put that fucking gun away before someone gets hurt. I'm conducting important business here, so stop interfering! Get back to your room!" He clenched his fists and aggressively started up the stairs, causing her to shrink back with a look of fear in her eyes. I wondered what the dynamic was between them. Was she nuts? Did he control her with beatings and other intimidation?

There was a lock on the upstairs door, and he turned it before returning to talk to me. "Sorry about that," he said. "My wife was a Navy nurse in World War II and had to treat Navy and Marines for wounds and burns. She hates Japs and goes crazy at the sight of them. I should have locked her in before they got here. I really need to sell her clocks because we need the money. Please ask your buddies to come back here so we can come to an agreement."

That explained the woman's bizarre behavior, but not why she had access to a gun. I wondered if this was a tactic by the owner to intimidate the Japanese men and if he was really smart enough to work a scam like that. I was also unsure about his mental state—the clocks could have driven him over the edge. I decided it would be better to not ask about the gun.

I walked out the front door and looked down at the five men who were staring up at me from the sidewalk, wild-eyed and taking deep drags on their cigarettes to calm their nerves. They appeared ready to run at any moment. I walked down the stairs and attempted to calm them, but they refused to go back to the house, and the owner wouldn't come down to meet them, telling me it would be construed as a sign of weakness.

So, I went up and down the stairs between them, making multiple trips with offers and counteroffers over prices and inventory. My knees were quaking with exhaustion by the time they finally reached a deal. One last trip up the stairs with a contract for signatures, and we were finally finished.

We piled back into the van heading north out of San Diego, and when we left the freeway at Encinitas, I hoped it was for lunch. Did they know a Japanese restaurant in the area? Hunger was driving me to visualize plates of delicious sushi and sashimi and bowls of steaming noodles.

To my disappointment, we parked in front of an antiques store, which like our first destination, was full of clocks. I became the front man again, but this time the negotiations were on a per-clock basis. The Japanese men would make a show of carefully inspecting each one, discuss it amongst themselves, and make an offer. The shop owner would haggle back, insisting their price was too low and that he had paid far more for such a rare clock. Eventually, there would be an agreement, but the process took several hours, and it was late afternoon before we left.

We merged into heavy rush hour traffic on the 405, and cigarettes lit up. Once again, the Japanese men talked with each other, leaving me out of it. I gloomily watched with burning eyes as the sun began lowering to the west. I couldn't tell if the orb's reddish hue was natural or caused by the cigarette haze.

There was one more round of buying to go. We pulled off the freeway and drove down through Laguna Canyon into Laguna Beach, stopping at a store whose owner had stayed past her closing hour. Thankfully, she only had eight clocks, and the negotiating tactics became politer, with each too-low offer accompanied by apologies.

"Mr. Bryan, please tell her that we are very sorry for such a low price. Our bosses force us to offer so little, and our hands are tied in this matter." Was it because she was a woman? Or because she turned out to be a very adept and hard-nosed negotiator?

"I am not interested in giving my clocks away," she said after one offer, looking angrily at me. "You are insulting me with that puny amount. These clocks are masterpieces and worth a hell of a lot more than the pittance you're offering!"

By the time the Laguna clock purchases were finalized, the amounts paid for each of them were definitely higher than those given to the other sellers.

Several hours later, we arrived back at the Nippon offices. I was exhausted. It was almost 10 p.m., and we had been gone fourteen hours without eating. Unlike so many other clients who expected me to work under punishing conditions, the Japanese men endured them with me. I still wonder: Were they superhuman? Did smoking cigarettes quell the pangs of hunger? Probably not because I had been breathing copious volumes of their second-hand smoke, and my stomach was agonizing for food. I also realized not one of them had gone to the bathroom on the entire trip. Iron bladders, for sure.

Raids, Repatriations, and Shady Dealings

Nataraja

ART HANDLING CAN PUT US in the center of sensitive dealings with foreign governments and shipping agents when art is stolen or ill-gotten and sent back to its rightful owner. Or if a smuggling ring is broken and works need to be moved for repair, return, or safekeeping.

It might seem that governments would be ideal clients—with access to the public purse and the authority to enforce their own rules. But working with the local embassies and consulates who generally handle the details can be sticky. For instance, they enjoy diplomatic immunity, which can embolden them to avoid paying their bills.

I learned about that particular pitfall when I did a sizeable crating project for the Korean consulate in Los Angeles, which agreed to pay us before delivering their cargo to LAX. After we finished the packing, a contingent of thugs showed up at our shop and tried to seize the crates without giving us a check. We locked the doors to keep them out while they milled around outside for over an hour, yelling in Korean and pounding the door before they finally left. By holding firm, we did get our money, and since then, I've generally asked to be paid in advance by government clients. But there's no way to plan for the political shenanigans and complications that can arise when art, politics, and commerce overlap.

I walked into the middle of a political tangle in 1986 when I received a call from Andrea Clark, the head registrar at the Norton Simon Museum, asking me to assist with returning an artwork to India. The work was *Nataraja*, the bronze masterwork that had been the linchpin of a deal made with the Indian government a decade before. Simon had built a prime collection of Indian works, many of them, including *Nataraja*, shipped to him from out of the country under dubious circumstances. *Nataraja*, a graceful work depicting the Hindu god of creation and destruction, was a particularly prized piece. Simon had cannily brokered an arrangement that let him keep the rest of the items in his sketchily acquired Indian collection if he would send that single precious sculpture back after ten years. The time had come to give it up, and Clark said the Indian government would be contacting me to make the arrangements for repatriation. Payment, she said, would come from them.

Several days later, I received a call from the Indian consul general in San Francisco. He introduced himself as Kumar, and as he began asking questions, it became apparent he was worried that my loyalty to the Norton Simon would interfere with the safe shipping and return of the sculpture. It took me twenty minutes to persuade him I would serve his needs in good faith, and at last, he set a date and time for us to meet at the museum. He said there would be paperwork to sign, and then I could take the sculpture back to my warehouse for crating. Before hanging up, he also asked me to hire security guards from Pinkerton to escort the sculpture. This request gave me pause. I had hired Pinkerton previously to escort a high-value painting to LAX for an international shipment, and the guard they sent didn't speak English. He arrived disheveled, his uniform shirt hanging cockeyed because the buttons were in the wrong holes, and a Pinkerton sergeant who came to brief him rebuttoned the shirt, much as a parent would straighten their child's attire. When the sergeant asked the guard where his firearm was, the guard shrugged his shoulders and gestured that he didn't have one. It did not inspire confidence to see the sergeant hand his own police-issued .38 caliber revolver to the bewildered-looking guard and then use hand gestures to pantomime proper use of the gun. The sergeant wished me a sarcastic "good luck!" as he left, and I drove to the airfreight terminal with the guard riding in the passenger seat next to me. The entire way there, he held the gun in his lap, the barrel pointed toward my chest and played with it. I hoped to see a little more competence from Pinkerton this time.

At the appointed day and time, I checked in with security at the Norton Simon and stationed a Pinkerton guard on each side of *Nataraja* with instructions that no one be allowed to touch it without my okay. A few minutes later, Kumar arrived wearing a dark suit and conservative tie. He introduced the man who accompanied him—and dressed similarly—as the Indian ambassador from their embassy in Washington. Four large, bearded, turban-wearing Sikhs followed and stood looking down disdainfully on the Pinkertons before surrounding them and the sculpture. The Pinkerton guards, for their part, seemed very uneasy.

Kumar glanced around nervously and, in a low voice, asked, "Do you think Norton Simon will release the sculpture to us?" I assured him Simon was a man of his word. But it was worrisome that no one from the museum was on hand to greet us. Considering the Indian ambassador was standing in the lobby, it would have been good manners to have someone welcome him. I figured Simon was violating protocol to keep the Indians off-balance in any final negotiations.

Forty-five minutes passed before a secretary arrived to escort the two diplomats to the museum offices. More time went by, and

I wondered if the deal was falling apart. I was also becoming concerned that we wouldn't have enough time to pack and crate the sculpture back at my warehouse. We were scheduled to deliver it mid-morning the next day for an outbound flight. Three more hours passed before Kumar and the ambassador emerged from the office, looking relieved and carrying a folder of documents. They instructed me to quickly move the sculpture to my truck, and we drove it back to my warehouse.

The sculpture was visible inside a partially finished crate sitting on the shop floor at 5 p.m. when my craters and office staff departed for the day, and I began shutting down the warehouse and offices. I told Kumar and the ambassador that I needed to turn on the alarm system and would walk them out and see them at eight the next morning.

"We are not leaving," Kumar insisted.

I told him I couldn't turn on the alarm if they remained inside, but he refused to budge, so I called the alarm company to let them know the system would be off for the night. I locked the front door and rolled down a steel door in front of it, leaving both men locked in with *Nataraja* for the night.

Around 3 a.m., an officer from our security patrol service called my house, freaking out. "Mr. Cooke, there are a bunch of weird-looking guys wearing turbans sitting in front of your warehouse! It looks like they're casing the place! What do you want me to do? Should I call the cops for backup?" I assured him it was okay, and I knew they were there.

I arrived early the next morning with coffee and pastries and found the Indian consul general and ambassador asleep on the concrete floor, lying on each side of *Nataraja*. Their suit jackets were folded to make pillows, and they were curled in fetal poses. Sleeping amidst the sawdust on the floor of my shop were men who had attended functions at the White House and talked with the president of the United States. They looked cold and uncomfortable.

As I stood over them, I realized how worried they had been that Simon would steal the *Nataraja* back. Perhaps they even feared I would allow him to come and remove it in the dead of night.

My crew finished packing the crate, and I drove it to Indian Airlines at LAX with Kumar sitting beside me. We followed the ambassador's black limousine, with diplomatic plates and Indian flags fluttering on each fender. A car with the four Sikhs was tucked in close behind my truck. We must have made quite a scene because the neighboring drivers stared as we went by. But a little fanfare was fitting. The sculpture would finally be returned to its home, a temple in Sivapuram in southern India.

Moche

As Norton Simon had shrewdly deduced, there is substantial value in acquiring art and artifacts from archaeological sites—if it can be done within the bounds of the law. On the other hand, there is a substantial risk of prosecution if it's done illegally, which it often is. In the late 1980s, I became involved with recovering Moche cultural artifacts, pre-Columbian objects stolen from the Sipán archaeological site in Peru. Discovered in 1987 during a UCLA-sponsored exploration, Sipán is considered one of the most important discoveries of pre-Columbian archaeology. Almost from the beginning, the site was systematically looted, with important artifacts finding their way into underground trafficking networks.

US investigators learned that one of the major trafficking participants was David Swetnam, an antiquities dealer based in Santa Barbara, California. Swetnam provided the financing his partner in Peru, Fred Drew, used to purchase the Sipán objects. They smuggled many of the larger artifacts into the United States by disguising them with coatings of clay to mimic low-fired clay tourist curios, stamping the bottoms with *"Hecho en Bolivia"*—made in Bolivia. News reports and court documents later revealed that those pieces were sent from Peru through Bolivia and then shipped to Vancouver, Canada, where they were carried across the border into the US. Other shipments were sent through London, brought by a smuggler named Michael Kelly. Kelly's cover story was that the objects belonged to his recently deceased father, who collected them while traveling in South America in the 1920s. It was a particularly useful fiction because objects collected that far back were exempt from later international treaties intended to curb illicit trafficking in artifacts.

Many of Swetnam's clients were in Southern California, and an important group of eighty Sipán artifacts, many of them gold and jade jewelry, arrived at LAX in a footlocker. The shipment cleared Customs as personal effects and was taken by Swetnam and Kelly to the home of a third member of the team, Ben Johnson, who lived in Santa Monica. By coincidence, Johnson's house was just a block from mine. I also knew him from his tenure as chief conservator at the Los Angeles County Museum of Art. Johnson, an expert authenticator of pre-Columbian artifacts, verified the Swetnam haul and allegedly purchased several pieces for his own extensive collection. The remainder went to Santa Barbara with Swetnam, where he sold additional items to other collectors in the area, with some ending up in the Santa Barbara Museum of Art.

Subsequently, Michael Kelly got cold feet and confessed to United States Customs. In exchange for immunity, he agreed to be an informant and assist in identifying the other perpetrators and stolen objects. Customs officials planned a raid on the Swetnam operation, and in March of 1988, they contacted me, wanting to hire Cooke's Crating to assist with the packing and inventory of the objects being seized in the raids. We were to hold the objects in our art storage warehouse until criminal trials concluded and the court determined the rightful owner of the artifacts.

In late March, my employees and I drove to Oxnard, forty miles south of Santa Barbara, for an 8 a.m. planning and strategy meeting. It was hosted by US Customs but also included DEA agents and the Santa Barbara County Sheriff's Department. Oddly, Santa Barbara city police were not on hand, perhaps in an effort to keep the operation secret from the local press.

We made our way to the federal offices on an upper floor of the only skyscraper in Oxnard—a small, scruffy farming town in a prominent strawberry growing area just inland from the Pacific. Chalkboards and lectern were set up at the front of our meeting room, and since the twenty-four available seats were already taken by men in uniforms, my crew of six and I lined up along a sidewall. The DEA and Customs agents wore Kevlar vests and carried sidearms, the sheriffs' personnel were in khaki uniforms with green jackets, and my team stuck out in our blue jeans and an assortment of shirts, T-shirts, and denim jackets.

A federal agent in a suit and tie started the briefing by outlining the crimes committed and describing the individuals and locations being raided. The first target would be a conservation studio in downtown Santa Barbara, where David Swetnam and his wife were removing the clay coatings used to disguise the artifacts. Once the Swetnams were arrested and the central target secured, the agents were to divide into two groups and simultaneously raid the residences of two Santa Barbara collectors, as well as the Santa Barbara Museum. The agent emphasized to the sheriffs that they couldn't use their radios because, in a small city like Santa Barbara, word could get out to the collectors, who might hide or remove their artifacts.

He was beginning to discuss the arrest warrants when his eyes focused on us. "Who the hell are you guys? What are you doing here?"

All the heads in the room swiveled toward us, and I tried to stay cool under the sudden scrutiny by twenty-four law enforcement officers. I started to explain that we had been hired to pack the seized objects, but before I could finish, he ordered: "Take your asses outside and wait!" We hastily retreated into the hallway.

Half an hour later, we were driving our three trucks behind a phalanx of black sedans and sheriffs' cars heading north to Santa Barbara. The entire group arrived in front of a small commercial building, and the sheriffs closed off the street while a dozen customs agents walked in the front door and arrested the Swetnams, who were perp-walked out the front door in handcuffs and taken away in a sheriff's car.

I stepped into a pristine, professional laboratory equipped with white cabinets, magnifying instruments on extension arms, and trays of tools. Sitting on tables and shelves lining a wall were several dozen large figures and pots, some of which were restored to original condition, with others beginning to appear from under their camouflaged layers of low-fired clay. I turned one over and read, "*Hecho en Bolivia.*"

The head agent told me his team needed time to photograph and catalog the lab for evidence and asked me to divide my crew into two groups. One was to follow several agents to a large estate in Montecito owned by a retired banker, while the second contingent was to raid the Santa Barbara Museum of Art. After that, a small, Victorian house in downtown Santa Barbara where a large number of artifacts were believed to be located.

I went with one of my trucks to the museum, where we removed a small group of artifacts. Then we drove to the Victorian, situated on a residential street corner. It was a sweet little house with pale yellow clapboard siding and blue trim, and its wooden stairs led up to a wooden porch and a paneled front door with etched glass panes. The agents rang the bell, and a wide-eyed, elderly man in rumpled slacks, a floppy T-shirt, and slippers answered. He looked confused and frightened. They arrested him and his partner, another elderly man, and sat them on the front steps in plain sight wearing handcuffs. Many of the neighbors came outside to see what the commotion was about, staring incredulously at the two bedraggled old guys, who must have been deeply embarrassed. Four agents went into the house and for the next hour searched it without finding anything.

While waiting for something to do, I sat on a couch in the small living room next to the front entrance hall. The room was full of clutter, with newspapers, magazines, and McDonald's wrappers piled on the coffee table, on the chairs, and on the floor. I riffled through the pile on the couch next to where I was sitting and finding an out-of-date *Time* magazine, I began turning the pages. Suddenly a large, gold ornament fell into my lap. I looked through more trash and discovered a gold figurine underneath a grease-stained McDonald's bag containing mummified french fries. I went to show one of the agents what I'd found.

After a brief meeting, four agents went up to the master bedroom and took everything out, leaving the room and closets bare. They closely examined each piece they removed and tossed every "clean" item back into the bedroom. The floor piled up with dresser drawers, clothes from the closet, bed linens, and shoes. They repeated this process room by room, carrying large pieces of furniture into the master bedroom, along with trash cans full of filtered clutter or kitchen goods. When they finished, the entire house had been emptied into the master bedroom, which was stuffed floor to ceiling with furniture, household goods, and enormous piles of trash. If the old guys got out of jail, they would be spending many days digging out that room. What they wouldn't find was the sizable haul of artifacts, many of them gold ornaments that the agents had removed from their hiding places.

I carefully cataloged the contraband, placing the smallest gold jewelry and gold artifacts in a large zip-sealed bag. While I was still inventorying, one of the Customs agents walked up and asked for the bag, saying he needed to take it for an "evidence check." I had already listed the contents on my inventory and was reluctant to let him take it because I would be responsible if it went missing. But he insisted, and I lacked the authority to refuse. As the day wore on, I became anxious about getting it back, and my concern intensified as darkness fell and the agents began finishing up. The bag of gold items still had not been returned.

"Where is the bag of gold the Customs agent took? I need it back immediately," I started yelling. "We can't leave until I get it, and I won't sign any custody receipts without it!" There weren't many streetlights nearby, and the area was dimly lit and gloomy, but from the corner of my eye, I saw a figure dart out from behind our truck, staying in the shadows while running down the street. I walked behind the truck and found the full plastic bag sitting on the liftgate. This pissed me off because a dishonest officer tried to damage my reputation and career to enrich himself. I was glad, at least, that he hadn't gotten away with it.

We held the Sipán objects in our warehouse under a US government contract for a year. We were then instructed to crate and ship them back to Lima, Peru, with me accompanying the goods and assisting with unpacking the objects, and verifying they had all arrived in good condition. With Peru still under siege from the murderous Shining Path Communist guerrilla movement and a virtual police state, it was a riskier than usual assignment. In Lima, I saw few Americans and felt conspicuous wherever I ventured. All over the city, businesses were surrounded by twenty-foot steel or concrete walls and even higher guard towers made from five-foot-diameter concrete storm drain pipes buried in eight feet of dirt to keep them standing upright. The towers overlooked parking lots, restaurants, and even private residences. In each one, an entry hole was cut at ground level and a ladder placed inside for access to a platform at the top, where guards carrying AK-47s sat in front of gun slots that gave them views of the property they protected. At night you would see a red glow up in a gun slot as a guard inside pulled on his cigarette.

Peru was economically depleted and short on resources. The government had forbidden the importing of paper products, apparently hoping the shortages would foster the building of domestic paper mills in the Amazon region of the east side of Peru. But the strategy meant there was no fax paper in Peru—at a time when faxes were central to communication—so the company receiving the Sipán crates asked me to smuggle some in for them. There was a certain irony involved in transporting illicit goods inside a government shipment that was returning other smuggled goods, but I sent a couple of cases of fax paper. The recipients were so grateful that they offered an employee, Nancy Leigh, to drive me out of Lima to visit some archaeological dig sites in her old, beat-up Volkswagen bug. She insisted I ride in the back seat. We had an enjoyable day, and in the late afternoon, we headed back to Lima, driving along a wide boulevard bordered on each side by identical stone walls that stood around six feet high and stretched ahead for several miles. There was no other traffic as cars were scarce and expensive, and not many of them were on the roads.

As we started down this long stretch, I saw that someone had flattened out a cardboard box to make a sign and taped it to one of the walls. An arrow drawn in black marker pointed back the way we had come. I thought this was strange until a hundred yards ahead, three guys dressed in black uniforms and ski masks jumped over the wall and aimed AK-47s loaded with banana clips at our car. Nancy urgently whispered, "Police! Don't say a word or do anything. Just sit quietly and let me do the talking."

The three advanced toward our car, still pointing the rifles at the windshield, and stopped ten feet away, yelling in Spanish that we were driving the wrong way. Nancy bravely answered back, and three sets of wolfish eyes focused on me in the back seat. More angry Spanish flew, and I understood enough to know they were asking about the "gringo" she was driving. Nancy said something about a US government official and hearing that they stepped back and consulted with each other. One walked up to Nancy's window, lowering his head to get a closer look at me as she urgently told him, "No!" She handed over her purse to distract him, and he took it back to the others. They rifled through it, taking money and coins before he walked back and contemptuously tossed it through the open window at me. Then they jumped over the fence and disappeared. Nancy was nearly in tears as we drove away.

When we got back to Lima, we realized how narrow our escape had been. We learned that the curator who had planned to join us at one of the sites we visited—but never showed up—had been assassinated by the Shining Path on his way to meet us. We calmed ourselves, and I tried to give Nancy money to cover her losses because I knew she was struggling, but she adamantly refused. Thirty years later, I would see Nancy and her daughter at conferences. I was happy to learn that the two of them owned an art moving business in Peru.

Ace

There is an element of danger that makes court-ordered raids and seizures fun and exciting for us—whether we were there to recover stolen art as a thief was being arrested or helping a court seize items from the losing party in a civil suit. As in the Swetnam raid, our involvement usually began with a phone call from a superior court clerk or a government agency asking if I would be willing to send art handlers and a truck to inventory and pack the art being seized. They'd ask me to be discreet because they didn't want their targets to have advance warning and time to hide the art, and they'd always assure me there wouldn't be any danger to my employees.

The operations generally followed the same script. My truck and employees were ordered to meet with law enforcement officers at a discreet location near the target address. When we arrived, the cops would give us a suspicious stink eye, because most art handlers tend to be scruffy artists and musicians. They'd reluctantly give us instructions to wait for a signal that court papers had been served or the crook arrested before driving to the site. Then, they'd repeat the instructions, an indication that they didn't trust us to follow orders. At the site, we'd find a dejected individual in handcuffs or an angry collector or art dealer about to lose a valuable asset.

I participated in several raids on Ace Gallery in Los Angeles in the 1980s. The first raid, an uneventful one, was to seize enough art to settle a litigation judgment against Ace's owner Douglas Chrismas. Doug had a brilliant eye for art and a talent for nurturing up-and-coming artists, but also an unfortunate proclivity for bending the rules. He was the target of numerous lawsuits by collectors and some of the artists he represented. He lived on the edge, taking big risks, often using other people's money. It was as if his DNA wouldn't allow him to follow the rules. I truly believe he could have become one of the world's most powerful and wealthy art dealers if he had just played the game straight instead of devoting so much energy to cheating.

I didn't have any compunction about helping the court go after him because he owed me money for services my company rendered and wouldn't pay. Not that I intended to be vengeful, but if a court wanted to hire me to recover something from him, I was going to accept because I didn't owe any loyalty to Chrismas or his gallery.

There was a personal element to the second raid, though, which came many years after the first. For years, Chrismas sold paintings to a wealthy Canadian collector, who stored them at Ace. One of the pieces was an important Robert Rauschenberg painting measuring 120 inches by 60 inches. Several years after selling it to the Canadian, Chrismas sold it again to a couple living in New York City. The couple contacted me to ship it to them, telling me how excited they were about owning the piece, which was beautiful and one of Rauschenberg's best. I informed Ace, which was located in a former Bank of America building in Venice at the time, but when my drivers arrived, the gallery wouldn't release the painting. The buyers expressed consternation and alarm when I told them, and over the ensuing months, they scheduled me to pick up the painting several more times. Each time they told me that Chrismas had agreed to hand it over, but when we got there, the gallery wouldn't let us take it. Eventually, the couple sued Doug in federal court, and though it took several years, they won a judgment giving them the Rauschenberg. The court contacted me to pick up the painting and said it was sending two federal marshals to serve papers and enforce the seizure.

On the morning of the operation, the marshals arrived at my office. They looked like Notre Dame linebackers, big guys in suits and shoulder holsters, rippling with solid muscles and ex-military crew cuts. This instilled confidence that we wouldn't encounter any problems, but I decided to accompany my employees—just in case. We took a truck and drove to Venice with the marshals' black government sedan trailing behind.

The marshals and I walked through the gallery's front door and immediately bumped into Chrismas, who was leaning over the front desk talking to the receptionist. A look of alarmed recognition flashed in his eyes, and he took off running toward the back, where there was a large walk-in bank vault. The round vault door was open, and I could see paintings leaning inside. Sprinting with the uncoordinated gait of someone who didn't often exercise, he reached the vault, grabbed the big, round steel door, and slammed it shut, spinning a spoked wheel to lock the safe. Walking back toward us with a look of satisfaction, he said: "The safe is on a timer and cannot be opened for forty-eight hours."

It was a dramatic ruse. I had already told the marshals about the layout of the gallery and suggested that since the Rauschenberg was too large for the vault, it was likely stored in the gallery's storage annex, across the square in a single-story office building. They handed Doug the court orders and told him, "If we can't look in the vault, we will look in your storage across the street." Chrismas looked alarmed. "I didn't bring my keys," he said.

"That's okay," one of the marshals replied, taking a step toward him. "We'll just kick down the door."

We followed a sullen Chrismas to a door in the side of a small stucco building. He reluctantly unlocked it and let us into a room where the Rauschenberg painting lay face up on a table. He stood glowering at us with his hands in his pants pockets while the marshals stared back with their arms crossed on their chests. The space between the walls and the sides of the painting was tight, and I needed to do a condition report before we took it away. But I knew Chrismas was touchy about condition reports and would refuse to sign one. I pulled out a blank report sheet anyway and began carefully examining the painting while writing notes. There was a scratch in the paint.

"Look at this," I told him. "There's some damage."

Chrismas made a guttural choking sound before screaming, "you sonofabitch!" and coming after me with his arms swinging punches. I backed away around the painting, keeping it between me and the attack, but Chrismas pursued me around and around the Rauschenberg, his face contorted with rage. Each time he passed, he brushed against the two wide-eyed marshals, who had their backs pressed to the wall and didn't move. I was shocked. They easily could have grabbed and subdued him, but they seemed paralyzed with fear.

I noticed Chrismas beginning to tire and saw an opening to move in to punch him in the nose, but decided that would complicate things and possibly give him grounds to file assault charges. I back-pedaled one more time, and Chrismas bolted out the door and disappeared. I finished the condition report, and we took the painting back to my warehouse for storage. Neither marshal would look me in the eye.

Getty

The operations to relieve people like the Swetnams of their looted Moche artifacts—or retrieve disputed works from the likes of a Doug Chrismas—were small potatoes compared to the battles over Greek and Roman antiquities that erupted between many major American museums versus the Italian and Greek governments. The most prominent museum being the J. Paul Getty.

I got periodic glimpses of trouble afoot at the Getty because Cooke's Crating has a long association with the Getty Museum and its affiliated entities, including the Getty Research Institute, which gave us unusual intimacy with some of the Getty's principals. Before the Getty Villa and the Getty Center were built, we delivered paintings and antiquities to the "Farmhouse'"—the original Getty Museum—in a small canyon above the Coast Highway at the southern end of Malibu, land owned by John Paul Getty. The main building, which was used for storage and had an excellent conservation studio, looked out on a courtyard with a large, circular fountain at its center. Bronze cherubs sat on the fountain's outer wall, spouting gentle arcs of water into the center. I always looked forward to making deliveries there, not only because of that beautiful setting but because often, Bertrand, the museum's head curator, would remove a cold six-pack of beer from the lab's freezer and invite us to sit along the low fountain wall to relax a minute after our work was done. The beer was okay, but the real treat was that the museum's three conservators, who likely were the smartest, most beautiful women on the planet, would join us in the warm sunshine. It was moments like those that made living the California dream feel like such a glorious adventure.

Getty was living as a recluse in England and had not actually visited Malibu in years when I was making those early deliveries. He passed away in 1976, and it was a shock when the enormous fortune he left was bequeathed to the museum in 1982. Suddenly, the Getty Museum had infinite possibilities to expand its collections and develop as an art institution. Bringing that dream to life required up-to-date facilities, which started with the Getty Villa—its design based on a Roman villa discovered in Pompeii excavations. This was a design choice that made sense because for years, Getty had been collecting Roman and Greek antiquities, and now they could be displayed in an appropriate environment. And while it might've seemed odd to put a modern version of an ancient Roman villa next to the Pacific, it fit with a playful California culture that embraced fanciful designs like those of Grauman's Chinese Theater, the Brown Derby, or those enormous donuts rising above shops—which inevitably made all of these places California icons. It was fitting too that, mirroring Getty himself, the original Villa had been built and lived in by one of ancient Rome's wealthiest Roman families.

For the enormous Getty Center, whose construction began in the mid-1990s, any theme-park traces faded away as architect Richard Meyer gave Getty's collections and legacy a fully modern home. When the center was completed, we moved all the collections there, including the antiquities, so the Villa could be remodeled. And once that was done, we moved all the antiquities back and assisted the Getty staff with installing them throughout the center.

Those antiquities collections had issues. As it happens in the antiquities trade, a certain percentage were fakes. It is often difficult to determine the age of an object carved from stone, and there were stories about how dealers used that to their advantage as they scrambled to satisfy Getty's desires. He traveled to Europe by passenger ship in the era before transatlantic flights, and before departing, he would wire his itinerary ahead to his favorite antiquities dealers. Some of them, in turn, were said to bury freshly made fakes and dig them up, dirty and earth-stained, for Getty, who was frequently fooled. Later, there were other problems, such as when the Getty acquired important pieces—real ones—that had been illegally excavated and smuggled out of Italy or Greece to be sold by dealers in Switzerland or other European cities.

A colorful curator of antiquities named Jiří Frel was linked to some of the dubious transactions. In the days before the Getty Center was constructed, he'd ask us to unload crates from the ocean freight containers he periodically had shipped to the Villa—generally on weekends or in the evenings when other Getty staff weren't present. Frel would have us unpack antiquities and place them on shelves in the Getty storage vaults. I wondered why the regular Getty preparation staff wasn't handling this work and why those tasks weren't being overseen by Getty registrars. Each time we unpacked a crate, Frel would get excited, as if seeing the contents for the first time and as if he had no prior knowledge of what was coming. It was Frel who later told me about Getty purchasing faked antiquities, a story that may have been intended to cloud the provenance of his own sketchy acquisitions.

He was known to work frequently with a couple of dealers tied to antiquities trafficking. But what led to his departure from the museum was the discovery of a scheme in which he arranged for dealers to sell pieces to collectors who agreed to donate them to the Getty—in exchange for inflated appraisals that would give them higher tax write-offs.

In recent decades museums have faced increasing pressure to repatriate important antiquities to the countries they originated. *Aphrodite*, a magnificent and powerful representation of the Greek goddess—once described as the single greatest piece of ancient art in the Getty's collection—was long a focus of contention. After years of negotiations and Italian criminal charges lodged against Getty curator Marion True, the Getty finally agreed to send the sculpture, which it had purchased for $18 million, back to the small town in Sicily where it was excavated. Cooke's Crating built the inner and outer crates for this sculpture, and the Getty preparators packed it, using space-age cushioning materials including Sorbothane, an expensive black rubber compound generally used for protecting delicate electronic components during shipping. The crated *Aphrodite* was flown to an Italian airport, trucked and ferried to Sicily under heavy security, and greeted by the excited townspeople of Aidone, who were dressed in their Sunday best. A brass band played as the mayor, police chief, and other town officials stood in front, wearing their sashes of office. The truck from a Rome-based art moving company pulled up, the crate was carefully lowered on the liftgate, and the art handlers used a pallet jack to roll it toward the local museum's front door as the crowd cheered and applauded.

The road was surfaced in cobblestones, and the crate, which the Getty had so carefully designed to protect the sculpture from shock and vibration during its overseas journey, began bouncing and lurching. Things got worse when, much to the welcoming contingent's chagrin, it was discovered the crate was too large to fit through the door. The crate was jostled back down the cobblestone street, around a corner, and over another rough road to the museum's rear entrance. By a miracle, *Aphrodite* arrived safely despite her rude and rough landing. Justice was done—the goddess was finally home.

Magui

Smuggling artifacts isn't the only criminal activity that uses art for financial gain. Forgery is another route to making substantial returns, something I saw more than once when the authorities called us in to handle the fake goods they'd seized. In 1990, the Federal Trade Commission asked us to participate in a raid on Magui Publishing, a company owned and run by a French national named Pierre Marcand. Marcand had been convicted of art fraud and jailed in Italy before showing up in Beverly Hills, where he allegedly produced and sold up to $44 million worth of Dali, Chagall, and other prints of dubious authenticity. These were mostly commercially printed images having no real value. But Marcand was selling them as "originals" to art galleries in tourist destinations throughout the United States at discounted wholesale prices ranging from several thousand to six thousand dollars each. The galleries, in turn, sold them to the unwitting and gullible for prices as high as twenty thousand dollars.

The flourishing trade in fake Dali's had been facilitated by Dali himself in the last decade of his life when he settled accounts with his dealers by signing an estimated 50,000 sheets of blank, art-quality printing paper, which could be used to mint a fresh supply of works. FTC representatives told me stories of how the artist sat at a desk while an assistant placed the blank paper sheets in front of him. A template with a rectangle opening was pulled over the sheet so Dali would consistently sign in the same location. This practice is said to have continued while Dali was suffering from dementia, possibly from the effects of syphilis. His dealer in Paris, who had accepted thousands of the signed sheets in payment for Dali's debts, sold them to Magui Publishing and possibly others with dishonest intentions.

The FTC called me as it was preparing to shut down Magui Publishing by seizing its inventory and attempting to recover the other prints from gallery inventories and private collectors. Marcy Tiffany, who was in charge of the commission's Los Angeles regional office, asked me to send trucks and art handlers to a Beverly Hills mansion, explaining there would be a raid on the place, but circumspect about who the target would be. They weren't sure what they would find, she said, but she wanted us to be prepared to handle "very many works on paper." Those would be going into our storage warehouse, and it was possible that similar works from other locations could also come to us for safekeeping.

We arrived at the gated driveway as scheduled and waited while the FTC, with assistance from the Beverly Hills police, took control of the site. The driveway behind the gate curved downhill out of sight, and the house wasn't visible from the road above.

After thirty minutes, we received word to drive down and entered a large motor court in front of an eight-car garage. The stone and brick mansion was impressive, and the wooden doors of the garage were beautifully made and painted with glossy white enamel. The garage doors were open, and I walked into a spacious interior with pristine white walls, and a floor painted a glossy blue-gray. Fluorescent fixtures hung from chains illuminating a work area with two printing presses and eight tables that held freshly printed "Dali's." The entire operation was clean, organized, and professional.

One of the presses had part of a print emerging—a sign that the process had been interrupted—and an open crate filled with a stack of blank paper sat next to the printing presses, each sheet bearing a Dali signature scrawled in pencil. The presses were commercial grade, the same kind used to print posters or books.

I saw one of the prints on a table and remarked out loud that it looked good—like a real Dali. An FTC officer explained that was because the counterfeits were made by altering images from various actual Dali works using photography and combining them. The familiar Dali motifs made these prints appear authentic to uninformed buyers who were naïve and easily duped, and even, at first glance, to people like me, who theoretically should've been harder to fool.

Stacks of crates stood at the back of the garage, and a dozen more stood against the right wall. We opened the crates in the smaller stack first and found they contained completed prints. The crates from the larger stacks were full of signed paper. Each of the crates contained two-hundred-and-fifty sheets, and there was a total of forty crates.

We packed them all and took them back to my warehouse. Several weeks later, we picked up additional crates from a van and storage company. The haul remained in storage for three years while Marcand fought the FTC through the courts, attempting to have the prints returned. Ultimately, an appellate court ruled against him, and the FTC destroyed all the prints and blank papers.

Despite those efforts, though, many fake Dali prints have remained in circulation, their owners unaware that their investments are worthless. Years after the federal government succeeded in putting Marcand out of business, I saw one of the counterfeit Dali's hanging for sale in a gallery in Maui, where I was vacationing. It was tempting to tell the owner his print was bogus, but he likely would have reacted badly. Or probably he already knew. There were, and are many, many fakes. Even after Dali stopped signing blank sheets himself, his signature continued to appear on blank paper. So not only are there fake prints with a genuine signature but there are other fake prints that have a fake Dali signature. Caveat emptor—let the art buyer beware!

Desmond's

Not long after I helped chase down the disputed Rauschenberg at Ace, the gallery relocated to the second floor of Desmond's, the 1929 art deco building on Wilshire. Desmond's was a marquee Los Angeles department store in the 1920s, but it had fallen on hard times and went out of business by the 1970s, leaving the edifice largely empty for many years and the blocks around it in decline. This area of the Miracle Mile district had been morphing into Museum Row, home to LACMA, Craft Contemporary, the Page Museum at the La Brea Tar Pits, and the Petersen Automotive Museum. The Ace opening was big news, but it would've been out of character for Doug Chrismas if something weren't a little off about it—and of course, there was.

Ace's second-floor space was a city block long, providing a huge exhibition area with multiple galleries and operations rooms. Its inaugural show featured artists in Doug Chrismas's stable, including Gary Amico, one of my former employees. Gary asked me to help deliver several paintings from his downtown studio to the gallery using one of my trucks. We carried his works up the back fire escape and through an open door into the galleries, leaning them on the walls where they'd be installed. There were track lights on the ceiling, and it was still daylight, but a crew was standing on ladders and stretching extension cords throughout the galleries and attaching clip-on floodlights. This seemed odd, given the track lighting, and when I asked Amico about it, he told me Chrismas was having a rent dispute with his new landlord, who retaliated by shutting off the gallery's power. Chrismas was tapping into a neighbor's electric meter, possibly without their knowledge, to run the lighting for the opening. The meters and circuit breaker boxes were near the elevator lobby, and I walked over to take a look. Someone had rigged up the power by cutting off the plug of the extension cord and twisting the bare wires around the positive and negative terminals in the circuit breaker box. But the wires had been attached ahead of the fuses, meaning the fuses would not provide any safety if the extension cords became overloaded. Typical of Doug's fast and loose style, the setup appeared to be extremely dangerous.

At the grand opening that evening, there was a line waiting for the elevator, so I walked up the narrow stairs and past the electric meters on my way into the galleries. The fuse box was partially open, and the extension cord was still there. Out of curiosity, I touched it, and it felt hot, hot enough to burn my hand.

Hundreds of people were packed into the gallery from the entrance lobby to the back, the movers and shakers of the Los Angeles art community dressed in cocktail attire and holding drinks. The throng was so thick it was difficult to move. Each gallery was dimly lit by two or three overhead clip-on floodlights, and it was hard to see the paintings hanging on the walls, but the crowd didn't seem to care. Alcohol flowed, and conversations roared.

When I reached the gallery displaying Gary Amico's paintings, I couldn't find the fire escape—it had been walled over. I felt a sudden rush of claustrophobia, remembering stories of how fires had turned packed nightclubs into death traps. If the extension cord blew out, the galleries would be pitch black, leaving everyone fumbling and panicked trying to get out. A fire could wipe out dozens of art cognoscenti, artists, and collectors and change the tenor of the Los Angeles art scene forever. I needed to get out, and I pushed through the crowd toward the exit. In hindsight, I regret that I didn't call the fire department. Happily, though, fire wasn't what would bring Ace Gallery down, and Doug Christmas's party made it through the night.

Thefts

Jawlensky

THE MOST IMPORTANT GROUP of paintings owned by the Long Beach Museum of Art is the Milton Wichner collection, sixty-one paintings by the Blue Rider group of the early twentieth century. The artists—including Alexej von Jawlensky, Paul Klee, Wassily Kandinsky, and Lyonel Feininger—were interested in the expansive idea of the spiritual in art, but the works are all small, most measuring under twenty inches. Wichner, a Los Angeles lawyer, built his collection in the 1930s through purchases from art dealer Galka Scheyer, who was buddies with those artists when they were actively painting in Europe, hanging out with them and financially supporting them by selling their paintings.

I came in contact with the works when the Long Beach Museum of Art temporarily stored its permanent collections with my company. It continuously kept the Blue Rider paintings in my storage warehouse for many years because of their high values. The paintings were housed in three ugly yellow crates constructed by a company that went out of business soon after. Although poorly built, they were custom fitted to hold all the Wichner paintings, with each framed artwork in its own slot, making it easy to spot anything that was missing. We always stored these crates separately from the museum's main collections in a locked, temperature-controlled room.

When the museum loaned Wichner pieces to other institutions, it fastidiously followed the same protocols. A registrar would come to our warehouse to oversee the opening of the crates and the removal of the chosen paintings. After completing a condition report, we would crate and ship the paintings to the borrower. When the loans were returned, the registrar would oversee the unpacking and watch us replace the pieces in the storage crates. We were never to open the crates unless a registrar was present.

But in 1998, there was a change to the longstanding procedures. Eight pieces from a Jawlensky series of thirty-five faces were loaned for an exhibition in Europe and shipped through Masterpiece International. We made padded foam-core boxes for each work and grouped these into a single crate, with all our packing work overseen by the Long Beach Museum registrar. But when the pieces returned to our warehouse months later, it was the museum's curator, not the registrar, who called me. The registrar was busy, he said, and we should go ahead and repack the Jawlenskys in the yellow crates by ourselves. This was very unusual, and it bothered me. To protect ourselves, I personally did condition reports and supervised my employees as they replaced the paintings in their crates. When all the Jawlenskys were accounted for, and all the slots filled, I called the curator to tell him we had finished.

In 2000, the museum opened a new wing with exhibition and art storage spaces. I was asked to deliver the Wichner crates to Long Beach so they could display a portion of the collection in the new wing's inaugural exhibition. Then, in early 2001, the registrar phoned me to schedule a meeting at our warehouse. She arrived looking pale and stressed, saying the museum was missing two Jawlensky paintings. I could tell by her demeanor and her inability to maintain eye contact that we were under suspicion. I took her to the area where we had stored the crates, and when she saw we had kept the foam core boxes for possible reuse, she got very excited. But she was disappointed to find all of the boxes empty.

After she left, I told my storage manager to make copies of every document relating to the Wichner storage, including all the visits by museum personnel, notes, invoices, shipping documents, condition reports, and most importantly, a signed copy of our bill of lading for returning the crates to LBMA. These documents filled a fat folder, a sign of the thoroughness of our record-keeping during the many years we stored the collection.

Several weeks later, the museum's executive director, Hal Nelson, walked into my office unannounced, aggressively accusing us of losing the Jawlensky paintings. I knew Hal because he lived with Bernard Jazzar, the curator of the Lynda and Stewart Resnick art collections, one of our clients, so I calmly asked him to sit down. Once he did, I asked the key question: Had the registrar opened the yellow crates, conducted a piece count, and done condition reports when we delivered the crates? He didn't know. I pointed out that this was standard procedure for all museums and should be documented in their files. When I mentioned how the curator switched the normal procedures, he said the curator had quit and moved to Hawaii.

I asked if the museum had kept the yellow crates. Hal answered that they had been discarded after being unpacked when the paintings were placed on shelves in LBMA storage. I pointed out that this, too, was a change in the longtime safeguard that ensured if any painting were missing from its designated slot, it would be immediately apparent as soon as the lid of the crate was opened. Who had unpacked the paintings? He didn't know. Had all the paintings been unpacked before the crates went to a landfill? He didn't know that either.

He also revealed the museum had hired temporary employees to help with the installation, and they had unaccompanied access to the vault for days. I asked if he had looked at the paperwork trail in the registration files, as we routinely sent the museum our invoices along with backup documents after completing every transaction. He replied that the file was virtually empty. Did he have a copy of our receipt for delivering the crates? He admitted there was a lot of missing paperwork. I gave him the folder of document copies we had prepared, and he appeared stunned by its size. I thought he looked deflated and worried when he left.

Several years passed without any follow-up, which I thought was irregular. Considering the high values and a loss from the complete collection of Jawlensky's heads, certainly some authority, either lawyers or insurance companies or the police would have contacted me.

I found out what happened a few years later at an insurance seminar for Los Angeles area registrars and art movers at the Museum of Contemporary Art. There, Victoria France, a specialist in museum art insurance, reminded the audience to always promptly inform their insurers of any claims for losses or damage. She said that a local museum had lost two Jawlensky paintings and waited over a year to make a claim. The wait had exceeded the policy's contractual limits, and the claim was denied.

In 2007, the city of Long Beach initiated an audit of its finances, which included inventorying the art collections. The new director, Ron Nelson—no relation to his predecessor—revealed to the *Los Angeles Times* in June 2008 that the museum was missing two Jawlensky paintings worth hundreds of thousands of dollars, adding they had disappeared after being sent on a tour to Paris in 2000. What is interesting about those two paintings is they are both monochromatic, painted entirely in white, gray, and black—unlike the normal palette of bright primary colors used for the vast majority of Jawlensky's faces. What are the odds of losing two similar paintings, both of which were so different from the remaining thirty-three in the series?

Laguna

Another strange painting disappearance occurred after the Laguna Beach Art Museum contracted with me to crate and ship a group of paintings to a college art museum in Pennsylvania for an exhibition. The Laguna Museum owns a large collection of paintings by Edgar Alwin Payne, Guy Rose, and William Wendt, among other Impressionist plein air painters working in Southern California during the early 1900s through the 1930s. The show included some fine examples of their work. It was further enhanced by additional loans borrowed from collectors in Orange and San Diego counties. Most of the paintings had ornate and often fragile original frames, and to protect them, we decided to pack each in a custom foamcore box with fitted foam interiors. We standardized the dimensions of the boxes to better group them into crates, using additional foam inside the boxes so smaller paintings would fit snugly. Each box was numbered and labeled with both the artist's name and the owner's, and a color photo of each painting was glued to the box lid. We packed four or five boxes into each crate and shipped the crates to Pennsylvania.

After the exhibition finished, the show returned to our warehouse. We decided it would be safest to return the paintings to each collector by leaving them packed in their custom boxes and doing condition reports while they were being unpacked in the collectors' presence. Everything worked smoothly until one of the collectors called to say we had delivered the wrong painting. The box was labeled with his painting and name, but the painting inside didn't match. We opened all the boxes and discovered others were also packed with incorrect paintings, and someone had altered the inside foam to make the wrong paintings fit inside. Then we discovered one of the boxes was empty. We verified with the collectors we had already returned paintings to that theirs were correct, and by matching our original packing list with all the ones we'd returned, we determined which one was missing.

I called the college museum and asked to speak to the registrar, hoping the painting had been inadvertently left behind, and was told the registrar had quit, as had the museum director and other key staff members. There was no one still at the museum who knew who had actually packed the paintings, and there were no records of condition reports or inventory lists. We notified the director of the Laguna Beach Art Museum, Bolton Colburn, and he told the painting's owner what had happened. The collector got an insurance settlement, but it was little compensation for losing a beautiful painting.

Emery

Over the years, some of the most treasured pieces of Hollywood history have passed through my hands—important and irreplaceable props and costumes used in landmark movies like *Citizen Kane*. There are myriad stories about how props like one of the Rosebud sleds built for that film wound up in trash bins, only to be rescued by a studio watchman. But much care was taken when such survivors—including that very sled—reached us. We also handled the camera used by Cecil B. DeMille to shoot *The Squaw Man*, a silent 1914 western, as well as the tablets carried by Charlton Heston in *The Ten Commandments*.

When we packed and shipped the contents of Jack Warner's office at Warner Brothers Studios to the Pompidou Museum in Paris, I got a good look at objects like the original script for *Casablanca*, annotated with notes by Warner, and Academy Awards statues including those for *Casablanca* and *Key Largo*. Of particular interest to me was Warner's personal address and telephone notebook. It listed all of the great movie stars of the '30s and '40s, with notes beside each one—the names of wives and kids as well as reminders like, "Don't call before 10 a.m., she needs time to sober up." Locked up at the time of his death and preserved exactly as he'd kept it, the office was a wonderful piece of Hollywood movie history.

We also crated and shipped the DeLorean used in *Back to the Future* and a full-scale Batmobile. Plus, many of the props and costumes from George Lucas's *Star Wars* and *Indiana Jones* archives, which we gathered at Lucas's stunningly beautiful Sky Walker Ranch north of San Francisco and sent to Japan.

A Beverly Hills dentist and memorabilia collector, Dr. Gary Milan, owned the piano used to play *As Time Goes By*, in *Casablanca*, and the namesake Maltese Falcon of the famous Bogart film. Multiple prop falcons were made for that movie, but by studying outtakes from the film, Milan was able to determine precisely which one Bogart held during the famous scene in which he strokes it and calls it "the stuff dreams are made of." In one sequence, Bogart accidentally dropped the heavy lead statue, narrowly missing his toes, and exclaimed, "Oh shit!" as he jumped back. So, Milan bought the falcon with a distinctive dent in its corner. The dentist had close ties to Warner Brothers Studios, which occasionally borrowed the piano and falcon for exhibitions, and when it did, we helped with moving them. We also packed Milan's large collection of Bogart memorabilia for storage. Unfortunately, he thought our storage fees were too high and instead put the collection in a "you-store-it" place in Van Nuys. He learned the true cost of cheap rent months later after the Los Angeles Sheriff's Department called me, saying they had raided a meth house in the desert near Lancaster and found several crates there with Cooke's Crating stencils. They mentioned the numbers written on the crates, which I knew corresponded with our storage inventory system, and looked them up on our computer. I verified they belonged to Dr. Milan. We sent a truck to the meth house on a dusty gravel road in a rural part of Lancaster and rescued the crates, returning them to Milan, who didn't know they were missing.

Other pieces of the Hollywood firmament, its literal stars, passed through our warehouses when we stored many of the terrazzo plaques from the Hollywood Walk of Fame sidewalk—which honor the entertainment industry's biggest names—during a renovation on Hollywood Boulevard. The general contractor hired us to remove and crate them, and they remained in storage for several years until one morning I received a phone call from the Los Angeles mayor's office asking if we had them. The city had fired the contractor, who disappeared with all the job files, and they had been trying to track down the stars for several months.

Some of the most important movie items, iconic parts of American cultural history, have been added to the collections of the Smithsonian Institution. We saw that the Smithsonian received not just Dorothy's ruby slippers from *The Wizard of Oz* but the costumes of the Tin Man and Scarecrow, which I found unceremoniously stuffed into cardboard boxes stored on dusty shelves in a Hollywood prop house. It was amazing they'd survived for decades because anyone could have rented them at any time.

The Smithsonian also contacted me about shipping some items donated to them by the estates of Mary Pickford and Douglas Fairbanks Jr. This inventory included Mary Pickford's dress and shoes from Charlie Chaplin's *The Little Tramp*, an annotated script from a Fairbanks swashbuckler, a Robin Hood costume, and some antique weapons including a world-class samurai sword with a particularly beautiful example of folded and hammered steel patterning in the blade. It was perfectly balanced.

Concerned about possible theft because of the weapons, I decided to pack everything into a single, coffin-sized crate to give it heft, making it difficult to move by hand so it wouldn't suffer a "grab and run."

The Smithsonian registrar sent instructions to use Emery Air-freight for shipping to Washington D.C., but before I sent the shipment, I happened to read a small article in the back pages of the Wall Street Journal that mentioned Emery was experiencing a rash of cargo thefts from their New York and D.C. terminals. I called the registrar to tell her I wanted to use another service or send the crate on ground transportation, but she insisted on Emery, even after I explained my concerns about theft. I tried one last time to persuade her, but she said the Smithsonian had a government contract with Emery for all their shipping, and that was that.

The best I could do was to ask Emery to send their truck for a last-on, first-off service, figuring that would keep the crate from being exposed to multiple stops before it arrived at LAX. It was after five and dark outside when the Emery truck arrived at my warehouse. The driver was in his thirties with dark hair, and something about him, maybe something in his eyes, didn't seem quite right. I debated holding back the shipment but was uncertain how the Smithsonian registrar would react since the shipment was supposed to be delivered the next day, and all I had to go on was a nebulous feeling in my gut. This was the classic service provider's dilemma: obey the client's instructions or go with honed instincts that could upset them. I decided my concerns were probably irrational and helped the driver load my crate inside his truck and secure it. When he rolled down the door, I noticed he didn't have a lock, so I grabbed a heavy-duty, stainless-steel padlock from one of my trucks and gave it to him along with one key. Locking the door, he casually asked, "What's in the crate?"

I felt a twinge of unease and didn't want to tell him the truth. "It's just auto parts," I said. I immediately regretted it. Auto parts could be an attractive target thief, and giving him my lock suggested that something important was in the crate. But he was heading directly to the airport, and I thought he surely wasn't stupid enough to steal something off his own truck, particularly when theft of interstate commerce is a federal crime investigated by the FBI.

The next morning, though, the FBI called to inform me the shipment had been stolen. They said the driver had stopped at a liquor store near LAX to get a Coke, and while he was inside, someone had cut the lock off his truck and stolen my crate. I was momentarily stunned, and then I got pissed off. That goddamned Emery driver actually *did* have the temerity to target his own load. I told the FBI the driver had to have done it—not only was the padlock one of the best made, but the crate was as big as a coffin and weighed nearly 250 pounds. Anyone stealing it would have needed a truck and help to load it.

When I called the Smithsonian registrar to give her the bad news, I felt like saying, "I told you so!" But I decided it wouldn't be received very well. I also ran ads in the *LA Times* for several weeks, offering a $5,000 reward for the safe return of the crate, no questions asked. Unfortunately, the Pickfair artifacts were never seen again.

Coins

Years later, we encountered another theft issue involving a crate that supposedly contained rare coins. It was consigned to us by Gander and White in London for Bruce McNall, a high flyer who ostensibly made his fortune dealing in rare coins. He owned the Los Angeles Kings hockey team and produced numerous movies, including *Weekend at Bernie's*. He also had two rare coin investment funds with Merrill Lynch, called Athena 1 and Athena 2, which allowed investors to purchase shares backed by the values of the coins. McNall eventually began having financial difficulties and wound-up spending nearly six years in jail for fraud.

Word was just beginning to circulate about his sketchy finances when our truck went to retrieve the crate Gander and White sent us, only to find it had disappeared from the British Airways customs cage at LAX. When the crate didn't turn up in an hour-long search of the carrier's warehouse, I figured something was going on and decided to file theft reports with both LAPD's airport division and the FBI. I also placed an ad in the *LA Times* offering a reward for information and had one of my office staff calling the police and FBI daily for reports, hoping that if we were pests, they would pay more attention to the theft.

I was fairly certain that if the crate had been stolen from a secured Customs cage, it must have been taken by someone inside. So I prepared flyers outlining the FBI and LAPD investigations and asked British Air to post them around their facility. A week later, the FBI notified me that the crate had mysteriously reappeared in the Customs cage. When they checked it for fingerprints, there weren't any—the crate had been wiped clean. My guess is that the disappearance was related to an insurance claim for coins that weren't actually in the crate or that it contained lesser coins being insured for highly inflated values. When we kept pushing for an investigation, the thief got cold feet and returned it. In any case, we never saw the contents. We just picked up the rediscovered crate and delivered it to McNall.

Parrish

The thieves who got into the Edenhurst Gallery in West Hollywood were patient and professional. They accessed the gallery's security system, triggering alarms at odd hours of the night for a week. The security company's central station would wake the gallery owners to notify them and send West Los Angeles sheriffs to investigate. Each time the thieves had a chance to watch from afar, noting the sheriff's response times and the way officers walked the building's perimeter, shining flashlights through the large storefront window to illuminate a group of paintings by Maxfield Parrish. The gallery owners assumed something was haywire with the alarm panel and complained to the company, but its technicians couldn't find anything wrong with the system. Finally, after nights of interrupted sleep, the owners stopped arming the system.

Once the thieves knew the coast was clear, they struck. They waited until the gallery closed for the weekend on a Saturday evening, then cut through the roof and dropped inside, where they sliced two of the Parrish paintings out of their frames, rolled them up, and disappeared. The stolen pair were part of the matched set of six paintings, each measuring five by six feet, once owned by Gertrude Vanderbilt Whitney, who had commissioned the artist to paint them. After the theft, the insurance company of the paintings' owner, Texas oil billionaire J.P. Bryan, placed the remaining paintings in my storage warehouse. We also stored two empty stretcher bars, fragments of painted canvas forlornly hanging off their edges as a reminder of barbarians who would debase a work of art by cutting a painting from its frame to steal it.

The paintings had been consigned to the gallery for sale on the condition the gallery would carry an insurance policy covering their values. But because the gallery stopped paying the insurance premiums and the insurance lapsed, the company refused to pay the claim. Several years later, we shipped the remaining paintings and the two empty frames back to the Bryan Museum in Galveston, home to the thousands of paintings in J.P. Bryan's collection. The two missing Parrishes haven't been seen to this day, despite repeated attempts by the FBI to get a response by publicizing them. The crime is still listed as one of the FBI's top ten art thefts.

Sharks and Hustlers

Irwin

ANDY WAS AN AMBITIOUS young hustler who began working as a gallery attendant for Larry Gagosian back when Larry was first venturing into the art world under his own name in West Hollywood. Gagosian's first venture was the Brockton Gallery in Westwood, which had its genesis—legend had it—when Larry was parking cars for a Westwood restaurant and struck up a conversation with a wealthy elderly widow. When he learned she owned a building on Brockton Street with an inner courtyard, he talked her into letting him manage the property and wound up opening the Brockton as a photography gallery in one of the empty storefronts. I did my first work for him at that gallery, and he paid me with photographs by Eggleston, Hockney, and Avedon, which I still own. One of my favorites is Avedon's portrait of Andy Warhol, lifting his black leather jacket to reveal his surgery scars after being shot by his girlfriend.

Gagosian soon realized he could make more money by selling paintings than dealing in photography. When he asked me about possible clients, I introduced him to Douglas Cramer, the *Love Boat*, and *Fantasy Island* producer. Soon Larry was building an important collection for Cramer and making inroads into the entertainment industry. He closed the Brockton Gallery and opened his first Gagosian Gallery in a space behind Trumps Restaurant on the western end of Melrose, a popular hangout for studio execs, who could drop by the gallery after lunch to look at the art. Gagosian was the consummate hustler, a guy who would identify a goal and always find a way to make it happen. He was relentless and utterly focused, and he let nothing keep him from achieving spectacular success dealing art on a global scale. I was once at lunch with Larry Bell and Ruth Bachofner at her hillside home in Santa Barbara, where Ruth owned a gallery. We were sitting on a patio overlooking the Pacific when Gagosian showed up, totally unannounced and uninvited. I don't know how he found out about our meeting, but he sat down and inserted himself to figure out what we were planning. Even if we were just talking about the details of an upcoming show, he needed to know.

Andy, his gallery attendant, did his best to model himself after Larry and latched hard onto his coattails, copying his moves and hoping for an opportunity. I saw his ambition firsthand when I was at the gallery installing the first show of Basquiat paintings on the West Coast. A show I still look back on with regret—having turned down Larry's offer to pay me with one of the paintings. I thought, why would I want a painting of graffiti when I live in the inner city surrounded by it? It was the worst decision I ever made.

As I was installing the show, Andy walked over from behind the front desk and asked me if I would be willing to do jobs in the evenings. A week later he phoned and asked for two of my employees and a truck. Andy wanted them to pick up a painting from a residence in Laguna Beach at 8 p.m. and deliver it directly to him at the gallery. He said he would be waiting there until the painting arrived.

When I asked who the artist was, he told me it was Robert Irwin. That raised the job's level of difficulty because Irwin's paintings were similar to eggshells, with surfaces of built-up paint that easily cracked. He applied layers of paint until the canvas was evenly covered with a single pastel color, bifurcated by thin, horizontal lines of raised paint. The paintings had a luminescent quality, not from any transparency, but from the way light was directed by the brush strokes. Light has always been an essential element in Irwin's art, and he was a master of using it. Those paintings are Zen beautiful, glowing, and mesmerizing in their simplicity. From an art movers' perspective, though, the highly fragile paintings are anxiety-inducing. Any damage cannot be adequately repaired.

When the scheduled evening arrived, I told my employees to do a detailed condition report and wrap the painting. I also told them to get signatures and have the parties print their names on our documents as well. They were to unwrap the painting when they arrived at Gagosian and have Andy inspect it before signing our paperwork. My crew drove off, and after locking up, I went home.

When I got in the next morning, the red light was blinking on our company answering machine. The message was from Andy, expressing outrage that incompetence and improper handling by my drivers had ruined the Irwin painting. He demanded I immediately file a claim with my insurance company. This complaint was unnerving, and for a few uneasy minutes, I thought my drivers had actually mishandled the Irwin.

They hadn't come into work yet, so I looked at their paperwork from the evening before. Andy had signed it without any exceptions and with no mention of any damage. When I looked at the Laguna Beach pickup address, I realized I had been there several years earlier while delivering a Larry Bell painting. It was Sterling Holloway's home. Holloway was a screen actor who had also been a voice actor for Disney as Winnie the Pooh, Jiminy Cricket, and other animated characters. He had a wonderful collection, primarily of Southern California artists, and made purchases directly from the artists as well as Santa Monica's Asher Faure Gallery. Betty Asher had recently told me Sterling was suffering from dementia and that someone connected to the family had a drug habit and was attempting to sell his art to support their addiction. I now understood what Andy was doing, and his likely reason for wanting the painting picked up at night.

I called him at Gagosian and asked him to describe what happened. He indignantly insisted that my drivers damaged the Irwin so severely that it would cost him a sale to a collector in Miami. Why had he signed for a damaged painting without noting the damage on our paperwork, I asked. He said it was dark in the gallery, and he hadn't noticed the damage until the next morning. Gagosian was upset, he added, and I would lose his business if I didn't pay. I said I would think about it.

I immediately drove to the gallery. Andy wasn't there, but the painting was hanging on the back wall, and even from across the room, I could see an area of spiral cracks twelve inches in diameter. I walked closer to examine the damaged area and noticed the surface of the canvas was bulging outward from beneath the cracks. This meant it had taken impact from behind, unusual because most art gets damaged from the front. The backs of paintings are inset behind stretcher bars and further buffered by cross bracing. A high-quality stretcher frame should include a backing board to protect a painting from behind, and dampen vibration and movement of the canvas, which can cause long-term damage to the painted surface.

Andy walked in, and when he spotted me, a moment of indecision crossed his face, a tell that he hadn't expected me to show up. He composed himself, rushed over, and began demanding that my insurance pay for the damage caused by my employees. From seeing the cracks and bulge, I knew that I needed to look at the back of the painting and told him to help me lift it off the wall. He protested, saying that attempting to move it would place it at greater risk of damage, but I grabbed the left side and insisted he take the right and help lift it off the wall. He reluctantly complied, and we took it down, exposing a broken wooden cross brace in the back, with the two splintered portions tilting inward against the area of damage. I knew then that Andy had tried to hang the painting by himself, grabbing the cross brace in his left hand while his right hand pushed against the side of the painting. As he lifted the painting toward the hooks, the cross brace snapped under pressure, breaking inward and causing Andy's fist to smash into the back of the canvas. I fought the urge to punch the sleazy little rat in his nose. He may have sensed my anger and retreated behind the reception desk. A few weeks later, he called to say he had sold the painting to the Miami collector.

Electric Chair

After many years of working for Gagosian in Los Angeles, the world economies turned downward, and the American dollar gained strength against most European currencies. Taking advantage of that, Larry went to Europe and brought back a small Andy Warhol *Electric Chair* painting and had me store it. Several weeks later, he called and asked me to act as an escrow holder between him and a potential buyer. The buyer would hand over a cashier's check to pay for the purchase, and after examining the painting, they could take it, and I would deliver the check to Larry. I had some misgivings about doing this, but Larry assured me it would be okay. The buyer arrived with a man he announced was a Warhol expert, but who ignored me when I introduced myself and extended my hand. It was unusual for him not to identify himself, and I wondered if the two of them were keeping something from Gagosian. The expert carried two large briefcases filled with books and catalogues, which they laid out on our large worktable. They spent nearly two hours examining the painting under magnification and black light, comparing it to photographs in their books. When they left, the buyer said the painting was definitely a fake, and he didn't want it. He forgot about his check. An hour later, Larry called me and demanded the check. I said the buyer rejected the purchase and that I was responsible for returning his money. He wanted me to deliver the check immediately. I told him that if I acquiesced to his demand, I would be breaking my word as escrow holder, and the purchaser would likely sue me for the amount. Larry said that was my problem. I could either give him the check, or stop doing business with him. We'd worked together from the beginning, but that unraveled the relationship.

Carson

One tactic con men and scammers use is to rush you so you won't have time to figure out what is happening until it's too late. I stepped into one of their high-pressure scenarios one afternoon when a call came in from a man who identified himself with the generic American name of "Peter Smith" but spoke in a heavy Eastern European accent. His voice was serious and businesslike. He described owning an important Peter Paul Rubens oil painting, which needed to be taken from his home in the San Fernando Valley and delivered to the *Johnny Carson Show* that evening. His original movers backed out at the last moment, he said, and he had called the Los Angeles County Museum of Art to ask for the name of a replacement company. They highly recommended Cooke's Crating. He went on to explain that the show's taping began at 7 p.m., and he wanted the painting picked up at 5:45 p.m. "to limit the window of exposure for possible theft or damage." He emphasized how important it was to deliver the painting on time and said he'd want me to stand by during the show so I could return the artwork to his house immediately after the taping.

He probed and prodded: Could I provide the requested services? Was I qualified to handle a rare and exceedingly valuable painting by such an important Old Master? Without damaging it? "After all, it is very fragile and has been in our family for generations," he told me. "It is priceless!"

I assured him we would take good care of his painting, and could be there in a few hours.

We arrived on time to find that Peter Smith lived in a small, cookie-cutter tract house on the flats of the San Fernando Valley, north of Ventura Boulevard. This was a surprising location for a painting potentially worth millions, and I worried I had written down the wrong address. The sun had set, and oddly, there were no lights on inside or outside the house, and no streetlights. It was pitch black outside. We cautiously went up the walk, being careful not to trip over some unseen object, and as we neared the house, the door suddenly flew open. Smith rushed out from the dark interior wearing a suit and tie, and a woman in cocktail attire followed. They hurried past us toward a Mercedes sedan parked at the curb.

"Can't wait!" Smith called to us. "We have to get to the Carson Show. My mother is inside, and she will show you the painting. It is extremely important for you to arrive on time. Don't be late! The painting has been in my family for generations and is an irreplaceable masterpiece. Please handle it with great care. Do not damage it!"

With that, they jumped into their car, made a U-turn in the street, and roared off.

We edged up to the front door, but I couldn't find a doorbell in the darkness, so I knocked, waited, and knocked again. After a long five minutes, the door opened a crack, and I heard a "thunk" as a chain prevented it from opening more.

"Who is it? What do you want?" mumbled a raspy old woman with an accent even thicker than Mr. Smith's. It was so dark inside that we couldn't see her.

"We're here to get the painting for the *Johnny Carson Show*, ma'am," I replied.

The door slammed shut, and I could hear the muffled sounds of a chain being fumbled. This continued for a minute or so until the door opened wide. Standing in the gloom was a small, stooped figure dressed in a housecoat or frock.

"Come this way," she said as she turned and shuffled down the dark hallway.

Before I followed her, I quickly glanced around at the living room and dimly saw that the walls were covered with dark paintings in heavy frames. When the woman reached the end of the hall, she opened a bedroom door, and as my eyes adjusted, I could see more painting-covered walls. Artworks were also stacked together on the floor and leaning against a bed. What was going on here? It was totally weird. What tract home has Old Master paintings stuffed all over the place?

"It's that one," the woman announced, pointing to a large painting hanging above the bed. I cautiously threaded my way through boxes and around artworks to get closer and see how we were going to take the painting down from the wall. I couldn't make out the painting's image or surface—it only appeared as a black rectangle—but I could tell it had a large, ornately carved frame, which was going to make it very heavy.

I tried turning on a table lamp next to the bed, and when that failed, I walked over and flipped the light switch. Nothing worked. "Excuse me, ma'am, but could we get some light so we can see what we are doing?" No response, so I asked again.

"No electricity!" she said, shuffling back down the hall.

We carefully moved cartons and artwork to make a pathway to the bed and then took off our boots and climbed up to take the painting down. Once we carried it into the hall, we moved everything in the bedroom back to its original position because I didn't want the owners to claim any damage. The old lady hadn't stayed behind to watch us, and we would deny touching the other paintings if an issue arose. It felt as though we were being set up in some manner, although I hadn't yet figured out how.

I couldn't see my watch to know how much time we had left to get to the Carson set, but feeling our way through the darkness put us behind. We needed to get moving, but I also wanted to condition report the painting before leaving a signed receipt with the crone, certain that we'd need a detailed report to protect ourselves.

We took the painting outside, and once we'd leaned it carefully against the garage doors, I drove our truck into the driveway and turned on the high beams. Bright light washed over the painting, and even from inside the truck cab, it was immediately obvious that it was a mess. There were several holes in the canvas, including a six-inch, V-shaped tear with a flap of canvas hanging inside its face. A large area of concentric circular cracks in the paint indicated something had hit the surface, and there were a dozen scratches and gouges in different quadrants. The frame also had missing chunks, some as large as a golf ball. This painting looked like it had been through a war.

I drew a rectangle on our bill of lading, noting all the damages on the margins with arrows pointing from the descriptions to the damaged areas. I was careful to report every condition problem no matter how small, and after finishing, I went back into the house looking for the old lady. I groped around in the darkness for several minutes before I found her standing outside on the back patio, smoking a cigarette. "They don't allow me to smoke in the house," she complained. She spat on the ground in disgust. "Bastards!"

I handed her my clipboard and held my thumb on the paperwork to show her where to sign. In the darkness, she wouldn't be able to see the condition report, so she'd have no reason not to sign it, but in any event, she probably didn't care.

We secured the painting in the truck and checked the time. We'd just make it if we drove as fast as we could.

A very agitated Peter Smith met us at the soundstage entrance. "Where have you been? You're very late! You must hurry!" he said. "They begin in only moments. Hurry up!"

We grabbed the painting and quickly followed him down several hallways and through giant curtains onto the stage. The ornate frame was heavy, and we were out of breath when we arrived. Johnny Carson was sitting behind his desk, and several aides with clipboards were discussing something with him. The stage was brightly lit, and I wondered how the Rubens would look on TV. Would the damage be apparent to the average home viewer? As the large audience sat expectantly waiting for the segment to begin taping, someone stood facing them and wise-cracked jokes to keep them revved up. Next to Carson's desk was a big easel, and we were told to place the painting on it.

Peter Smith was beginning to look nervous and distracted. I took advantage by giving him our delivery paperwork and a pen to sign. We were also handed a lucky break because, at that moment, the stage manager arrived and told him he was on next. He quickly scribbled his signature without noticing the condition report and rushed over to his seat next to Carson's desk. A stagehand ushered us offstage, and we watched from the side as Smith told Carson about the Rubens and how valuable it was. His family had hidden it from the Nazis during the war, he said, and later smuggled it out of Eastern Europe under the noses of the Russians after the war. If Carson noticed the damage, he never mentioned it. He appeared to be impressed, and the audience clapped loudly in appreciation.

After the taping, we put the painting back on the truck as Peter Smith and his wife stood by watching. When we finished, they left, saying they would meet us back at the house. When we drove up, the whole place was ablaze with lights. Every window was brightly lit, and floodlights illuminated the entrance and driveway. As we carried the painting into the living room, Smith and his wife confronted us, and a middle-aged man in a suit and tie walked in carrying a briefcase. In what appeared to be a choreographed scene, the three stared at the painting in a state of feigned shock.

"Oh! My god! My god! What have you done to our beautiful painting?" Mrs. Smith cried out. She held her hands against her face. "You've ruined it! Generations have protected it with their lives, and now you've negligently destroyed our family's heritage!" She acted as if she were about to faint as Mr. Smith grabbed her elbow and led her to the couch, where she collapsed.

The man with the briefcase walked aggressively toward me, saying, "I am the attorney representing this family, and I have some documents for you to sign accepting full responsibility for your irresponsible and inept handling of this priceless masterpiece."

He opened his briefcase and pulled out four or five pages of prepared documents. With a flourish, he handed me a gold pen. I stood quietly for a moment without showing any emotion and then held up our bill of lading.

"As you can see, there is a complete condition report on my document," I told him. "It was signed by Smith when we delivered the painting to the Carson Show, and his mother signed it too. If you can find any additional damages to the painting, I will be happy to discuss them. Sign here, please, for the delivery."

I wanted to keep the expensive gold pen, but before I could clip it in my shirt pocket, the attorney snatched it out of my hand, shoved the claim papers in his briefcase, and walked out the front door. Mrs. Smith, who just moments before had been lying faint on the couch, stood up and marched out of the room toward the kitchen. Mr. Smith signed our delivery receipt without saying a word, his eyes downcast to avoid looking me in the eye. I couldn't tell if he was ashamed or disappointed.

We left the painting leaning against the couch without offering to rehang it over the bed.

Rembrandt

I watched from my office window as a Ford station wagon pulled into our parking lot. It was one of those oversized, Rust Belt-manufactured dinosaurs from the '70s, with beige paint that was oxidized and faded from too many years in the sun. Its faux Woody vinyl siding had faded too and was beginning to peel. And where the left front fender had crumpled in a long-ago accident, the sheet metal was rusting along the sharp edges of dents that had cracked the paint.

Two men in their late forties got out of the car and argued as they walked toward our office entrance. The skinny one was preppy, dressed in chinos, boat sneakers, and a short-sleeved shirt. The other was attired in suggestive leather-boy style. He wore a black leather motorcycle jacket covered with studs, a motorcycle cap with a small Marlon Brando brim and little chains, tight jeans, and even tighter black leather chaps that appeared under stress as they strained around his plus-size body. Together, the two looked like a perverse Laurel and Hardy.

Our receptionist called me on the intercom and said the men wanted to store a valuable painting, so I walked out and introduced myself. The leather man looked me over from behind black-rimmed glasses with thick lenses.

"Can you store an extremely valuable painting?" he asked.

"That's no problem," I said. "Who's the artist?"

"It's a Rembrandt!" the skinny one blurted in a sing-song voice.

The big man angrily whirled toward him, hands on hips, and shouted, "Shut up, you idiot! I'm doing all the talking because the painting belongs to me. Just shut up!"

The skinny guy stood on his toes to increase his height and leaned toward him. "It's not yours! Mommy left it to me when she died!"

The big guy took a step toward him. "She left it to me because she was always embarrassed that you are such a scrawny little faggot!"

"Mommy loved me more than you!" the skinny guy sputtered in outrage.

"That's untrue," said the big man. "Take back what you said! Take it back!"

Concerned that they were coming to blows and not wanting their bickering to disrupt my office staff, I decided to intervene. "Excuse me. Could I see your painting please?"

They turned toward me with tense lips and hurt looks in their eyes, and the leather guy waddled out the front door and went to the station wagon, leaving his brother to sulk. I watched his ass-cheeks doing the hula as he crossed the parking lot—two pigs fighting in a sack. He opened the rear hatch and bent forward to retrieve something inside the car, pulling out a large, black portfolio box, which he carried back into our office and laid flat on the counter. It was four feet square and six inches deep, covered in thin, black leather that was well-aged and worn, particularly along the edges. The box's corners were protected from wear by metal angles that once had been plated brass, but the plating was losing its finish from age and repeated handling. Worn, brass spring clips held the hinged lid closed on three sides, and there was a single black plastic carrying handle on the top. A long, distinctive scratch diagonally crossed the center of the lid.

The big guy began releasing the hardware clasps and opened the lid to reveal the portfolio's threadbare red felt lining. A frameless canvas was inside, facing upward. It was attached to a stretcher with rusty round tacks, indicating it belonged to a time before staples were used. I immediately could tell that although it wasn't a Rembrandt, it had been painted by an artist with some talent and skill. The canvas depicted a battle among dozens of rival mounted horsemen, who carried pikes, battle flags, and other weaponry. Would Rembrandt have portrayed mounted horsemen doing battle when Amsterdam was in the midst of canals and harbors? The composition was awkward and off-center, and after looking at it for a minute, I realized it was a fragment from something much larger. I wondered if it survived a catastrophic event that destroyed the rest of the painting or if someone had cut apart a stolen work to make smaller scenes that would be easier to sell.

The brothers continued to bicker and whine at each other, finally agreeing to store the painting with us, with a caveat that they both needed to be present to view or remove it. We drew up an agreement and had each sign it, and then I watched as they got into the wagon, shouting and angrily pointing fingers at each other as they drove away.

Two weeks later, the skinny brother arrived in a taxi by himself and demanded custody of the painting. He argued and cajoled, but we refused, and he finally left. Several days later, the fat brother drove up in the station wagon and wanted to talk to me. He was dressed exactly as he'd been on the first visit and said his brother was an idiot who had no rights to his painting—their mother definitely left it to him. He, too, demanded we hand over the painting and threatened to call his attorney if we continued to refuse. But when I told him that we'd be upholding the custody agreement and he was welcome to have his attorney look at the paperwork, he stalked out in a huff, got into the station wagon, and floored it out of the parking lot, leaving a cloud of blue smoke trailing behind.

The next time I saw the brothers was several months later when they came in together to show the painting to a specialist from Sotheby's. They were both excited and in a good mood, smiling and laughing in anticipation. But as we opened the portfolio for the Sotheby's man, I saw a brief look of incredulity cross his face. He studied the painting with a magnifying glass, holding a flashlight for illumination, and after fifteen minutes, he departed without saying anything. Several weeks later, the brothers returned to meet a representative of Christie's. This time their mood was somber, and I took this as an indication that their hopes of making millions had been dashed when Sotheby's told them the painting was not a Rembrandt. The Christie's representative rendered his verdict quickly after looking carefully at the painting, lifting it out of the portfolio, and examining the reverse. It had definitely not been painted by Rembrandt, he said, and it was not a complete painting. Both brothers looked stricken as they walked away.

Over the ensuing months, they kept scheduling auction houses and appraisers, none of whom would authenticate the painting as a Rembrandt. Then one day, they arrived together and removed the portfolio from storage. With sad faces, they loaded it into the station wagon and drove off.

A decade later, a woman called me and asked if Cooke's Crating could store a valuable painting. She said she represented VIP clients and was looking for highly secure art storage for a masterpiece they owned. When I asked her who the artist was, she replied she was not at liberty to reveal the names of either the artist or the owners of the painting. She said she would call back later, and after a few weeks, she did, asking if I would come to Pasadena at eleven the next morning to look at the painting in their boardroom.

I drove from downtown LA to the address on Colorado Boulevard, a real estate office in a rundown storefront, where the sun came in through dusty windows. I had expected a modern office building with a fancy boardroom, and I waited a minute, thinking I'd come to the wrong place. But finally, I walked inside and announced myself. A woman sitting behind a worn wooden desk pointed toward steps in the rear and went back to typing a document on her Selectric typewriter.

I walked up the stairs and into a small, windowless room, likely a storeroom, harshly illuminated by a two-bulb overhead fluorescent light. A woman rushed up to me and grabbed my hand. "Mr. Cooke! How nice to meet you! Thank you for coming. We are so grateful. We didn't know what to do and are very worried that something bad could happen to our painting. Your storage comes very highly recommended."

I looked over her shoulder and saw four men in suits and ties, two facing pairs sitting at a plywood table with their hands folded on top. They looked straight ahead, not acknowledging my presence or even glancing up at me. Warning bells pealed in my brain. The woman gestured toward the table. "There it is, our masterpiece!" As she moved aside, I saw the black Laurel and Hardy portfolio, complete with the distinctive scratch across its lid, lying on the table. These people were definitely working a scam.

Concerned for my safety, I immediately blurted, "I'm not interested!" and hurried down the stairs, through the store, and out into the bright sunshine. I was loping toward my car when a clatter of footsteps rushed up behind me. I prepared to defend myself and turned to find the woman, along with one of the men. "Mr. Cooke! Mr. Cooke. Please help us! We have no place to turn, and we're worried about the welfare of the painting. Please agree to store it for us!"

I gazed past her at the man who was now looking me in the eye with a big, friendly grin across his face. I backed away. The woman grabbed my arm, and the man, who was bigger than I was, came too close for comfort. "Please, Mr. Cooke," the woman pleaded again. "I implore you to help us! Won't you please take the painting?"

I wrenched my arm from her grip and spread my shoulders wide in an aggressive stance. "Don't touch me! Leave me alone. I don't want anything to do with that painting." They backed away with a momentary look of uncertainty, and I dashed to my car, where I sat for a few minutes to collect myself. I debated getting lunch before driving back to work—I love an old-fashioned drugstore counter in South Pasadena with delicious milkshakes and hamburgers—but seeing the Rembrandt again and dealing with those con artists killed my appetite. Instead, I drove through the twists and turns of the Arroyo Parkway toward downtown and into our parking lot, where I noticed a black sedan parked at the entrance to our offices.

When I walked inside, the black portfolio was sitting on the reception counter, and three of the men from the realty office surrounded the desk of my storage manager Jeffery, practically leaning on him while shoving papers and a pen into his hands. "We just met with Mr. Cooke, and he agreed to accept this painting into your storage," one of them was saying. "We need you to sign this safekeeping receipt." Jeffery looked bewildered and frightened. I was outraged at the mendacity of these crooks, invading our offices and intimidating my employee.

"Get your goddamn asses out of my office right now! Get the hell out, or I'm calling the cops!" I yelled at them. Their faces turned sullen, and they grabbed the portfolio on their way out, but they left one of the papers behind. It was a safekeeping receipt stating that Cooke's Crating agreed the painting was a Rembrandt worth ten million dollars and was guaranteeing the value. Jeffery knew I had gone to Pasadena to look at the painting and could have believed their assertions. If I had gone to lunch, he very likely would have signed the papers. It was a close call.

Pollock

Agnes was a middle-aged woman obsessed with two paintings she purchased for fifty dollars at a garage sale. Convinced the paintings were by Jackson Pollock and would make her wealthy, she brought them to our warehouse in a U-Haul truck and opened a storage account. They were clearly not Pollocks. Someone had mimicked his sweeping gestures of arced and splattered paint, but the canvas was coarse, more like burlap than the linen canvas Pollock used, and the choices of colors and symmetry were clumsy. Agnes, though, wanted to believe. She followed the usual pattern of trying to find an expert willing to verify the authenticity of her paintings, wasting the time of numerous knowledgeable specialists, who took one look before saying no. And when those efforts failed, she began calling on lower-tier gallerists and auction houses, again with no luck. Finally, she came for the paintings, telling me our $65 a month storage charge was "outrageous" and that she found a "much more economical place to store them."

Nearly a decade later, she called again, requesting a truck and two art handlers to meet her in Topanga Canyon to pick up her treasures, which she decided to return to our storage space. She gave directions involving several dirt roads and told us, "When you see the big oak tree, park and walk up the trail to the right." She also asked us to send along wrapping materials and some cardboard.

My drivers found the oak tree and walking up a path, they came across the twenty-foot sea container in which Agnes had been storing her "Jackson Pollocks." What Agnes hadn't told me was that a month earlier, a brushfire had swept through the area and turned the sea container into a red-hot oven. The "Pollocks" were baked, charred and scorched, curled up like burned potato chips. Portions of the wooden stretcher bars had burned away, with the remaining wood converted to charcoal. She had my drivers make cardboard trays and gently load the remnants into them. The paintings, once six-feet square, were now grotesque remnants a quarter of the size. When she called me to reopen the storage account, she wanted to insure them for an outrageous amount, and—concerned about a possible scam—I refused. I was glad I did when I saw how pathetic the paintings were.

A month later, she arrived at my warehouse accompanied by a man she introduced as a "scientist from a nuclear physics lab in Saint Louis." He looked at the paintings but avoided making eye contact with me, a suspicious sign. A few days after that visit, Agnes called, sounding out of breath with excitement. "Oh, Mr. Cooke, I have such wonderful news! The nuclear physicist assures me he can completely restore my Jackson Pollocks, and I want you to guarantee you can ship them safely to St. Louis." I decided to avoid any further involvement with this farce, figuring it would inevitably come to a bad end, and politely told her she needed to come and remove her items promptly. If the "Pollocks" did eventually rise from the ashes, I never heard anything about it.

Joe

Sometimes innocent people get victimized by art dealers. I saw it happen—extremely and tragically—to Joe, who brought two crates to our warehouse in the back of his old Ford pickup truck. Painted white, they looked like poorly made museum traveling crates. While my storage registrar was preparing a receipt for him, Joe told me his story.

He enjoyed going to the monthly auctions that van and storage companies hold to sell the contents of unpaid storage lockers. He had attended one at a Bekins warehouse, bidding sight unseen on the contents of a locker he expected would be full of furniture or personal effects he could sell at swap meets for extra income. Joe was retired, living on Social Security with limited savings, and had a modest house in a poorer area of the San Fernando Valley, which he paid off after years of hard work and scrimping. The money he made from swap meets helped keep him going.

Joe won the bid, and when the storage locker was opened, he was disappointed to see it contained only the two small crates. He hauled them home in his pickup and asked the roofer working on his house for tools to open them. The roofer climbed down his ladder and helped Joe remove the lids. Looking inside and finding a bunch of framed photographs sitting in slots, he told the roofer he had made a lousy purchase. "Just look at this bunch of worthless photos," he complained. "They're even the old-fashioned black and white kind. Who is going to pay anything for those?" The roofer lifted one out of the crate for a closer look. "Dude!" he told Joe. "Them's not just any photographs! Them's Ansel Adams!"

Joe had never heard of Ansel Adams, so the next morning he called the Los Angeles County Museum of Art and asked if someone there could tell him what the photographs were worth. Joe thought he might've hit the mother lode and would soon be rich. The LACMA registrar directed him to a museum curator, who said the museum didn't do valuations but suggested he call G. Ray Hawkins, a photo dealer based in Los Angeles. I didn't have a high opinion of G. Ray because he had once attempted to ship a damaged photograph through my company, possibly with the intention of sticking us with a claim.

Joe asked if G. Ray would come to his home to look at the photographs—which turned out to be a fateful mistake. Hawkins immediately recognized the crates belonged to a client of his but didn't say anything to Joe except that the photos were indeed by Ansel Adams and very valuable. He promised to let Joe know what they were worth later. He also suggested that Joe find proper secured storage for the photographs as quickly as possible. The suggestion sounded altruistic but was likely a self-serving move to ensure the photos were kept safe for his clients. When G. Ray departed, Joe made a second call to LACMA, which recommended my company. That's what brought Joe to us.

We only had the crates for a couple of months when I received a court order telling me not to release the photos to any party without first getting court authorization. Joe was being sued by the original owners. Reading the documents carefully, I learned that Bekins was a co-defendant in the suit. The couple, who had not bothered paying their storage bills for over a year, had employed high-powered attorneys to allege that Bekins employees and Joe fraudulently conspired to take the photos and sell them for personal gain. Joe, who had no money, could not afford to hire a lawyer to mount a defense.

The suit took several years to conclude, and one morning Joe came in to sign over the crates to the couple, who had prevailed in court. He was a broken man. The couple won a large judgment against him and Bekins, forcing him to sell his house to pay his share. He lost everything. He looked terrible, but still apologized for being unable to pay his storage bill.

When the couple, who never paid us a thing, notified us they were sending one of our competitors to pick up the crates, we informed them about the past due charges and warehouse release fee, which they readily agreed to pay. They sent us a check, and it didn't surprise me in the least that they placed a stop payment with their bank as soon as the crates left our warehouse.

Endings

Gehry

SHORTLY AFTER THE RICHARD SERRA near-disaster at Marcia Weisman's, Frank Gehry became one of my regular clients. In those early years, while his architectural practice was small, he would contact me directly about crating and shipping his project models. But as his business and renown grew, he became aloof, and all business contacts went through his staff.

Like many great architects, including Frank Lloyd Wright and Greene and Greene, Gehry designed not just buildings but furniture and lighting fixtures. Frank's pieces weren't custom-designed for particular homes, as his predecessors were. His furniture, cleverly made of layered corrugated cardboard, Masonite, and wood, was manufactured for commercial sale to anyone who wanted it. He chose similar everyday materials for individual works of art he called "fish lamps." For those, white or colored Formica laminates were intentionally broken into pieces that resembled fish scales, then glued together with silicon to create the shapes of languorously swimming Koi. Lit from inside the process produced beautiful, glowing lamps that seemed to be alive.

In the mid-1980s, under the direction of Fred Hoffman, an LA art dealer, we crated and shipped a group of these lamps to Metro Pictures, a gallery in New York City. Our shipment consisted of twelve crates, each containing a single lamp and sometimes its base. I booked Atlantic Van Lines, one of the early interstate art carriers, for the cross-country delivery.

It was early morning as I watched two of my employees forklifting the crates onto Atlantic's trailer. The driver moved them inside and lined them single-file along one wall and then jumped down and began closing the doors. "Aren't you going to tie those crates off before driving away?" I asked him.

"Not necessary," he replied.

"Yes, it is," I insisted. "The contents are fragile, and I don't want them moving freely, or something is going to get damaged."

He jumped back up, and I watched to make sure each crate was individually strapped against the trailer wall. I could tell the driver wasn't happy about this extra work because after signing paperwork, he turned on his heel and walked away without a thank you or goodbye.

We were ready to close at the end of the workday when he called from a hospital in Flagstaff, Arizona, saying he had hit an ice patch, lost control, and rolled his truck into a ditch. He wanted me to know the accident location—a mile marker on I-40, a few miles west of Flagstaff—because I had been so concerned about the crates. I immediately feared the worst given the impact of the accident, which could have left the crates exposed to theft or inclement weather, so I asked my stalwart employee Rita Gomez if she would go with me to help rescue them. A quick look at a map showed the fastest way to get there that evening was to fly to Las Vegas, rent a car, and drive over Hoover Dam to I-40 and then east to the site. I booked a flight and rental car, and we got to Las Vegas by ten, spent the night in a casino hotel, and left at 6 a.m. Driving through a nasty sleet storm, we arrived mid-morning at the accident scene. The trailer was lying on its side next to the freeway, and it was no longer in a rectangular shape—the impact had distorted it into a parallelogram. Worse, it was wide open to the elements, with one door torn off and the other flopped on the ground. A large tow truck was busily winching the smashed-up tractor out of the ditch, and the trailer would be next. Before that happened, we needed to get the crates to safety.

Rita and I stepped into the trailer. Artwork was scattered about, some damaged, and we were careful to avoid stepping on any of it. Once our eyes adjusted, we could see none of that art was ours. The ten Gehry crates were still strapped to the wall, which was now overhead. They appeared to be undamaged, but we'd need help getting them down to keep them that way. Fish lamps aren't heavy, but with the added packing materials and wood, the crates averaged 100 pounds.

The tow truck driver finished pulling out the tractor, and as he was retracting his cable, preparing to right the trailer, I asked if he could help us lower the crates and if he knew somewhere we could keep them safe and dry. He told me he was operating out of an auto repair garage several miles down I-40 and volunteered to take the crates there. With his help, we loaded them onto his tow truck, setting them amid gas cans, automobile jacks, chains, and tools. We also scavenged some truck pads from the trailer to protect them from the sleet and rain.

We followed his flashing yellow lights through the sleet to a garage and unloaded, placing crates on either side of a hydraulic car lift. He left us to return to the wreck while we unscrewed crate lids. To our relief, nothing was damaged. On returning to LA, I arranged for another truck, which got the lamps safely to New York.

Gehry began developing his architectural style and philosophy by experimenting on his own home, an older Santa Monica bungalow.

In the process of working out ideas, he modified or tore out the walls, built new ones sheathed in corrugated metal, and changed the rooflines. I thought it was bold of him to risk devaluing his house as he developed the concepts and design skills he later used in grand projects, trying out new formations that showed early hints of his cubist architecture philosophy. His house experiments definitely paid off, but they were not without consequences—the changes caused stresses to the remaining portions of the original house, most noticeably the flooring, which wound up deformed.

That created problems when we went to install a two-glass panel Larry Bell sculpture we had been storing for Gehry. When I walked into the living room, I could see the center of its maple floor bulging, which would put the sculpture at risk. The two Bell panels, each measuring five feet by seven feet high, were attached with silicone at a ninety-degree angle. But the deformed floor made the panels sit unevenly, creating pressure points on the edges—and glass doesn't like pressure. It was impossible to install the sculpture safely. I called Gehry's office to explain the problem, and forty-five minutes later, a young architect showed up with a Skilsaw and proceeded to cut two grooves into the floor at a right angle, forming level slots that the glass pieces could fit into. It was an audacious solution, and I was struck by the way Gehry hadn't hesitated to ask someone to do it.

While the cutting was underway, I had an epiphany and went to a builders' supply for a bag of fine sand. We used the sand to fill the grooves, then inserted the glass panels in their silicone joint and slid them back and forth several times until they seated perfectly. Unfortunately, the sculpture was out of scale for the space and completely dominated the room. Several weeks later, we were called back to remove it because Gehry's infant son Alejandro kept running into the glass. The floor grooves may still be there.

Unlike most architects, Gehry didn't seem to work out his concepts and ideas with drawings. From what I could see, he didn't have much skill as a draftsman, or perhaps he simply didn't like working in that medium. His brilliance was in thinking like a sculptor as he formed his concepts and developed ideas, and his method was to use models because he realized they made it easier for his clients to envision their projects. Once they'd agreed on the final design, computer-generated drawings followed.

I got to know his process intimately because we were often called upon to move and store the models built at every stage. Gehry began projects using small cardboard cutouts and wooden blocks to work out the shapes and symmetries of structures. A team of model-builders produced dozens of these small concept assemblages before progressing to larger models, making a whole series of models for a project, each succeeding one having more detail or a different scale. In some instances, multiple components were combined into a huge single model measuring ten by fifteen or more feet. Model-builders working in teams put in long hours on these projects, often sleeping under their worktables. Most were young architecture school graduates getting their first experience working in an architect's office, and they were always rushing under time pressure and often cut corners to meet deadlines. As a result, portions of the models would occasionally collapse in transit because they were inadequately glued or had weak internal supports. These problems were made worse by Gehry's proclivity for making last-minute changes. A section of a model would be cut out and replaced, but in the process, access to the inside for proper reinforcement was often constricted, weakening the entire structure.

Because Gehry would lay off the model-builders when a project was completed and hire an entirely new group for the next one, no one got the benefit of experience. The new modelers had to relearn everything and repeated many of the same mistakes. Twice, after these problems became acute, I volunteered to give a talk to the model-making teams, emphasizing basics like the importance of constructing on a solid base instead of flexible cardboard or thin foam board, and building around a solid core to help stabilize and strengthen the structure. I also introduced them to hot-glue guns, which eliminated the drying time of white glue, sped up their work, and adhered better.

My company's biggest problems with Gehry involved last-minute scrambling to get models crated and delivered on time to a client's location someplace in the world. We often built crates in advance to meet the tight deadlines, using measurements provided by model-builders who were still at work on the ever-shifting designs. If the final dimensions changed, we were forced to abandon the original crate and hastily build a replacement. Timing was particularly critical when the models were for a competition, with architectural firms vying for a large project. If the models arrived late, Gehry would lose the chance to be considered for a project worth millions of dollars. With so much at stake, my employees often stayed late into the night, shivering in a cold airfreight terminal while riding herd on the crates to make sure they got onto an outbound flight. But even this didn't guarantee they would leave on time. A shipment could go asunder because flights were canceled, or a shipper had to give priority to shipments such as perishables, flowers, or even bodies packed inside waxed cardboard boxes dropped off by hearses. On more than one occasion, I watched crated artwork being loaded on a pallet alongside a body box.

On shipping days, we descended on the Gehry studio with truckloads of crates and a large packing team, along with a forklift, compressors, and power saws. We'd set up in the parking lot and feverishly try to meet the airfreight cutoff. This was delicate work because the models were so fragile. No matter how carefully we packed them, they were likely to arrive at the destination with several parts coming loose from inadequate gluing or because someone had forgotten to attach a component. If the model-builders hadn't completed portions of a model on time, we quickly made foam core boxes they could take on a flight the next day.

There were occasionally significant damage issues, as happened with four twenty-four-foot trucks full of model crates we shipped to France for Gehry's design of the Louis Vuitton Museum. I consigned the shipment to Chenue, a Paris member of an international shipping group called ICEFAT, the International Convention of Exhibition and Fine Art Transporters. A month later, as I was preparing to leave the office on a Friday evening, our fax machine spat out a notice from a French court. Luckily it arrived while one of my employees, who was fluent in French, was still in the office to translate the news that a hearing would be held in two days. At nine Monday morning in Paris, the court would determine financial responsibility for damages caused to the Louis Vuitton models—which Chenue had never mentioned to me. If we failed to appear at the appointed time, the notice said, Cooke's Crating would lose any right of defense in the matter. The Friday evening timing of the fax seemed like it was intended to prevent us from hiring a French attorney to represent us in the hearing. I immediately sent a reply contesting the notice and demanding a delay in the proceedings. Nothing came of it, but I felt betrayed. To add insult to injury, Chenue stole my French client. The one positive outcome of this unfortunate incident was that it made me aware of a need for better ethical guidelines in our field. I wrote rules of ethics requiring ICEFAT agents to represent the financial interests and protect the reputations of fellow agents by immediately reporting any damage issues and by not stealing the clients of a consigning agent. These rules were voted into the ICEFAT articles of association and are now the standard operating procedure for our group's seventy-six member companies from thirty-seven countries worldwide.

Early on, Gehry began storing his models with my company. As his commissions grew larger, the project storage archives at his offices in Santa Monica filled up, with hundreds of banker's boxes of small study models taking up several rooms. Frank saved everything down to the smallest, seemingly insignificant item. His office manager, Jill Auerbach, asked me to estimate the cost of moving and storing the boxes and negotiated a per cubic foot price that was lower than our regular rate. As the years progressed, Gehry put more and more models in storage, and although my warehousing costs steadily increased through inflation and annual lease increases, I continued to honor the original price. We also hired a full-time registrar to oversee the Gehry account. Eventually, we had to lease a 26,000-square-foot warehouse to provide space for the crated models. It had ceilings twenty-five feet high, and we set up pallet racking to stack crates almost to the top. As the models grew larger, we built oversized twelve-by-five-foot pallets and stacked crates fourteen to eighteen feet high, securing them with ratchet straps. Eventually, the entire warehouse was packed solid, and we added 5,000 square feet in another warehouse. Overall, the scope of Gehry's model storage was nearly 25,000 square feet stacked sixteen feet high, or around 400,000 cubic feet.

Years into the relationship, some artists we worked for who were also friends with Gehry began telling me he thought he was being overcharged. No one ever bothered to come see firsthand the scale of what he'd asked us to store, so hearing this was disheartening, given that we were actually undercharging by a significant amount. I tried to get an appointment to meet with him to discuss the storage issues but couldn't get past his management team.

Then suddenly, one day, his project manager called to let me know they were going to move everything to a building in El Segundo, an industrial area near the Los Angeles International Airport. He also said Gehry hired an architectural historian and a team to photograph, condition report, and catalogue the models. I asked to see the building to determine loading dock access. When I met the historian there, it was immediately apparent the building wasn't nearly large enough to accommodate all the models, especially since its ceiling clearance was only twelve feet. I suggested to the historian that we deliver models grouped by the projects they represented, for example, all the Disney Concert Hall models and related archival materials. We had comprehensive inventory records and could easily locate the appropriate models, but she casually dismissed the chance for easy organization. "Just deliver all the models," she said without discussion.

So, we did as she asked. The biggest model crates, representing multiple projects, were stacked on oversize pallets lining our storage aisles, and we pulled and delivered those first. As a courtesy, I stationed one of my forklifts at the site, and to maximize the El Segundo space, we used it to stack crates within inches of the ceiling. But by the time we delivered a third of the models, El Segundo was full. The historian hired a registrar and two others to help with the cataloguing but soon realized they needed our help to move and unpack everything. After a year passed, Frank abandoned the project, and everything returned to our storage warehouse. This fiasco seemed to have been a colossal and avoidable waste of money and effort. But the customer, of course, always has the right to ignore good advice.

Several years later, Meaghan Lloyd, Frank Gehry's right-hand administrator, called to tell me that Frank would be coming in a week to look at what we were storing for him. When she arrived at our offices, she said Frank was waiting outside in an SUV. Some guy wearing a suit and tie was driving, and Frank was in the passenger seat, so I got into the back seat with Meaghan. No one acknowledged me when I said hello, an ominous sign. I took them first to the warehouse holding the smallest group of crates. Then, we got back in the car and drove around the corner to the large warehouse, which was packed full of hundreds of models. When Meaghan and the suit went inside, Gehry turned to me with a friendly smile and said, "So you calculate my storage by the volume being stored?" I replied that we entered the dimensions of each object, and the computer gave the totals to determine the charges. I was about to explain the reduced charges when he snarled, "Go to hell!" and stalked through the door. But once inside, he stood with his mouth wide open as he realized for the first time the true scale of what he'd amassed.

He didn't apologize. After all, "a servant must know his place," and what was I but his servant?

Sollie 17

My final encounter with Ed Kienholz occurred years after his death and made me wonder if his ghost was hanging around to haunt me. During my early years working for Ed, he told me he didn't trust any art moving company to properly crate his assemblages because too often they had arrived damaged. He cannily safeguarded against that by making this work in sections. When being prepared for shipping, the tableaux were turned facing each other and fastened together using hardware clasps and bolts. The backs of those sections became the fronts and sides of what were essentially crates. Then the assemblage floors were built on joists, which created access for forklift and pallet jack blades. This contrivance was exceptionally clever because it reduced the sizes of the large sculptures for storage and also protected them in transit. But the system broke down over time as the original wood aged and the fittings used to close the tableaux became sloppy from repeated usage.

One of Kienholz's best assemblages was a bleak piece called *Sollie 17*, which used materials salvaged from a rundown residential hotel in Spokane to capture three moments in the day of a forgotten old man. It arrived at our warehouse by sea container shipment from a museum in Korea, and when we unloaded it, I saw that parts had been damaged. It was obvious to me the sculptures were becoming rickety with age and increasingly prone to future breakdown. Fortunately, Ed's wife and artistic partner, Nancy Reddin Kienholz, had worked with him in an artistic collaboration for years, and even though he was gone, she had the knowledge and skills to restore his original pieces. She came in to do the repairs.

Not long after, a registrar from the Whitney Museum contacted me about shipping *Sollie 17* to Berlin, and I told her my concerns over the fragility of the sculpture. After I recommended crating the two components, she consulted with the museum's director and asked for an estimate. She called several days later to say that the museum's budget didn't include the additional costs of the crating, so they would forgo it. But they changed their minds when I said that my worries about the piece were so strong that I was willing to do the work at my cost, which reduced the estimate by twenty percent. My employees packed the Kienholz components into two crates, and we shipped them to Berlin by ocean freight container service.

Six weeks later, the Whitney registrar called me. She was upset. At first, I was alarmed because I thought *Sollie 17* had suffered some damage despite our efforts. Instead, there was another problem: Nancy Kienholz was angry that we were "besmirching the memory of Ed Kienholz and had dishonored his vision and workmanship by crating his crates." Nancy had called the Whitney's director from Berlin and raised hell, demanding the museum not pay me for our services. The director, in turn, called the registrar.

Upsetting a museum registrar is a nightmare scenario for any art moving company. Registrars are a close-knit bunch, and if you piss off one, it will adversely affect relationships with many more. But I wasn't sure what to do. Why would Nancy be so upset that I was trying to protect the sculpture? It seemed especially punitive of her to demand the museum not pay for my services when the money was not coming from her.

Six months passed, and all was quiet until I received a curt phone call from Nancy demanding I meet her at the Museum of Contemporary Art, Los Angeles, at ten the next morning so she could show me "all the problems with your crates." I arrived to find two crates sitting unopened in the center of the gallery, along with a large crowd of the museum's staff, including registrars, curators, and preparators. Nancy Kienholz stood with Kienholz's dealer Peter Gould and Henry T. Hopkins, the influential former director of the San Francisco Museum of Modern Art and later the Hammer Museum. Henry worked closely with curator Stephanie Barron in 2008, raising a million dollars to purchase Kienholz's *Illegal Operation* for LACMA's collections. Henry, always the proper gentleman, looked uncomfortable, and I sensed that this was to be a public shaming.

Nancy launched into a tirade about how cumbersome and difficult it was to unpack my crates and how I should be ashamed to charge for them. I waited until she finished talking, and then, without saying a word, I handed one of the preparators the socket wrench I brought with me and pointed to the top of the crate. In a matter of moments, we removed the top, and a few minutes later, we had completely taken the crate apart to reveal *Sollie 17* safe inside. I asked two others on the museum's staff to help, and the four of us easily lifted the sculpture off the crate's bottom and set it gently onto the floor. The crowd dispersed as we started uncrating the second component. If they'd come expecting drama, there was nothing to see.

My company has moved many Kienholz pieces in the years since as part of our routine services to museums, collectors, and auction houses. Those endeavors have always gone smoothly, so I know that Ed has finally stopped haunting me.

Hammer Dies

I moved art for Armand Hammer until the end of his life. My final task came when his son, Michael, called and asked me to immediately go to Hammer's house in Westwood and remove all of the art. I drove a truck there, and as I waited for Michael to arrive, I walked across the porch to the front door, looking around to see where the Jewish Defense League's protest pig had been tied so long ago. Michael pulled up, jumped out of the car, and rushed down the sidewalk. "We need to hurry. There are some estate issues I don't want to go into now, but it is important to get the paintings removed quickly."

I had expected a mansion with maids and servants, but the house was small, and inside, it was depressingly dingy and rundown. The window drapes looked dusty, the window glass was dirty, and the carpets were stained and worn. Why would such a wealthy man live in those conditions, with his collection of Old Master paintings hanging in gloom? The works he'd kept around him were mostly small canvases by sixteenth-century Dutch painters, similar to the piece I had prevented Hammer from removing at the USC galleries years before. Perhaps he had also removed these from Fischer Galleries after donating them. I was surprised not to see a Monet or Renoir or even a Van Gogh. He had many beautiful and important paintings but apparently didn't want to enjoy them in his home. Perhaps his real tastes favored sixteenth-century Dutch maritime scenes, and he'd collected all those other paintings for prestige or the investment value.

Michael was still rounding up boxes of documents and loading them into his car when we finished packing and drove away. It was good timing because a few minutes later, lawyers representing Joan Weiss, the niece of Hammer's deceased wife, showed up to block the removal. Joan was suing Hammer in an attempt to get a portion of his estate, which she claimed her aunt had been entitled to. I knew Joan and her husband, Robert, because they collected contemporary art, and I installed a complicated Michael Heizer wall sculpture in their Brentwood home along with other paintings.

I couldn't help them then, though, and they weren't fated to win. Though Joan's lawyers presented 250,000 exhibits and 5,000 pages of depositions and documents in an effort to get a share of Hammer's $200 million in paintings and assets, the judge in the case ruled against them in just one day.

Picasso

The last time I saw Norton Simon was just before he died. Andrea Clark, the Norton Simon Museum's registrar, scheduled me to pick up a Picasso arriving from Paris on Air France, asking me to meet the flight at LAX in the early evening, and deliver the painting directly to the museum. But on the afternoon of the flight, she called again and told me to take the painting first to Simon's home in Malibu. "Mr. Simon wants to view the painting. Please uncrate it and let him look at it. But under no circumstances are you to leave the painting there," she emphasized. "It belongs to the museum, and you must deliver it to us."

That evening we drove to the airport and waited in a line of trucks for a space to open up at the Air France loading dock. Eventually we got our turn, and we sat by the loading door while forklifts zoomed back and forth on the warehouse floor. One of them rushed toward us, balancing a thin, four-foot-tall crate on its fork tines, which were raised three feet above the warehouse floor. The Picasso crate rocked back and forth and looked like it was on the verge of falling off. I held my breath.

After the operator set the crate down and roared away, we inspected it carefully for damage, loaded it up, and drove north on the Pacific Coast Highway toward Malibu. Simon still lived in the same wealthy enclave, the Colony, where I delivered and installed his Indian sculptures many years before. A large, muscular man wearing a suit and tie—likely a bodyguard and someone who spent a lot of time lifting weights—answered his door. He gave me a cold stare, which he held for a good twenty seconds, waiting for me to avert my gaze, and then demanded to know what we wanted. "We're delivering a painting from the Norton Simon Museum for Mr. Simon to look at," I answered. He looked at the crate for a moment and disappeared down a dark hallway.

A few minutes later, he returned, accompanied by another tough-looking fellow, also dressed in business attire. "Well? Don't just stand there," he barked. "Mr. Simon is waiting and doesn't have all day. Open the crate." We complied, removing the wrapping materials to reveal a beautiful Picasso, a Cubist portrait of a woman, perhaps one of his lovers.

"Bring the painting," the first guy ordered. We grabbed it and followed him down the hallway while the second guy followed us. Norton Simon's bedroom was at the end of the hall.

He was lying in a hospital bed in the dim light, with an intravenous bottle hanging on one side and tubes from an oxygen tank inserted in his nostrils. Various wires connected him to quietly beeping monitors.

I saw his eyes focus on us. He waggled a finger, and the bodyguard leaned over to listen, his ear only inches from Simon's mouth. Simon's lips moved, and I heard mumbling. The guard straightened up. "He wants to know who the hell you guys are." This was disconcerting, but I began explaining I was the owner of Cooke's Crating and that the museum had instructed us to bring the painting so he could see it for a few minutes before we delivered it to Pasadena.

Before I could finish, the finger wiggled again, and this time the guard said: "He wants you to hold the painting up so he can see it." He turned on the gooseneck lamp that sat on Simon's nightstand and twisted it toward us to illuminate the painting, which we lifted above Simon's toes, holding on tight. Again, the finger and another order: "Move the painting closer so he can see it better." Because of the medical equipment surrounding the bed, we couldn't stand on either side of the bed to hold the painting close to him, so we leaned over from the end, bracing our knees against the foot of the bed to keep from falling on top of him as we tilted the heavy painting toward his face. He stared at it for minutes, and my back began to ache from the strain of holding it in that awkward position. As more time passed, a tremor passed through my arms and I began to have a difficult time breathing. The finger waggled emphatically, and the bodyguard leaned over.

Straightening back up, "he said to leave the painting here and get the fuck out!"

Shocked by the rudeness, I blurted, "But our instructions are to return the painting to the museum." I caught Simon's eyes watching my reaction and saw the satisfaction in them from my weak response. I immediately realized I had been outplayed.

The finger waggled again while Simon continued staring at me. This time the guard stepped aggressively toward us. "What part of *get the fuck out* don't you understand!" he roared. He and the other big guy marched us down the hall, pushed us outside, and slammed the door in our faces. Simon may have been dying, but his mind was still a steel trap and, even on his deathbed, he was mentally maneuvering to be the winner.

I called Andrea the following morning to report what had occurred. "I was afraid that could happen," she said. "I know you did your best."

Princess

The art moving business is both a blessing and a curse. It is a blessing for an art lover because it provides a daily feast of paintings, sculptures, and rare artifacts. There are opportunities to view private collections the public could never see or visit artists' studios—allowing us to witness their works in progress firsthand, and therefore, better understand their thinking and processes. And of course, we visit museums and galleries to view close-ups of what is hanging on their walls and what's stored in their backrooms and basements. It is a privilege to be able to handle a rare painting or sculpture because the intimate, tactile contact evokes a deeper sense of the object. We can turn a painting upside down, which may reveal more about the artist's composition and method of working. We can tilt it to allow light to rake across the surface, revealing brushstrokes, subtle techniques, and raised paint covering something underneath, a place where the artist changed his mind. Shining a black light on an Old Master painting exposes repairs and conservators' in-painting. Looking behind a painting reveals how the artist stretched and primed the canvas. And often, there is a collection of labels and tags cataloguing the piece's history and provenance—where the painting has been exhibited and who owned or sold it.

A painting captures the moments of a place and an artist's creative intellect. To closely examine a masterpiece is to commune with the artist and become closer to the art. What a privilege it is to hold a Monet or Picasso knowing they once held it, too—and perhaps spent days or weeks painting it, while making creative decisions and changes involving colors and light. This continuous immersion in art develops connoisseurship, a discerning eye that makes it possible to immediately distinguish an exquisite artwork out of the hundreds or even thousands of ordinary to mediocre ones.

The curse of having this access and hands-on relationship with great art is becoming infatuated with pieces that are unaffordable, falling in love with something out of reach. It's bittersweet to briefly have a wonderful work of art in your custody before delivering it, knowing your moments with it will soon end, and the next time you see it—if you do—you may be kept behind a barrier with the rest of the public, told you cannot touch.

One of my clients, the film producer Tony Ganz, asked me several years ago to help his sister ship her art collection to New York City. I made an appointment and went to her Hollywood Hills home to scout the collection. She wasn't there, and her housekeeper let me in, pointing out where the paintings and drawings hung. She left me alone, and while walking around, I noticed another framed drawing just inside a hallway off the living room. It was dim there, and I thought it might've been hung as an afterthought, but I was immediately attracted to it. It was a color portrait, the profile of a young woman who wore a distinctive crocheted hairnet held by a single yarn around her forehead. This feature seemed familiar, and I thought I had seen it in a painting once before but couldn't remember where. The drawing was done by a skilled and talented artist, and I was infatuated with it.

The New York shipment was postponed, and months later, I was asked to return to the house to survey a different group of artworks, including the drawing. Ganz's sister was home this time, and when I asked her who the artist was, she told me it was by an "unknown nineteenth-century German artist." I again found myself infatuated by the drawing and debated asking her if she would sell it to me. But Tony Ganz had asked me to help her, and I thought he might take offense if I crossed the line from being a service provider to buyer.

We picked up her art and temporarily stored it, and several times each day, I would go and admire the drawing. There was a mysterious quality about it that kept pulling me back, and I verged on asking to purchase it, though I never did. We shipped all the art to New York, and although the drawing was gone, I continued to wonder why I had been so drawn to it.

I next saw it several years later, when I was looking through the pages of a Wall Street Journal over breakfast. I turned a page and was stunned to see a small photo of the drawing with a caption that read: "Previously unknown drawing by Leonardo da Vinci discovered!" The article said that Ganz's sister had it on display in a gallery she owned in New York, and someone had purchased the drawing by an unknown nineteenth-century artist for $25,000. Following a hunch, the buyer sent it to a Leonardo expert in London who was soon convinced it was authentic. Additional tests by a French imaging lab in Paris gave further credence to the belief that the drawing was an authentic Leonardo worth millions.

National Geographic magazine did a fantastic article about the research establishing the authenticity of the drawing, and a book has since been published about the discovery. It noted that the unusual hairnet was in style at the Milanese court for only a few years, which coincided with Leonardo's time working there. After reading that, I remembered when we moved the Huntington Art Museum collections, I had seen a painting by another artist showing men and women of the Milanese court during the same period—the women wearing the same distinctive netting over their hair.

Had I known Ganz's sister was an art dealer and that the painting was for sale, I would have asked to purchase it, and after living with it, could possibly have figured out it was by Leonardo. But even if I never had, I would have enjoyed its beauty. It is one of those rare works that brings much happiness and joy every time you see it, a work of art that never loses its magic. On the other hand, if I had found out it was a Leonardo da Vinci valued at $50 million, would I have left it hanging in my house? Would I have continued to enjoy it if I were always worried about it being stolen? Or the house burning down? We bear an enormous responsibility for protecting brilliant works of art for future generations. Perhaps the prudent thing would have been to lock it in a vault for safekeeping. But then, what good is a painting if it is locked out of sight in a locker? Art is made to be seen and enjoyed.

Buying art for the love of having it in your life is the only thing that makes sense to me, and a twist in the story underlined the point. Not long after the drawing was authenticated and the book about it came out, a British art forger published a book of his own, in which he said he wanted to set the record straight. *He* had created the portrait in his teens, he said, when he decided to try his hand at making an "Old Master drawing" he could sell. The subject wasn't a Milanese princess, as the experts claimed, but instead "a girl called Sally who worked on the checkouts" at a supermarket. The author of the book that painstakingly described why it is an actual Leonardo stands by his claim. The drawing's official status remains clouded, but I would have been happy to own it. I saw it, felt the power it held for me, and I could enjoy it with no regrets, even if the princess were an ordinary checkout girl.

I'm under no illusions that love trumps money in the art world, though. In recent years I've seen art commodified to the point where people use it to hedge their investment portfolios and flip it when they've made their profit. And lately, some have rushed to buy NFTs—non-fungible tokens—which can perform the magic of using digital systems to "add value" to an infinitely reproducible image file by making it "one of a kind." It's a good day for artists when they can sell an NFT for $69 million, and maybe for some people, that's the future of art.

But I came into the art world for the love of tangible, fragile, irreplaceable work that carries life and stories through time. To see and handle a masterwork or a brilliant experiment is to come in contact not just with beauty or provocation or history but with the scars and traces of all the human foibles it has somehow survived.

I know without a doubt that in my business, art can kill. But for good or ill, I'll keep taking my chances—because it makes me feel so alive.

THE END